How to Rig an Election

Praise for *How to Rig an Election*

'Democracy is great, unless it can be undermined, manipulated and rigged. This eye-opening and important book is essential reading for everyone who wants to get democracy right again, so that it acts as it should: in the genuinely best interests of each and all.'

– A.C. Grayling, author of *Democracy and Its Crisis*

'Clear, punchy, and potentially revolutionary, *How to Rig an Election* should be read by every voter, civil society activist, opposition politician, election monitor, journalist and diplomat who has ever come away from a voting booth or tallying centre feeling angry, worried or frustrated.'

– Michela Wrong, author of *It's Our Turn to Eat*

'Cheeseman and Klaas hit the nail on the head: in many countries elections are a sham. The problem is getting worse, while the international community connives at being deceived. The implications for public policy are profound and will take years to digest. An excellent book.'

– Sir Paul Collier, author of *Wars, Guns and Votes*

'Rigging elections has become an art to which an impressive array of resources is brought to bear in even the poorest countries. This work is a most timely addition to all who care about this important piece in the great democratic jigsaw on which so many basic freedoms depend.'

– John Githongo, anti-corruption campaigner and CEO of the Inuka Kenya Trust

'A concise, penetrating examination of why and how a growing number of governments are rigging elections, brimming with telling examples and practical recommendations for how concerned international actors can do more to help reverse this disturbing global trend.'

– Thomas Carothers, Carnegie Endowment for International Peace

'A timely wake-up call to the greatest political paradox of our time. Although more elections are being held than ever before, we are witnessing a worldwide undermining of democracy and democratic processes. A must-read for anyone fighting for democratic governance and for the voices of citizens and ordinary people.'

– Winnie Byanyima, Executive Director, Oxfam International

How ☐ To ☐ Rig ☒ An ☐ Election ☐

Tricks Despots Play

Nic Cheeseman and Brian Klaas

HarperCollins *Publishers* India

First published in 2018 by Yale University Press

First published in hardback in India in 2018 by
HarperCollins *Publishers*

Building 10, Tower A, 4th Floor, DLF Cyber City, Phase II,
Gurugram Haryana – 122002, India
www.harpercollins.co.in

2 4 6 8 10 9 7 5 3 1

P-ISBN: 978-93-5302-472-7
E-ISBN: 978-93-5302-473-4

Set in Adobe Caslon Pro by
IDSUK (DataConnection)

Printed and bound at
MicroPrints India, New Delhi

CONTENTS

INTRODUCTION
How do you solve a problem like elections?

The greatest political paradox of our time is this: there are more elections than ever before, and yet the world is becoming less democratic.

Nowadays, elections are held almost everywhere. The vast majority of governments at least go through the motions of election campaigns, and are rhetorically committed to allowing citizens to cast ballots to choose the leaders who will govern them. However, in many places, that choice is little more than an illusion: the contest is rigged from the start.

Take Azerbaijan's 2013 elections, when the highly repressive government of President Ilham Aliyev sought to boost its democratic credentials by launching an iPhone app that enabled citizens to keep up to speed with the vote tallies as ballot counting took place. Touting its commitment to transparency, the regime said that the new technology would allow anyone to watch the results in real time. But those who were keen to try out the new technology were surprised to find that they could see the results on the app the day *before* the polls opened.

In other words, anyone with the app could see who had won, who had lost, and by how much, before any ballots had even been cast. When journalists asked how the government had managed this act of political time travel, the authorities back-pedalled, claiming that these were results from a previous election. However, this explanation did not stand up to closer scrutiny: the candidates listed were those contesting the current poll. Inadvertently, the regime had shone a digital light on the fraud they intended to carry out in the shadows.[1]

It is tempting to think that Azerbaijan's egregious election rigging is an outlier. We want to believe that elections are truly transformative political institutions and that the case of Azerbaijan is the exception that proves the rule. However, in other authoritarian states in which leaders hold elections despite not being committed to democratic values, rigging is the norm rather than the exception. Since the end of the Cold War, the *majority* of elections held in such states have featured some form of electoral manipulation. Partly as a result, authoritarian leaders win elections in such contexts about nine times out of ten.[2] Despite the impression of competition and choice, then, these elections deliver more continuity than change.[3]

If you think that these kinds of poor-quality polls are a small proportion of all of the elections held around the world, think again: on a scale of 1 to 10, in which 10 reflects a perfect election and 1 reflects the worst possible, the average election around the world scores just 6. In Asia, Africa, post-communist Europe and the Middle East the figure is closer to 5 (see appendix 7).[4] Moreover, even if we move away from a specific focus on authoritarian leaders to consider the entire universe of all elections globally, only about 30 per cent of elections result in a transfer of power.[5] In other words, incumbents win seven times out of ten – and this figure has not moved much since the early 1990s.

The picture changes little if, for a moment, we shift the focus from elections to the broader context in which they are held. As the Cold War ended, some scholars and politicians were seduced by the belief that we were nearing the 'end of history'[6] – that all countries were on a slow but inevitable march towards liberal democracy. In hindsight, that prediction appears to have been naïvely optimistic. Instead, the last decade has witnessed a gradual decline in the quality of democracy in the world. Moreover, there is little evidence that this trend is easing. According to Freedom House, the American pro-democracy think tank, in 2017, seventy-one countries suffered net declines in political rights and civil liberties, with only thirty-five registering gains.[7]

This represented the worst annual democratic recession in quite some time, but the pattern is consistent: in each of the last twelve years more countries have experienced democratic backsliding rather than democratic consolidation. Significantly, this process is not concentrated in only one part of the world and does not appear to reflect specific regional dynamics. Instead, the erosion of democracy can be identified in all of the regions caught up in the 'third wave' of democratization – Latin America, Eastern Europe and Africa – as well as areas that have yet to democratize, such as the Middle East. This is reflected in the fact that the five countries that suffered the biggest democratic decline in 2017 were, in order of magnitude, Turkey, the Central African Republic, Mali, Burundi and Bahrain – with Venezuela and Hungary not far behind.[8]

These developments are particularly striking when stacked up against the other major trend of recent times: the growing prevalence of multiparty elections. How is it possible that the flourishing of elections has coincided with a decade of democratic decline? The answer is that dictators, despots and counterfeit democrats have figured out how to rig elections and get away with it. An increasing number of authoritarian leaders are contesting multiparty elections, but are unwilling to put their fate in the hands of voters; in other words, more elections are being held, but more elections are also being rigged.

This part of the story – global democratic backsliding and the inability of elections, on their own, to deliver democracy – has already received considerable academic attention and media coverage.[9] Although international policymakers continue to demonstrate a remarkable faith in the transformative power of elections, even those held in the most difficult of contexts, such as in Afghanistan and Iraq, recent experience has shown the enduring capacity of leaders to subvert multipartyism.[10] What is less well known is that in many countries elections do not simply fail to topple dictators and despots; they sometimes actively help them shore up their grip on power. This is because reintroducing elections typically enables embattled governments to secure access to valuable economic resources like foreign aid, while reinvigorating the ruling party and – in many cases – dividing the opposition. Consequently, a number of authoritarian regimes that appeared to be in their death throes have, with the help of the ballot box, proved able not only to win consecutive elections, but also to re-establish their political dominance.

To put it another way, if authoritarian leaders can hold elections without losing, they can have their cake and eat it – boosting their resources and legitimacy while retaining their grip on power. This is not to say that autocrats welcome elections: most fight the reintroduction of multiparty politics tooth and nail, in part because they do not see dissent and opposition as legitimate political activities. But once competitive elections have been reinstated, these regimes often prove to be remarkably adept at manipulating them for their own purposes. As a result, authoritarian systems that hold elections but do not allow opposition parties to meaningfully contest them prove to be more durable than those that do not.[11]

This book is about why this is possible and how it happens. While a small number of authoritarian governments win elections through legitimate means, the majority adopt a range of strategies to ensure that they cannot lose. Thus, in many countries around the world the art of retaining power has become the art of electoral manipulation.

This is not to say that all elections are rigged, or that authoritarian leaders rely on rigging alone to win. In reality, savvy autocrats understand that it is far easier to fix the election result if they enjoy significant public support, and that small amounts of rigging are far easier to hide. Election rigging is therefore only one of the tools used by effective dictators. However, this caveat notwithstanding, it remains an essential weapon in the despot's arsenal.

For many years, both of us have travelled extensively to understand the paradox of more and more elections of worse and worse quality. We have closely monitored elections in a number of different contexts, and draw heavily on many months of field research in eleven countries across sub-Saharan Africa, the Middle East and Southeast Asia. Between us, we have interviewed more than 500 elite figures in these states, ranging from prime ministers and presidents who have rigged elections to lower-level election officials; from ambassadors to local aid workers; from opposition candidates to rebels and coup plotters disillusioned with democracy.

In this book, we combine these on-the-ground interviews from hundreds of thousands of miles of travel with a global data set of all elections held between 1960 and the present day (see appendix 1 for more details), along with the latest analysis in political science research to construct a rounded picture of the strategies used to rig elections – and the failing attempts to stop them. In contrast to important recent publications that have focused on quantitative data analysis,[12] we place greater emphasis on revealing the lessons that can be learnt from those cases of electoral manipulation that we have observed at first hand; thus, we draw most on the countries we know best, including Belarus, Kenya, Madagascar, Nigeria, Thailand, Tunisia, Uganda, the United States and Zimbabwe.

What counts as rigging?

Because 'rigging' is such a contentious term, it's essential to separate out election strategies that are simply part and parcel of democratic politics. In this book, we intentionally distinguish election *rigging* from the use of election promises to generate support. While campaign promises can confer an advantage on the incumbent, who typically has far greater access to resources than opposition parties, they are also a common and legitimate feature of democratic politics. We also distinguish rigging from other standard advantages of incumbency, such as the ability of the ruling party to time government programmes so that they launch during election campaigns, and the fact that presidents and prime ministers tend to receive more media coverage than opposition leaders in between elections. The bottom line is this: rigging represents an *illegitimate* and *undemocratic* means of tilting the playing field clearly in the favour of one party or candidate at the expense of others.

Election rigging can be broken down into six subcategories of manipulation. The first is *gerrymandering* (chapter 1), in which leaders distort the size of district boundaries so that their parties have a head start in legislative elections.[13] By these means, opposition parties can end up with fewer seats even if they receive more votes. The second is *vote buying* (chapter 2), which involves the direct purchase of citizens' support through cash gifts or, as it is often referred to in Africa, 'something small'. This can be an effective way to secure votes that could not be earned, but it is an expensive strategy and – when the ballot is secret – one that is difficult to enforce. Voters may be able to take bribes from one candidate and then vote for another without consequence.

Autocrats may also employ a third type of rigging, engaging in *repression* to prevent other candidates from campaigning (chapter 3), deny them access to the media, and intimidate rival supporters in order to stop them going to the polls. If these strategies don't work, counterfeit democrats have two main options left open to them: digitally *hacking the election* (chapter 4) in order to change the debate and, in some cases, to rewrite the result; and *stuffing the ballot box* (chapter 5) – adding fake votes or facilitating multiple voting in order to improve a given candidate's performance. To get away with such tactics, they may also need to *play the international community* (chapter 6), duping donors into legitimizing poor-quality polls. Because the latter three options can easily backfire, the most effective autocrats don't leave election rigging to the last minute.

These strategies generate different costs and benefits, and so their use varies depending on how vulnerable a position an authoritarian leader finds themselves in. Most obviously, ballot-box stuffing and repression are the most eye-catching forms of election rigging. That makes them risky; they are also easier for election monitors, foreign governments and citizens to spot.[14] As a result, sophisticated authoritarian regimes begin manipulating the polls well before voting begins. If these efforts work well, vote tampering and political violence never become necessary because the result has already been determined.

Although a great deal has been written about problematic elections around the world, not many authors have considered the full range of options available to leaders, and how different combinations of strategies create new possibilities. To put it another way, existing analysis has often focused on only one of the various tools at the incumbent's disposal, rather than considering the full extent of their toolbox, and the ways in which tools can be substituted for each other when one becomes unavailable, or too costly.[15] By looking at the entire toolbox, we highlight the ability of incumbents to draw on a range of different strategies to turn the reintroduction of multiparty elections to their own advantage, using the image of democracy to entrench authoritarian rule.

But in order to understand why this process is happening at all, we must first explain the increasing prevalence of multiparty polls, the reasons why despots are so keen to retain power, and the full scope of the options at their disposal.

The rise of multiparty elections

Many people assume that the task of sustaining authoritarian rule has become harder over the last thirty years.[16] It is easy to see why. In the 1970s and 1980s, global superpowers such as the United States placed less emphasis on promoting democracy abroad and more on maintaining allies in power, whatever their reputation. Under the intense pressure of the Cold War, and fearful of losing ground to the Soviet Union, even states that were democratic at home were willing to sacrifice democracy abroad on the altar of security or 'containment'. As a result, a number of Western governments became involved in propping up authoritarian regimes in Africa, Asia and Latin America, facilitating the flow of funds and weapons to leaders who were – in some cases at the very least – morally and economically bankrupt. At the same time, the Soviet Union sustained a series of 'puppet states' and allied authoritarian regimes throughout Eastern Europe, which often took the form of highly coercive one-party systems in which opposition was fiercely repressed and political space tightly controlled.

The first of these states to make major democratic breakthroughs were the Latin American nations that began to democratize in the late 1970s and throughout the 1980s – spurred on by similar processes occurring in the region's main former colonizers, Spain and Portugal. By the 1990s, what the political scientist Samuel P. Huntington called 'democracy's third wave' began to lap against the shores of Eastern Europe and sub-Saharan Africa as the Cold War began to thaw.[17] On the one hand, the internal collapse of the Soviet Union led to a brief moment of American hegemony in which it appeared that democracy and market capitalism had triumphed over one-party states and economic socialism. On the other hand, the rise of 'post-materialist' values in the West,[18] whereby citizens began to place greater importance on issues that did not personally impact on them (such as the protection of the environment and human rights) made voters more sensitive to the foreign-policy decisions of their governments. At the same time, the World Bank and the International Monetary Fund – the major international financial institutions to which many authoritarian governments were and are indebted – began to use their leverage to promote the 'good governance' reforms that they believed were necessary to turn economies around and ensure that their loans would one day be repaid.

Taken together, these shifts changed the international political landscape, if only for a brief moment. Now lacking in international support, authoritarian regimes in both Africa and Eastern Europe became far more vulnerable to popular criticism, which had always been present but had previously struggled to gain traction. As domestic pressure to open up political systems began to mount, popular discontent spilled over into the formation of new civil society groups and mass protests in favour of political reform. Lacking the coercive capacity to repress these movements, and the economic capacity to co-opt them, many of the world's authoritarian governments were forced to accept a degree of democratization in the shape of its most common modern incarnation: multiparty elections. Indeed, over time, even the strongest strongmen – like Zine al-Abidine Ben Ali in Tunisia – began to introduce ostensibly democratic contests.

As a result, more national multiparty elections are being held than ever before.[19] From an average of thirty a year in the early 1950s, there has been a constant upward trend, which accelerated in the early 1990s with the political liberalization of sub-Saharan Africa. Today, around seventy national elections are organized every year, more than double the number just thirty years ago (appendix 3).[20] It is important to note that this increase is not simply driven by one region or type of state. Rather, there has been an increase in the number of national polls held pretty much across the board: Latin America is the only region in which the number of elections held in 2012 was lower than in 1946.

The rise of multiparty elections has significantly changed the nature of the challenge that authoritarian leaders face. Thirty years ago, the main aim of the average dictator was to avoid holding elections; today it is to avoid losing them. Given this, the notion that it is tougher to be an authoritarian leader now than ever before rests on an assumption that often goes unspoken: that winning elections is harder than banning them.

There are some good reasons to think that it should be difficult for authoritarian incumbents to retain power at the polls. After all, despots are not usually beloved unifiers. During their time in office, authoritarian leaders typically alienate significant sections of society through their policies. A quick look at the pro-reform movements that brought down African one-party states in the early 1990s demonstrates this point well: they were almost all made up of people who had been beaten, frustrated or excluded by the government over the previous thirty years.[21] The same is true on many other continents, where opposition to despotism rests not on a shared ideology or platform but on a common rejection of the leader and the things they have done during their time in office.

At the same time, the breakdown of the old system of authoritarian rule, whether military, one-party or personal dictatorship, also implies a degree of weakness on the part of the establishment. Thus, when multiparty elections are reinstated, pro-reform and opposition groups usually appear to be in the ascendancy. Consequently, the early media coverage of founding elections often conveyed the sense that the incumbents were destined to lose, unable to make themselves relevant in the new democratic landscape. However, while alluring, the assumption that it has become harder to sustain authoritarian rule turns out, for the most part, to be false. Instead, authoritarian governments have proved to be highly adept at findings ways to 'win' elections even when they enjoy limited support among the population.

In many cases, elections were introduced in the absence of other political reforms, leaving autocrats in control of their political systems. In turn, the legitimate and illegitimate advantages of incumbency to which this gave rise made it extremely difficult for opposition parties to compete. Indeed, in those countries that we term counterfeit democracies, elections very rarely generate a transfer of power.[22] Instead, incumbent presidents win the vast majority of the polls that they contest.[23] As a result, we have entered an era in which only a small proportion of elections deliver political change.[24]

Another way of putting this argument is that many of the countries discussed in this book did not experience a moment of high-quality democracy and then gradually fall back into authoritarianism; rather, in most cases they simply shifted from one form of authoritarianism to another. Thus, for some of the states we cover here, it is more appropriate to talk about how we can strengthen or build democracy, rather than rescue or defend it.

This is an important point, because it helps to explain why democratic consolidation has stalled in so many parts of the world. Most countries are neither full dictatorships nor consolidated democracies; they fall somewhere in the middle. However, the electoral advantages enjoyed by the ruling party are only half the story. It is not just that the introduction of multiparty elections has often failed to unseat established dictators – the bigger problem is that it has actually enabled them to consolidate their hold on power. By conferring a degree of legitimacy on the political system, allowing incumbents to open up access to international financial assistance, and removing one of the main demands of opposition parties and civil society groups, the introduction of multiparty elections can actually extend the life of authoritarian regimes. This is why we find that dictatorships that hold tightly controlled elections prove to be more stable than those that do not.[25]

In other words, so long as autocrats can tightly control the political process, their regimes have a better chance of survival if they hold elections and rig them than if they avoid holding elections altogether. That is the unsettling reality at the heart of this book.

Defining democracy

The discussion of different types of political system means that it is time to say something about how we define the key terms that we use in our analysis. Typologies are often dull – the kind of thing that makes people stop reading books written by academics. But it is important to quickly clarify what we mean by these labels, in part because the type of regime has significant implications for the way in which elections play out.

We recognize four basic types of political system, existing along a spectrum of democracy. The first are *pure authoritarian* regimes in which no elections are held at all, as in China, Eritrea and Saudi Arabia. The second are *dominant authoritarian* states in which elections are held in a context of extremely constrained political rights and civil liberties such that the opposition is barely able to compete, for example Russia, Rwanda and Uzbekistan. The third category on our scale features *competitive authoritarian* states, in which elections are hotly contested but the opposition nonetheless competes with one hand tied behind its back.[26] This is the kind of political system that holds in countries like Kenya and Ukraine. Finally, there are *electorally democratic* states, in which polls tend to be reasonably free and fair, although there may be some discrepancies, as in the United States and United Kingdom.[27] A full list of the countries we discuss and their level of democracy is provided in appendix 15.

The cases that mainly interest us fall into the second (dominant authoritarian) and third (competitive authoritarian) categories – where elections are held but they are neither free nor fair. For ease of reference and to avoid using clunky terms throughout the book, we refer to these countries collectively as *counterfeit democracies*. We have chosen this term because it highlights the core feature of these states, namely that they masquerade as democratic political systems though in reality are anything but. However, it is important to keep in mind that the prospects for opposition victories and long-term democratic consolidation vary considerably within this category.

For countries in both the second and third categories, 'regime continuity' – whether the same regime survives from one year to the next – is extremely high, at over 80 per cent.[28] Yet the evidence suggests that, as one might expect, the most stable systems are dominant authoritarian states that use high levels of repression to engineer landslide victories. Precisely because they are more open and tend to witness closer election results, competitive authoritarian states are considerably more likely to experience a transfer of power and a transition to more democratic political systems.[29] This is a theme to which we will continue to return throughout this book, most notably in the conclusion when we ask how, and where, democracy can be strengthened.

But before we discuss that, it is important to consider how these various regimes types come to be. Why do old authoritarians find it hard to give up power? What prevents the emergence of democracy? And which factors determine how repressive a government is, and whether it becomes more dominant or more competitive over time?

Should I stay or should I go?

When faced with pressure to democratize, authoritarian leaders must decide whether to use an olive branch or an iron fist. They can respond to such pressure either by conceding ground and appeasing their opponents, or by cracking down on opposition and sustaining the existing political system through force. The outcome of this choice is shaped by whether a given leader thinks that their interests will be best served by embracing reform or repression.[30] This will depend on a basic calculation: how much does each option cost, and what are its chances of success?[31] However, it is important to understand that costs are not objective but rather subjective. In other words, it is not simply a case of working out which strategy will cost more financially. How individual leaders feel about committing human rights violations and the ways in which they want to be remembered are also important. Despots are not always rational in the eyes of others.

Furthermore, the costs of repression can be significant, and include not only purchasing weapons, funding the security forces and co-opting the opposition but also the cost to a leader's reputation and international standing that they are likely to incur by using force against their own citizens. This, for example, partly explains why Egypt's Hosni Mubarak allowed the Tahrir Square protests to continue largely unabated during the Arab Spring rather than simply attempting to crush them. There were serious costs in using state violence, especially given the reluctance of the military to intervene against the demonstrators, and they kept his iron fist (somewhat) in check. Thus, as the economist Paul Collier has argued, in most cases the ability of leaders to deploy political violence depends on whether other countries are prepared to fund them, sell them arms, and look the other way.[32]

However, the costs of reform can also be high: genuine political liberalization increases the likelihood that the opposition will be able to defeat the incumbent in an election. Whether or not a leader finds this acceptable depends on their own personality, the benefits they gain from holding office and what they stand to lose by standing down. In other words, the decision to rig or not to rig is best understood as a cost–benefit calculation rather than simply the inevitable by-product of thuggish leadership.

Popular and media discussions typically focus on the more venal and corrupt aspects of this equation, making it tempting to think that leaders simply refuse to leave office because they are addicted to power and the personal benefits that they derive from it. After all, one feature of many authoritarian regimes is an attempt to build a cult of personality around the leader. The notorious Ugandan dictator Idi Amin was not content with being known just as 'President Amin'. Instead, he changed his title to 'His Excellency, President for Life, Field Marshal Al Hadji Doctor Idi Amin Dada, VC, DSO, MC, Lord of All the Beasts of the Earth and Fishes of the Seas and the Conqueror of the British Empire in Africa in General and Uganda in Particular' – not to mention, of course, the Last King of Scotland. In Togo, Gnassingbé Eyadéma went one step further, employing a troupe of dancing girls to follow him and sing his praises, and publishing a cartoon that depicted his numerous 'superpowers'.[33]

Similarly, if you go to the cinema in Bangkok, the preview trailers are preceded by a slick multimillion-dollar short film praising the glory of the Thai monarchy and its military ruler. Not to be outdone, Turkmenistan's former dictator, Saparmurat Niyazov, changed the word for bread in the local language to *gurbansoltan* (his mother's name), banned smoking nationwide so that he could kick his own habit, and unveiled in the opulent white marble capital city of Ashgabat a $12-million golden statue of himself that rotates so as always to face the sun.[34]

In short, there can be no doubt that many of the world's authoritarian leaders exaggerate their own importance and benefit handsomely from their control of the state. As Michela Wrong argues in relation to Kenya, when the system itself is corrupt, it is those at the top who tend to benefit the most.[35] Perhaps most notoriously, a succession of Nigerian presidents are estimated to have stolen at least $20 billion from public coffers over the past thirty years – more than the total OECD aid to Africa over the same period.[36] Tellingly, the personal value of staying in power is far higher for leaders in authoritarian systems than in democracies, and so the potential costs of reform, and of defeat, are greater. According to the Corruption Perceptions Index, counterfeit democracies in which elections occur in the absence of the trappings of democracy feature high levels of corruption. On a scale of 0 to 100, in which lower scores denote more corrupt states, the average counterfeit democracy scores just 29, suggesting that there are significant opportunities for personal enrichment for those who sit at the apex of the political system. In other words, the opportunities for corruption are often greatest where democracy is weakest.

That said, it is important to note that this pattern does not hold for all authoritarian regimes. We both interviewed the former president of Zambia, Kenneth Kaunda, who ruled over a one-party state between 1972 and 1991, and were struck by his relatively modest demeanour and lodgings. Kaunda can be accused of mismanagement and repression, and of course enjoyed a privileged life as head of state, but there is scant evidence that he amassed a personal fortune on the back of his time in office. Other examples of less personally corrupt authoritarian leaders can also be found, such as Singapore's first prime minister, Lee Kuan Yew (popularly known by his initials LKY).[37] However, in the universe of authoritarian rulers there are far fewer Kaundas and LKYs than there are Amins and Niyazovs.

Moreover, leaders also have a number of other important motivations for remaining in office. Two of the most significant are the need to protect their political legacy and self-preservation.

The first of these may sound self-serving – and often is – but it is also true that many presidents and prime ministers are committed to managing a process of national transformation of one form or another. Their visions are frequently deeply problematic and lead to considerable hardship for their people,[38] but it is important to keep in mind that many authoritarian rulers took power during, and have spent most of their time in office responding to, a period of political crisis.

In some cases, leaders headed rebel movements that overthrew the previous government during a liberation struggle or civil war, as in Uganda, Rwanda and Zimbabwe. In others, they took power through coups that toppled the previous leader during a period of economic or political instability, as in Thailand's 2014 military takeover or in Tunisia from 1987 until the Arab Spring. In yet other cases, leaders came to office in legitimate post-conflict elections, and only began to roll back democratic rights and freedoms after losing popularity. This has been the trend in countries like Angola and Burundi and, more recently, much of North Africa. Finally, in a small but significant number of states such as Belarus, the people entrusted government to a seemingly visionary leader during the post-Soviet power vacuum, only to find that he quickly transformed into a self-interested despot willing to employ the same methods as the Soviet regime from which he was charged with breaking free.[39]

What unites these cases is that presidents and prime ministers took power rather than inheriting it, often against a backdrop of widespread instability. Only in a relatively small number of cases has an authoritarian regime been in power for so long that we are now on the third or fourth generation of leaders, who no longer remember their regime not being in power and so do not fear the potential for political unrest.[40] As a result, many of the autocratic governments operating today understand one of their main roles to be maintaining political stability, and have embarked on state-building programmes in pursuit of this goal. Of course, many dictators have been predominantly destructive and do not fit this bill, and in a number of cases the pursuit of order has served to legitimize the repression of minority groups and dissenting voices. But for leaders such as Rwanda's Paul Kagame and Uganda's Yoweri Museveni, whose countries suffered brutal civil conflict in living memory, unity and stability are genuine concerns,[41] even if this does not justify the strategies that they use to stay in power.

This is an important point, because the desire for stability is not just a feature of old authoritarians; surveys tell us that this is also a key priority for citizens in many new democracies.[42] Thus, when leaders justify staying in office on the basis that they need to fulfil their mission and maintain order, it often strikes a chord with their people. This can lead to some fascinating paradoxes. For example, in Africa, a strong majority (67 per cent) of respondents to the Afrobarometer survey of political attitudes report supporting democracy and multiparty elections.[43] However, they also report having more trust in the president (62.3 per cent) than in any other political institution, and are typically particularly sceptical about the role played by opposition parties (only trusted by 38 per cent in southern Africa in 2015, for example).[44] In large part, this is because opposition parties are seen as being divisive and contributing to election-related unrest.

A further reason for leaders to seek to remain in power in countries that feature chronic political instability is self-preservation. Leaving office is a dangerous game in many parts of the world. Over the past sixty years, a significant proportion of leaders have suffered jail, exile or death upon standing down. Indeed, in the 1960s and 1970s this was the most common outcome for departing leaders in Africa and for more than 30 per cent of leaders in Latin America. In Africa, the risks of leaving office have declined significantly since the 1970s, but remain high despite two decades of multiparty politics.[45] The often deadly aftermath of losing power demonstrates just how great the cost of reform can be.

Against this backdrop, three factors make leaving office particularly problematic for authoritarian rulers. First, the use of physical force against opponents of the regime renders the rulers especially likely to suffer reprisals from rival leaders if they lose office. Second, assets built up under authoritarian rule are often illegitimate or at the very least of highly questionable origin, and so are prone to being appropriated by future governments. Third, the kinds of abuses committed by authoritarian leaders make them vulnerable to prosecution for past crimes, either in domestic courts or in arenas such as the International Criminal Court. Sudan's President Omar al-Bashir, for example, knows that he risks being prosecuted by the ICC for crimes against humanity if he leaves power. Partly as a result, he is determined to remain in office.[46] These three factors help explain why authoritarian leaders rarely leave power willingly and often rig elections to stay in office.

Significantly, the risks of losing power vary considerably across regions. The potential costs of leaving office are much higher where the level of trust between different elites and communities is low, and institutional checks and balances are limited: incumbents have few reasons to believe that the political system will protect their interests should a rival come to power. Consider the case of sub-Saharan Africa, which features a number of countries that have suffered high levels of political conflict, violent authoritarian rule, and particularly weak political institutions. As a result of these underlying conditions, incoming leaders often have both the motivation and the opportunity to either prosecute or persecute their predecessors. This explains why African leaders have been more than twice as likely to be killed, exiled or jailed after leaving office than those in any other part of the world from the 1960s onwards.[47] Understood in this way, we can see that the efforts of some

African politicians to become 'presidents for life' is not simply motivated by unrestrained megalomania; rather, it is a rational response to the political landscape. Their counterparts in other regions might well do the same if they faced similar risks.

Leaders' perceptions of risk also vary across countries within a given region, depending on their personalities as well as what happened to their predecessors. Consider the case of Haiti, where bloody deaths for former leaders are not aberrations but the norm. Between 1908 and 1915, Haiti's departing leaders were, in order, 'exiled, exiled, bombed and blown up, imprisoned, exiled, executed, exiled, and, particularly gruesome, "dragged from the French legation by an angry mob and impaled on the iron fence surrounding the legation and torn to pieces"'.[48] In such a context, those in power are less likely to be willing to contemplate defeat, whatever the cost of staying in office. Rigging becomes rational and understandable when the alternative could involve being impaled on a fence.

Unsurprisingly, leaders who have more to fear from leaving office are less likely to look favourably on the prospect of reform. This is one reason why those who occupy the executive for a long time become particularly likely to rig elections. Incumbents who have been in office for many years have had more time to engage in corruption and commit human rights abuses. They are also more likely to have faced popular movements demanding change. As a result, they tend to have a greater need and a greater desire to rig elections. It is therefore unsurprising that we find that rather than mellowing in their old age, the longer authoritarian leaders hold office, the more likely they are to manipulate the polls.

Of course, leaders who hold more-open elections are also more likely to lose power, and so this trend also reflects the fact that as time goes on the concentration of hard authoritarian states increases. But this caveat aside, the significance of time is nonetheless striking. Forty-five per cent of elections are rigged when authoritarian leaders have been in power for the equivalent of one term in office (roughly five years); for leaders who have served seven terms (thirty-five years), this figure rises to 65 per cent – a jump of some 20 per cent (see appendix 8).

However, even if leaders want to stay in power come what may, they can only do so if the costs of repression – such as paying the wages of the security forces – can be met. Governments generally find it easier to meet these costs if they enjoy a steady stream of revenue from natural-resource wealth, which insulates them from domestic and international pressure to democratize. This is one reason why there is such a high correlation between oil reserves and the quality of democracy. With the obvious exception of Norway and the United States of America, most of the world's oil-producing states are authoritarian.

To get a more precise sense of the impact that oil has on democracy, it is useful to compare how oil-rich and non-oil-rich states rate in terms of their political environment. To do this we divide countries into those that do and do not have significant oil reserves, and those that are more and less democratic. On a 20-point scale in which –10 is a pure dictatorship and +10 is a pure democracy, the average country with no or very low oil revenues scores +4.2, while the average country that secures at least 3 per cent of its GDP from oil scores –2.4.[49]

We find a similar story if we turn our attention to the specific issue of the conduct of elections. On a scale of 0 to 100, in which 100 represents the highest quality and 0 the worst, the average oil-producing state scores just 24, almost half the score of the average non-oil-producing state. Indeed, beyond summary statistics there are numerous examples of leaders who have been able to use oil – and other valuable natural resources – to insulate themselves from domestic and international pressure to reform.[50] The implication is clear: from Angola to Saudi Arabia, oil and democracy mix about as well as oil and water.

Other factors can also help leaders meet the costs of repression. The governments of countries that have geostrategic importance, such as being located in an area of particular strategic significance to the foreign-policy goals of external powers, have naturally been able to translate this into greater traction with the international community. Regimes as diverse as those in Uzbekistan, Pakistan and Thailand used security co-operation with the United States' 'war on terror' after the attacks of 11 September to blunt criticism of their undemocratic practices. At times, the hypocrisy was staggering; as Western powers cosied up to Uzbekistan over closer security co-operation, human rights watchdogs documented simultaneous abuses that in one case involved boiling political opponents of the regime alive.[51]

Similarly, American allies in Eastern Africa have been able to leverage their support for anti-terror activities in their own states and in the Horn of Africa to mute Western criticism of authoritarian backsliding.[52] In turn, this has enabled them to access international financial assistance and hence to meet the costs of repression. Finally, it is worth noting that leaders who enjoy unquestioned authority over more effective security forces are clearly better placed to contain dissent in the long run.

In contrast, periods of economic decline can fatally undermine the capacity of authoritarian regimes to fund their core activities.[53] This is particularly true in countries that are not geostrategically important and which are forced to rely on aid from Western actors that are (at times) keen to support good governance – such as the United States and the World Bank. Under these circumstances, the need to secure international financial assistance may constrain the authoritarian strategies available to despots. This is not to say that aid money itself cannot be diverted and manipulated, but simply to note that the imperative of sustaining the flow of funds can force recipient governments into reforms, such as the introduction of a new constitution, that subsequently constrain the options available to them.

Considering the collective impact of these various structural and individual factors suggests that leaders are most likely to try and stay in power: when they believe that their presence is essential to maintain political stability; in cases when they are less committed to plural politics; when they have engaged in high-level corruption and/or committed human rights abuses; when they lack trust in rival leaders and political institutions; when they have been in power for a longer period of time; and when they control geostrategically important states with natural resources, effective security forces, weak institutions and high levels of distrust.

In addition, it is important to keep in mind that while some of the costs of repression and reform are likely to remain the same over time, others can be shaped by the strategies of a range of domestic and international players and may rise and fall relatively quickly. For example, a more united opposition coalition may escalate the repression and manipulation that a leader needs to employ in order to retain power, significantly increasing the cost of these strategies. Similarly, more effective international election monitoring and clearer signals about the negative consequences that may follow from holding flawed elections are likely to increase the cost of authoritarian strategies in the eyes of incumbents, and hence make reform seem like a more attractive option.

In this way, the strategies of key domestic and international actors can shape the cost–benefit calculus facing presidents and prime ministers. It is therefore possible to design more effective political strategies and international interventions that can enhance the prospects for better-quality elections. However, as we shall see in the chapters that follow, this is not an easy task. Not only do authoritarian leaders have a number of strategies at their disposal to divide the opposition, they are also adept at manipulating foreign partners – even when natural resources and geostrategic influence are not at stake.

The authoritarian toolbox

In this book, we demonstrate how governments that are determined to pursue repression, rather than to reform, rig elections – and how some dictators are not only getting away with it, but are actually becoming stronger as a result. The great irony here is that in many countries the spread of elections has entrenched despotic incumbents rather than dislodging them. As we have already noted, and will explore in greater depth in the conclusion to this volume, this is because holding elections helps to legitimize governments, opens up access to international financial assistance, and facilitates the use of divide-and-rule politics.

Unless you are a seasoned election observer, some of the stories of electoral manipulation that appear in the next six chapters are likely to make you sigh and shake your head. The tactics are as innovative as they are infuriating. Elections have been rigged by not allowing the opposition leader's aeroplane to land (Madagascar); by announcing a final tally that includes seventeen times as many ballots as the number of registered voters (Liberia); by assassinating the most prominent challenger (Pakistan); by telling subordinates precisely what percentage of votes the dictator expects to win (Belarus); and by an election official being forced to sign off on an official result while a pistol was held to his head (Equatorial Guinea).

But as the analysis to come will demonstrate, subtle forms of election rigging are often most effective. It is therefore important to recognize that patterns of election rigging vary considerably across both time and space. For example, the percentage of elections that featured state targeting of the opposition with violence, intimidation or harassment is worrying, but has fallen from 30 per cent between 1992 and 1996 to 23 per cent between 2012 and 2016. At the same time, levels of vote buying have remained both stable and extremely high, barely shifting from 40.3 per cent between 1991 and 1995 to 39.9 per cent between 2011 and 2015 (see appendix 14). In part, the explanation for these trends is that, for leaders, overt violence is a particularly high-cost strategy in terms of their domestic and international reputation and the credibility of the elections, whereas vote buying is often so commonplace that it rarely draws condemnation in the media and election observation reports. As a result, authoritarian governments have a strong incentive where possible to swap violent forms of rigging for other, less blatant strategies.

Slicing our data in a different way reveals similar nuances when it comes to geographical variations. While vote buying remains frequent in most parts of the world, this varies considerably between sub-Saharan Africa, where over two-thirds of elections held between 2012 and 2016 featured substantial electoral bribery, and other regions in which the figure is considerably lower, such as the Middle East (29 per cent) and Latin America (36 per cent – see appendix 14). These differences relate in part to levels of socioeconomic development and the amount of money that voters expect to receive in return for their allegiance: the average cost of a bribe is cheaper in most African states ($1–5) than it is in Latin America ($5–15), and so African candidates find it is less financially draining to use this strategy.[54] However, these patterns are also rooted in the historical evolution of political processes; if local norms legitimize the giving of 'something small' – such that it is not necessarily seen to be a 'bribe' at all – then candidates have more to gain and less to fear from doing so.

As we discuss the different strategies available to counterfeit democrats in the remainder of this book, we explain their costs and benefits, and when they are most likely to be used. In other words, our aim here is not to argue that there is a single blueprint used by all authoritarian governments all of the time, but rather that leaders have a toolbox of options that they can select from in order to get the job done.

We demonstrate this by using the next six chapters to look at the main strategies that authoritarian leaders can use to turn elections to their own advantage, addressing the tactics in the order in which they are typically deployed in the real world. That is, we start with those that are implemented well in advance of election day, and finish with the last-resort tactics used to steal an election after the votes have been cast.

Our exploration of these tactics includes old strategies such as gerrymandering, which has been around for hundreds of years, and new frontiers such as the rise of online dissemination of 'fake news' stories to destroy a given candidate's reputation and tip the scales in favour of the incumbent. In some cases, we also point out that what is said to be new has a long history. For example, it is often said that the distribution of made-up information using social media began in earnest with the election of Donald Trump in the United States in 2016.[55] But this ignores the long history of the falsification of documents and news stories both in the West and beyond.[56]

What has often changed is not the methods themselves, but rather the ways in which they are deployed or weaponized to win elections. In short, the methods used have become more sophisticated and sinister. In the Kenyan election of 2007, figures seeking to discredit the main opposition candidate, Raila Odinga, went to great lengths to fake an extensive 'Memorandum of Understanding' that he was alleged to have signed with Muslim leaders to transform Kenya into a Sharia state. The document looked authentic, and came complete with the opposition leader's signature. In reality, it was an elaborate hoax, and Odinga had simply committed to investing greater government revenue in the coastal part of the country, which has historically been economically and politically marginalized.[57]

Clearly, old strategies are now being deployed in new ways. But it is also true that information warfare is going to be the new frontier of election rigging, and business is going to boom for these digital forces in the years ahead. From hacking to fake news, there is a rising digital menace to democratic integrity:

autocrats now have more ways than ever before to manipulate public opinion in order to shape how voters cast their ballots.

Most of our case studies are drawn from the category of counterfeit democracies in which it is clear that leaders depend on the use of election rigging to retain power. However, we also use historical cases of rigging in countries that used to be rife with electoral manipulation but now hold high-quality polls, and draw on examples of cutting-edge forms of electoral manipulation that have been identified in otherwise consolidated democracies. We do this for three reasons. First, a historical perspective is often essential to explain how certain kinds of rigging came into being and have evolved, and hence to build a full understanding of how they work. Second, providing this context also serves as a valuable reminder that there is nothing 'African', 'Asian' or 'Latin American' about election rigging – these are practices that have compromised democracy in all parts of the world at one time or another.

A third reason not to ignore the historical antecedents of contemporary rigging is that some of these issues continue to compromise the quality of democracy in Europe and North America today. Most obviously, the imposition of stringent requirements on the information that voters need to provide to register and cast their ballots in order to actively demobilize rival supporters continues to be a significant problem in the United States – and, in many ways, has been getting worse in recent years.

Indeed, while the focus of this book is on how authoritarian leaders retain power, it is worth keeping in mind that the current democratic recession has hit a wide range of countries – including consolidated democracies. Most notably, in 2016 the Economist Intelligence Unit (EIU) downgraded the United States of America from a 'full democracy' to a 'flawed democracy' on the basis of falling trust in key democratic institutions and elected officials.[58] Significantly – and as the report of the EIU was at pains to point out – this fall was not 'a consequence of Donald Trump', who took office after the end of the year under review;[59] even before he became president, American democracy was decaying. As a result, the lessons contained within the pages of this book are not just relevant for the 'developing world' or 'third wave' countries: pro-democracy campaigners in the United States and Europe may also, unfortunately, find them useful in the years to come.

A final advantage of framing our discussion in a more comparative and historical manner is that it opens up the possibility of learning about how countries that have become considerably more democratic over time have been able to bring election rigging under control, and the conditions that make it harder to sustain authoritarian rule.

Strengthening democracy

The findings of this book highlight the fragile nature of elections – and the importance of not conflating regimes that hold sham elections with regimes that are genuinely democratic. They also demonstrate the role that the international community often plays in legitimizing and sustaining authoritarian governments, despite the constant rhetoric of support for human rights.

The fragility of elections in so many different parts of the world raises one of the most important questions of our time: what can be done to strengthen democracy? If we are to prevent elections from being manipulated, we will need to develop a more sophisticated understanding of the toolbox of strategies available to authoritarian leaders, and to identify new tactics that can help to prevent the image of democracy from being used to sustain dictatorship.

Although this book highlights the manipulation of democracy to sustain authoritarian rule, our message is not a defeatist one. Not all counterfeit democrats are successful. Authoritarian leaders have lost elections in a number of countries, in large part either because they failed to follow the six strategies identified here, or because they were prevented from doing so. Indeed, as we noted earlier, more-competitive authoritarian states have been shown to be more likely to experience a transfer of power and a transition to more democratic rule.

Drawing on these case studies, we explain how the quality of elections can be enhanced and established autocrats challenged. Some of the lessons are familiar. Most obviously, economic decline reduces the capacity of regimes to keep their friends close, and so undermines their hold on power. A more coherent and focused international community can adopt a firmer line on the importance of reform, eroding the capacity of leaders to win elections in advance. And the formation of united opposition coalitions – pooling resources and supporters – can generate a more resilient political machine, undermining the effectiveness of divide-and-rule strategies.

Less obviously, even heavily manipulated elections can present a significant challenge to the ruling party under certain conditions. For example, elections are far more likely to act as 'vehicles for change' when the ruling party must run with a new leader.[60] This is because authoritarian parties often struggle to manage the process of leadership succession that occurs when their leader dies, suffers ill health, is made to step down as a result of term limits, or is forced from office as a result of a scandal. As a result, 'open seat' elections in which there is no incumbent president or prime minister represent a window of opportunity for the opposition.

Finally, outgoing presidents sometimes start to think about their legacy, and do not always enjoy good relations with their successors. This means that they may be less willing to use the full range of powers at their disposal to ensure the victory of their party in the way that they did when they were running for office. The combined impact of these three processes means that opposition parties are far more likely to win power when the incumbent does not stand. One implication of this argument is that the defeat of established authoritarians has as much to do with internal mismanagement within the ruling party as the strength and unity of the opposition. Elections are sometimes won by the opposition, but given the advantages of incumbency, they are most often lost.

Of course, there is no guarantee that a victorious opposition party will necessarily be more democratic than the government it replaces. But, in some cases, a change of government facilitates a period of political reform, with long-term improvements in the quality of both elections and democracy.

This is a fight worth engaging in even if one is ambivalent about the value of democracy for its own sake, or the importance of elections. As we discuss at greater length in the conclusion, a growing body of research has demonstrated that competitive elections may encourage a number of positive trends, such as state provision of education and investment in other public services, in regions as diverse as Latin America and sub-Saharan Africa.[61] Encouraging better-quality and more-open elections therefore promises to generate important benefits in areas ranging from human rights to development.

But before we embark on that discussion, we need to answer a deceptively simple and extremely important question: how do you rig an election?

Chapter 1

INVISIBLE RIGGING

How to steal an election without getting caught

The smartest way to rig an election is to do so before the ballots have even been printed. If you have to resort to rigging with henchmen and ballot boxes, you've already failed. Today, the most effective autocrats steal elections well before polling day.

Russia's politicians learnt this lesson long ago. In the 1998 St Petersburg local assembly elections, incumbent Oleg Sergeyev proved to be quite a thorn in the side of Governor Vladimir Yakovlev and challenged his political dominance. A populist operating in a semi-authoritarian political system, Yakovlev did not take opposition lightly. Knowing that the country's limited civil society and inconsistently implemented rule of law would not stand in his way, he allegedly moved to neutralize those who sought to oppose him. Thus, when Sergeyev launched his re-election bid, he was surprised to learn the names of two of his opponents: Oleg Sergeyev and Oleg Sergeyev. The former was a pensioner, the latter an unemployed man. Neither had any qualifications for the office they were seeking. But they had been handpicked for one key characteristic: their names. When voters arrived in the ballot box, they were unsure which Sergeyev was their candidate of choice. Many cast ballots for the 'wrong' Sergeyev, exactly as was intended.[1]

There is a sort of amusingly ingenious quality to this form of rigging, but pre-election rigging is rarely funny. As we will see in the chapters to come, counterfeit democrats use a wide range of strategies to hold onto power that have negative social and political impacts, including vote buying (chapter 2) and violence (chapter 3). Indeed, before the recruitment of the two decoy Oleg Sergeyevs, the tactics used against their namesake were far more sinister. Unnamed men attacked Sergeyev with rubber truncheons and left him for dead. He survived, barely, and spent two months in hospital recovering from broken ribs and a fractured skull. When the regime failed to kill him or scare him into withdrawing, it sought out people who shared his name.[2]

In the same election, the government also aimed to stop other candidates from qualifying for the ballot. Election rules required each candidate to provide sufficient signatures to show that he or she had popular support. This meant that to prevent a candidate from appearing on the ballot, all you needed to do was block them from obtaining enough names. To that end, thugs affiliated with the ruling party attacked a woman in a lift as she was collecting signatures on behalf of a poet who planned to run for public office. Knocked unconscious, when she came to she found that her ribs were broken but she still had her purse: all that was missing was the folder of signatures she had already collected.[3]

Such brazen attempts at election rigging continue to be employed in a number of countries where leaders face a particularly strong opposition or feel empowered to ignore domestic and international criticism, but they represent a high-risk and high-cost option because they are visible and obvious. Everyone knew that Oleg Sergeyev had been beaten; his wounds offered a visible testimony to the lengths that the regime would go to in order to win. Everyone voting, seeing the three Oleg Sergeyevs on the ballot paper, knew what game the ruling party was trying to play. And international election monitors do not have a difficult time condemning elections when innocent volunteers are getting beaten up in elevators.[4]

But counterfeit democrats have other strategies at their disposal that are less visible, and they use these to make sure that the opposition has to compete with one hand tied behind its back. To understand which approach such leaders choose to follow, it is important to think of the six strategies identified in the introduction as an interchangeable set of tools that can be deployed in various combinations to get the job done. Those seeking to rig elections have a number of different tricks up their sleeves, and tend to choose between them by calculating across two different axes. First, how likely is it that the rigging will be detected and punished? Second, how likely is it that the rigging will ensure victory?

When it comes to the sweet spot of pre-election rigging tactics, the optimal strategies are those that can be done subtly and legally but will nonetheless ensure victory. The worst forms of pre-election manipulation are easily detected, illegal, and have little impact. The savviest regimes stay away from these while continually reinventing new ways to tip the scales in their favour without anyone noticing. In other words, effective rigging ensures that you win and that you get away with it without losing legitimacy. Such tactics include manipulating the electoral register, blocking certain candidates from running in elections, and playing with electoral boundaries to maximize partisan gains. What all of these tactics have in common is that they can be deployed months in advance of an election when observers are likely to be thin on the ground, and they can be presented as technical or legal decisions as opposed to political skulduggery. When these mechanisms are effectively put in place, governments can win elections unfairly without attracting any of the negative attention – criticism, sanctions, international prosecutions – that inevitably result from the use of other, cruder strategies in the dictator's toolbox.

It is important to note that, like some of the other forms of malpractice described in this book, these forms of rigging have a long history. In many cases, the blueprint for how to abuse the advantages of incumbency enjoyed by ruling parties was laid down in Western countries that are now considered to be consolidated democracies.

'Rotten boroughs' – electoral districts that deliberately included a tiny number of voters who were all dependent on a single landlord – were common in the United Kingdom in the early 1800s. The most notorious example of these was Old Sarum, which had no resident voters at all. Instead, the owner of the land used his right to nominate tenants to reside in certain properties known as 'burgage tenements', which conferred on them the right to vote. In 1831, there were only eleven voters in the whole constituency.

The tiny electorate, and the fact that Old Sarum's voters were dependent on their landlord, ensured that the landlord would always be elected to parliament. For many years in the 1700s, the borough was owned by the Pitt family, and elected William Pitt the Elder, who was prime minister in the 1760s.[5] When the Pitt family finally decided to sell the land, it fetched £60,000, even though it was worth much less; in effect, this was the price not of the territory, but of the parliamentary seat that came with it.

As set out in the introduction, we discuss these historical cases not because these countries are counterfeit democracies today, but to explain how certain kinds of rigging came into being and have evolved over time. The past has much to tell us about how we can combat electoral manipulation in the future.

How to rig without getting caught

If you wanted to take a masterclass in subtle and legal pre-election rigging, you might want to travel to the United States. Despite being seen as the world's most powerful democracy,

America is where many of the rigging techniques used today were perfected, and continue to exert a powerful legacy. This is particularly true of two of the most tried and tested methods for establishing a pre-electoral advantage: gerrymandering and voter suppression.

Elbridge Gerry, after whom gerrymandering is named, was born in Massachusetts in 1744, decades before the United States broke away from imperial England. By the age of eighteen, he had become a cod trader, selling fish in the local market. Ten years later, though, talk of revolution prompted him to successfully angle for a spot on the colony's 'general court'.[6] In 1776, at the height of the Revolutionary War, Gerry participated in the Continental Congress in Philadelphia, the founding convention of the United States of America.

Over the next decade he played an important role in the country's political development, and in 1789 his presence in the Constitutional Convention was essential to the system of checks and balances that Americans still use today. Gerry refused to sign the original Constitution draft without a Bill of Rights. He lost that battle in 1789 when the Constitution was agreed without one, but he won the war two years later when the Bill of Rights was finally adopted. It is partly thanks to Gerry that Americans formally enjoy codified liberties like freedom of speech and freedom of the press.

Indeed, the future US president John Adams was so impressed by Gerry's performance in Philadelphia that he wrote: 'If every man here was a Gerry, the liberties of America would be safe against the gates of Earth and Hell.'[7] Perhaps, but later many people did copy Gerry when it came to their approach to elections, and the liberties of American voters have been far worse for it. Sadly for Gerry, his best-known legacy is not as the founding father of the Bill of Rights, but as the founding father of American election rigging. In 1810, he was elected governor of Massachusetts. At that point, the United States was still a very young and fragile democracy, and like many of the other countries that feature in this book, the rule of law was weak and vote buying was rife. Gerry's party, Thomas Jefferson's Democratic-Republicans, faced stiff competition in the 1812 elections from Alexander Hamilton's party, the Federalists. In anticipation of the election, the state party in Massachusetts came up with an electoral map that packed Federalists into a handful of areas to maximize the gains of the Democratic-Republicans in the state senate.

The district boundaries were so distorted, however, that people noticed. The 26 March 1812 edition of the *Boston Gazette* featured a cartoon of one newly created district in the form of a fork-tongued, winged salamander, captioned 'THE GERRY-MANDER: A new species of *Monster* . . .' The portmanteau word stuck, and would overshadow all of Gerry's other achievements – which was a bit unfair, as Gerry reportedly did not even come up with the district maps, and instead is said to have called them 'highly disagreeable' before grudgingly signing them into law.[8]

Nonetheless, the tactic worked beautifully – at least in the short term. Across the state, the Federalists received 1,602 more votes than the Democratic-Republicans. It was a narrow margin, but clearly a verdict against Gerry's party. Yet because of the distorted district boundaries, the Federalists won just eleven of the state's forty districts. In the longer term, however, the strategy caused Gerry considerable problems. Most notably, the high-profile attempt to distort the will of voters generated an intense backlash. Gerry was defeated in his re-election bid, largely as a result of having being tainted by this obvious attempt at manipulation. He bounced back, though, and went on to become James Madison's vice-president before dying in office in 1814 at the age of seventy.[9]

Gerrymandering subsequently became a feature of a number of political systems around the world, especially those in which lower levels of media coverage and public scrutiny have enabled it to pass under the radar. Indeed, even in the United States itself, a more sophisticated and subtle form of gerrymandering continues to operate, shaping electoral outcomes with significant consequences for the quality of American democracy.[10]

The problems caused by distorted electoral boundaries are well demonstrated by a paradox that overshadows every congressional election. Opinion polls consistently show that Congress is viewed favourably by just 10 to 20 per cent of the American population. That is about the same favourability rating as cockroaches (yes, polls have asked the public about their attitudes towards cockroaches).[11] But even with that dismal popular sentiment, only 8 incumbents out of a body of 435 representatives lost their re-election bids in 2016.[12] This is one of the lowest turnover rates in the world – much lower than the equivalent figure in legislatures in sub-Saharan Africa that are by other measures considered to be significantly less democratic.

This is, of course, partly due to gerrymandered districts drawn by partisan legislatures. Allowing those in power to determine the boundaries of the seats that they contest is the electoral equivalent of allowing foxes to guard henhouses. As a result, many district maps resemble inkblots rather than coherent geographical groupings. In Illinois, for example, the 4th congressional district is nicknamed 'the Latin Earmuffs', because it connects two predominantly Latino areas by a thin line that is just one road wide in parts.[13] In so doing, it packs Democrats as tightly as possible into a contorted district, giving Republicans a chance to win surrounding districts even though they are vastly outnumbered. The net result is a weakening of the power of the Latino vote and more Republican-electing districts than the electoral maths should reasonably allow.

The overall impact of these historical legacies is controversial. Some recent political science literature argues that the partisan composition of the United States House of Representatives is not swayed considerably by gerrymandering. This is not because it does not distort the will of the electorate, but because the distortion in favour of Democrats in some areas and Republicans in others balances out across the whole country, such that national political outcomes remain broadly fair.[14] Moreover, it has been suggested that calculating political design might have less of an effect on geographical clustering of voters than selection bias – the idea that like-minded people tend to live in partisan pockets partly because they do similar jobs and enjoy spending time with each other, which explains some of the differences between, say, rural New York and New York City.[15]

Economic factors, popular tastes and migration patterns are, of course, part of the explanation of contemporary election outcomes in the United States. It is also true that some of these abuses cancel themselves out. But to leave the story at that would be woefully incomplete and inadequate. Other more recent empirical studies, such as a May 2016 analysis from the Brennan Center for Justice, find that partisan gerrymandering actually does favour one side over the other. More specifically, electoral distortions deliver a net benefit of between sixteen and seventeen seats to Republicans that they would not otherwise win were districts drawn in a non-partisan fashion.[16] This is a major effect: the current Republican majority would become a Democratic one if just twenty-four seats shifted parties.

Moreover, these national impacts are generated by just a small number of states in which one party wields disproportionate influence. According to the Brennan Center's quantitative analysis, some of the most starkly gerrymandered seats come from just three states – North Carolina, Michigan and Pennsylvania. The remaining net seat gains for the Republicans come from Florida, Ohio, Texas and Virginia. On the Democratic side of the ledger, the worst offenders are Massachusetts, Maryland and, to a lesser extent, Illinois. However, the net shift from those three states is much smaller than the swings produced in the Republican states. In effect, then, less than one-quarter of American states are distorting the partisan composition of the national legislature.

These ten states have another feature in common: their redistricting process is solely controlled by one party. In other words, elected officials from the Democrats or Republicans get a chance to pick their voters. This is important because it highlights the fact that whether the net effect of gerrymandering in the United States is considerably skewed towards Republicans or not, the practice has dire consequences for the character of democracy. By drawing district lines in a self-interested manner, voters have far less of a say in who represents them and politicians are less accountable to the people they are supposed to represent.

That is bad news for democracy beyond the question of who wins power at the national level. For democratic accountability to work, voters must be able to 'kick out the bums'. In turn, this requires that most elections be competitive – if they are not, then politicians can carry on regardless, safe in the knowledge that they will not lose their seats. But in the 2016 election to the US House of Representatives, the average margin of victory was 37.1 per cent.[17] In other words, the average House election involved one candidate getting close to 70 per cent of the vote, with their rival finishing with just over 30 per cent. This is a remarkable statistic that seems more in keeping with sham elections in North Korea or Russia than those of the world's most powerful democracy.

The lack of competition in the 2016 election is brought home if we look at the number of races that were closely fought. Out of a total of 435 House contests, only 17 were decided by margins of 5 per cent or less, and only 18 others were within a margin of 10 per cent.[18] That means that 400 out of 435 representatives were elected in something approaching a landslide. Indeed, most outcomes were foregone conclusions before ballots were even printed. In some cases, there is effectively no contest at all, as in 2016, when there was no competitive House of Representatives election in forty-two of the fifty American states. This was not purely due to gerrymandering of course – America's urban–rural divide shapes this reality, while several states that have only one representative cannot be gerrymandered because the district's lines are just the state boundaries. But these caveats notwithstanding, it is startling to note how many American politicians can waltz to victory so long as they win the party primary.

Unsurprisingly, voter-turnout rates are low in US legislative polls; in the 2014 congressional midterm elections only 36 per cent of those registered went to the polls (see appendix 10 for global voter-turnout trends). This means that nearly two-thirds of Americans didn't cast a ballot in determining the composition of the United States House of Representatives and United States Senate. But to an extent, it's understandable in the context of uncompetitive elections. Why bother to vote if you already know who will win?

If politicians can get away with gerrymandering in a country in which politics is as open and well covered as the United States, it is hardly surprising that it has become a popular electoral strategy of governments in more-authoritarian contexts. One of the most striking examples of this comes from Zimbabwe, where Robert Mugabe spent much of his last twenty years as president – before being finally toppled by a military coup in 2017[19] – searching for new ways to defeat the opposition and consolidate his political control.

It did not start this way. In the 1980s, Mugabe was widely viewed as a stable and forward-thinking leader dedicated to getting the basics of governance right. Having won power as a result of a liberation struggle against Ian Smith's white minority regime, he was seen as both a nationalist hero and a leader willing to manage the demands of war veterans for land redistribution in a way that did not undermine agricultural productivity or economic growth. As a result, Mugabe was awarded a number of honorary degrees from respected universities, received an honorary knighthood from the British state, and even won an award from the Hunger Project – a New York-based philanthropic organization – for making Zimbabwe the 'agricultural success story' of Africa.[20]

However, by the early 2000s, Mugabe's government was coming under increasing pressure from both inside and outside Zimbabwe. Internally, older party leaders were accused of being out of touch by younger rivals. Externally, worsening economic conditions, criticism from veterans of the liberation war that land redistribution was proceeding too slowly, and the evolution of the Movement for Democratic Change (MDC) opposition, proved to be a potent combination.[21] Mugabe's government responded by implementing a number of different strategies including political violence (chapter 3), political exclusion and gerrymandering.

Ahead of the 2008 election, the MDC had built up a head of steam. Although it was fast expanding into some peri-urban and rural areas, the opposition's strongest support came from cities where people had greater access to information and education, and where the ruling party could not rely on traditional leaders to control voters.[22] Armed with this knowledge, the government attempted to manipulate the legislative elections in its favour. In January 2008, a delimitation report on redrawing legislative boundaries by the Elections Directorate was presented to parliament. It proposed redrawing the electoral map to increase the number of House of Assembly seats from 120 to 210. Of these new electoral units, the vast majority were located in rural areas. For example, sixty-two of the ninety new House of Assembly constituencies were located outside of the main towns, and while Bulawayo, the country's second-largest city, was allocated only twelve seats, rural provinces such as Mashonaland East, Mashonaland West, Masvingo and Manicaland all gained more than twenty.[23]

The impact of these changes was well understood by the opposition. According to Ian Makone, who helped to run the MDC's campaign, 'our elections directorate has established that of the 210 constituencies in the House of Assembly, 143 are rural constituencies while just 67 are urban and peri-urban constituencies. So technically speaking ZANU–PF already has the crucial two-thirds majority in the Lower House before a single vote is cast.'[24]

In the event, this prediction turned out to be false. The great momentum behind the MDC propelled the party to a slim majority in the legislature and a lead in the first round of presidential voting. But ZANU–PF ultimately prevented the MDC from taking power through a combination of political violence and its ability to reassert control over the legislature. In a free and fair poll, the MDC leader Morgan Tsvangirai would have won the absolute majority of the vote needed for a first-round victory, and his party would have secured a dominant position within parliament. In the event, brutal repression forced Tsvangirai to pull out of the second round of the presidential election, while gerrymandering enabled the government to win enough seats to prevent the opposition from using the legislature to create a fairer political system.

This was critical to the gradual reassertion of ZANU–PF hegemony. Although domestic and international condemnation of the widespread use of political violence ultimately forced the regime to enter into negotiations and accept a power-sharing arrangement, in which Tsvangirai was given the post of prime minister and the MDC was awarded half of the posts within the cabinet, ZANU–PF was able to use its control of the presidency and its disproportionately strong showing within the legislature to block investigations into the electoral violence and the reform of the security forces. Indeed, although Mugabe has now gone, the party remains in power today.

ZANU–PF is not alone in attempting to secure a pre-election advantage through gerrymandering. Indeed, this strategy is remarkably common across competitive authoritarian states, with notable examples in Kenya, Malawi, Zambia and much of Latin America, which, in the 1990s, featured 'some of the world's most malapportioned legislative chambers' including in Argentina, Chile, Ecuador and Venezuela.[25] In Asia, one of the worst offenders is Malaysia, which has used gerrymandering to systematically benefit the ruling party.[26]

Fixing the electorate

Although gerrymandering is widely used, there is a limit to the kinds of government that it can keep in power, because it is essentially a scheme for fixing legislative elections. If a president is elected nationally, it is impossible to gerrymander because the electoral borders are simply those of the whole country. Gerrymandering is therefore extremely useful in parliamentary systems in which the party that wins the most seats earns the right to form the government, but much less effective in countries where a directly elected president wields ultimate power. This is significant, because the proportion of countries in the world that are presidential has increased over time, from around 25 per cent in the 1970s to over 50 per cent today, in part because this has been the overwhelming choice of political system for new democracies.[27]

In these countries, gerrymandering can help the executive to ensure a more favourable legislature, as in Zimbabwe, but – unless some form of electoral college is used – it cannot secure the top job itself. This means that leaders must look for alternative strategies that can give them an edge without generating too much resistance. One option to supplement gerrymandering is voter suppression, another form of electoral manipulation that was perfected in the United States, where politicians have long understood that even if you cannot pick your voters, you may be able to determine who can make their voices heard. In particular, Republicans have shown themselves to be extremely skilled at limiting the voting power of impoverished minorities – citizens who tend to vote overwhelmingly for the Democrats.

This aspect of American democracy has an ugly history. After slavery ended, Jim Crow laws in the southern United States long ensured that black citizens were unable to vote. As recently as 1964, African American voters in Louisiana were subjected to a nonsensical twenty-three-question 'literacy test' that even well-educated people would fail.[28] The test was designed to be a string of 'gotcha!' questions: 'Print the word vote upside down, but in the correct order'; 'Draw a figure that is square in shape. Divide it in half by drawing a straight line from its northeast corner to its southwest corner, and then divide it once more by drawing a broken line from the middle of its western side to the middle of its eastern side.' A single mistake – even on a technicality – would result in an African American voter being turned away from the polls. In 2014, a group of Harvard students were given the same test used in the 1960s in Louisiana. All of them failed.[29]

Jim Crow laws are gone thanks to the 1965 Voting Rights Act but their modern equivalent is the voter identification laws that disproportionately disenfranchise minority voters. In the United States, voting patterns skew considerably according to ethnicity. This is true not just for turnout rates but also for party affiliation. For example, Hispanic Americans vote at much lower rates than white Americans; 48 per cent of eligible Hispanic voters cast ballots in 2012, compared to 64.1 per cent of white voters.[30] Estimates are similar for 2016.

There are also major partisan skews that occur with striking regularity. Most notably, African American voters overwhelmingly support the Democratic Party. In 2012, 95 per cent of black voters cast their ballots for Barack Obama. That figure dipped slightly in 2016, when 88 per cent of black voters backed Hillary Clinton, but Donald Trump still only earned the votes of just 8 per cent of that demographic group. This distribution holds true, although to a lesser extent, for Hispanic voters. In 2012, 68 per cent of Hispanic voters backed President Obama's re-election campaign; in 2016, their support for Hillary Clinton was estimated at 66 per cent.[31] With such clear-cut ethnicity-based divisions, it is obvious that Republicans benefit when minority groups stay home on election day; for Democrats, the opposite is true.

Enter voter identification laws. In the United States, thirty-four states have some sort of voter identification law, and eleven of those states have strict identification laws.[32] These are in place, purportedly, to stop fraudulent voting. However, audit after audit of voting in the United States fails to show any evidence of systematic or widespread voter fraud. In the 2016 presidential election, Donald Trump falsely claimed that millions of people voted illegally. This is simply not true. In a post-election audit in North Carolina, for example, the review uncovered only one case of fraudulent in-person voting out of millions of ballots cast.[33] Nonetheless, Republicans continue to press for ever-stricter voting laws that will do little to combat a non-existent problem, but will do an enormous amount to deter groups that tend to vote Democrat from showing up and casting their ballots.

In states with strict voter identification laws, it is impossible to vote without a valid photo identity card. This may not seem like a burden at first glance, but most Americans do not have an ID card unless they have a driver's licence or a passport. Poor people disproportionately have neither, because they are far less likely to own cars and far less likely to travel internationally. As a result, some poor voters may not be willing to spend the time or incur the cost of obtaining an identity card simply to vote. Therefore, strict voter identification laws, operating in tandem with a system that does not provide automatic and free identity cards to everyone, can act like a voting tax on poor people.

Recent studies have convincingly demonstrated that these regulations are indeed effective when it comes to suppressing minority participation. In general elections, Hispanic voters are 10 per cent less likely to turn out in states with strict voter identification laws than in states without them. Similar declines occur in primaries, where turnout is already often minuscule. These laws do not just serve to 'diminish minority participation but also to increase the gap in the participation rate between whites and nonwhites'.[34] In other words, such stipulations systematically amplify the power of white voices while diminishing that of others. Across ethnic lines, people who identify as Republican are significantly less likely to be adversely affected by voter identification laws than Democrats. In short, this system makes it more likely that Republicans will win elections.

We cannot say exactly how this has affected election outcomes, because it is extremely difficult to estimate precisely who would vote under more amenable conditions, but it is possible to get a sense of the kind of effect that restrictive rules have. Take Wisconsin, a state that recently enacted strict voter identification requirements. In 2016, Donald Trump won that state narrowly, by roughly 30,000 votes. However, 300,000 Wisconsinites lacked the voter identification necessary to vote on election day and so would have been turned away from the polls had they tried to vote.[35] Moreover, 60,000 fewer people voted around Milwaukee – an area with the largest concentration of black voters in the state – than participated in 2012, when more-open laws were in operation. Although it is impossible to say for certain what the result would have been, it is plausible that had these people voted, Trump would have lost the state.

Like gerrymandering, voter suppression is a strategy that has travelled around the world. In competitive authoritarian states across Africa, Asia, Latin America and the Middle East, governments deliberately make it hard to vote, using their control over identification documents to keep opposition supporters off the electoral register.[36] The classic way of doing this is to require citizens to hold a national identity card in order to be able to register and vote. Once this stipulation is in place, governments can restrict or promote the awarding of IDs, effectively acting as gatekeepers of electoral participation.

As in the US, such a strategy is particularly effective if there are clear socioeconomic groups and areas that can be expected to back the opposition. For example, in a host of African countries including Kenya, Malawi and Tanzania, opposition leaders have alleged that the government has deliberately made it difficult for their supporters to procure IDs by requiring them to do so in person, and locating registration centres far away from opposition strongholds.[37] This strategy can then be supplemented in the run-up to elections by implementing a similar strategy when it comes to voter registration, making it harder for those opposition supporters who have received their IDs to access registration centres and to make it onto the electoral roll.

Again, Zimbabwe offers a prime example of how the ruling party can block the 'wrong' kind of voters. In addition to gerrymandering, ZANU–PF has implemented a number of strategies designed to depress and punish opposition voters. Limiting the distribution of ID cards in opposition areas, while making these IDs essential for access to certain state services, undermines the capacity of the opposition to vote and thus their ability to be fairly represented. Although precise figures are hard to come by, civil society groups estimate that as a result of ZANU–PF's deliberate drives to increase the proportion of citizens with ID cards in its strongholds, those living there are considerably more likely to have an ID than those living in MDC-supporting areas – despite the fact that opposition supporters tend to be better educated and to live in more urban areas.[38]

Moreover, in the last few years there have been rumours that the quest for political dominance has led the ruling party to pursue more drastic measures. According to recent reports, one in three Zimbabwean children does not have a birth certificate, and there are some schools in pro-MDC areas where almost no children have birth certificates at all.[39] Given that these documents are required to gain ID cards, this would effectively disenfranchise an entire generation of opposition supporters. The rise in the number of children without documentation is partly related to a policy enacted in some hospitals that has denied birth certificates to mothers unable to pay a fee.[40] However, this leaves open the question of why birth certificates are given out in some areas and not in others.

In July 2017, the Registrar-General Mr Tobaiwa Mudede, who has overall responsibility for recording births and deaths, was forced to deny accusations that the government was refusing to give birth certificates to people in areas with a history of resistance to ZANU–PF rule.[41] Not believing that any ruling party could be quite so cynical and forward-thinking as to plan election rigging eighteen years (the legal voting age) ahead of time, on one visit to Zimbabwe Nic arranged a meeting with a former ZANU–PF official to investigate.[42] After hearing the allegation, the official rocked back in his chair, chuckled and said, 'That I can neither confirm nor deny . . . but, you know, you have to get up very early in the morning to beat ZANU–PF.'[43]

Beyond identification checks, political parties and the lobbying groups that sometimes work for them have attempted to suppress voting through disinformation campaigns. In the Kenyan election of 2017, candidates at a number of levels were alleged to have told opposition supporters that in order to correctly cast their ballots they needed to tick the box of the candidate they wished to vote for and place crosses against the names of all the others.[44] It is hard to know how many people fell into this trap, but anyone who did would have invalidated their ballot: in reality both ticks and crosses can be used to indicate who a voter supports, and so placing a mark in more than one box leads to the ballot paper being rejected.

Once again, the use of these strategies is not confined to the world's autocracies. Similar strategies have been employed in the United States by unofficial interest groups operating on behalf of specific parties. These manipulation tactics are often particularly appealing because they come with plausible deniability built in: the candidate or political party can easily claim that it did not orchestrate any misinformation campaigns itself. Take, for example, a 2008 effort in Virginia to suppress the Democratic vote. A flyer, printed on official-seeming paper with a fake letterhead from the State Board of Elections, told citizens that 'due to larger than expected turnout', Republicans should plan to vote on 4 November but Democrats 'shall vote on November 5 as adopted by emergency regulation of the Virginia General Assembly'.[45] The election, of course, was held on 4 November. There is no way of knowing how many people were duped by the flyers and did not show up to the polls. It was probably a fairly small figure, but it could have been significant. Similarly, in the 2010 governors' race in Maryland, the campaign manager for the Republican candidate sought to reduce the turnout in favour of his rival by approving calls to African American precincts urging residents not to vote by saying that their favoured candidate – a Democrat – was on track to win without their help: 'Everything's fine. The only thing left is to watch it on TV tonight.'[46]

Such misinformation campaigns are difficult to track, but they probably disenfranchise a small number of voters. As with many savvy manipulations, though, their low-profile nature means that it is difficult to say how effective they are at flipping outcomes.

Political exclusion

Voters are much more likely to be excluded from elections than candidates, but this does not mean that ruling parties do not also try to prevent their rivals from standing. Although you might think that it would be impossible to get away with excluding an election rival, this is actually a fairly common rigging strategy in states where authoritarian legacies live on and where more sophisticated strategies cannot be trusted to get the job done. Indeed, authoritarian incumbents often try to legitimize electoral exclusion by manipulating the rule of law, which helps to explain why it is not always condemned by election monitors.

Take Madagascar for example, a country with a democratic tradition far less robust than that of the United States. As one of the poorest countries on Earth, the Malagasy government is extremely weak.[47] Its ability to manipulate elections in sophisticated ways is hampered by the fact that even the provision of basic administrative functions on the rugged island poses a challenge. The government certainly does not have detailed computer models to help determine how best to gerrymander, nor do they need to.

Instead, Madagascar's self-serving politicians have frequently found new ways to use the letter of the law to undermine the spirit of democracy. In recent years, that effort has taken the form of an increasingly common type of election rigging: electoral exclusion, or the practice of illegitimately ensuring that a certain candidate is disqualified from being put on the ballot. After all, if your opponent's name is excluded, it is pretty much impossible for them to win.[48] In this sense, neutralizing a prospective challenger with a single disqualification ruling represents the most effective form of pre-election manipulation, and the cheapest.[49]

Perhaps nobody has learnt that lesson so well as the former president Marc Ravalomanana, who ruled the island from 2002 to 2009. Ravalomanana's rags-to-riches story was an inspiring one – a businessman who built a highly successful dairy empire from humble beginnings, selling yogurt off the back of a single bicycle. But in 2006, Ravalomanana's re-election prospects faced a stiff challenge from Pierrot Rajaonarivelo, a former deputy prime minister. Ravalomanana had previously forced Rajaonarivelo into exile for political reasons. While he was abroad, the president's rival had built up a core of political support in opposition to Ravalomanana. So when the elections approached, Rajaonarivelo announced his intention to stand as a presidential candidate in a bid to unseat the dairy kingpin. But first, he would need to return to the island.

Under Malagasy election law, candidates are only eligible to run for office if they have applied for candidacy in person – in Madagascar. As a result, Rajaonarivelo took the logical step: he booked flights home in an effort to end his exile and run for president. The deadline for filing the correct paperwork was 14 October 2006. On 6 October, Rajaonarivelo boarded a flight from Paris to Madagascar via the neighbouring island of Réunion. The second leg of his flight was supposed to land at Toamasina airport on Madagascar's east coast, an area of strong support for Rajaonarivelo's candidacy. Supporters turned up at the airport, ready to welcome their party leader home. Instead, they were confronted with tear gas. At the same time, President Ravalomanana unilaterally closed the Toamasina airport to all air traffic, and Rajaonarivelo's flight was turned back due to the 'security risk' on board.[50]

Five days later, Rajaonarivelo tried again – this time coming from the island of Mauritius. However, at the request of Madagascar's government, Air Mauritius refused to allow him to board his plane. As a result of direct intervention on the part of President Ravalomanana, Rajaonarivelo was unable to return in time to file the paperwork required for his presidential bid. His candidacy was officially rejected on 18 October by a court that simply upheld the strict letter of the law: nobody can run for president of Madagascar unless they file their paperwork in person and on time.[51]

With his main rival disqualified and once again exiled, Ravalomanana coasted to an easy victory. The election was a landslide: he beat his nearest challenger by a margin of more than 40 per cent. Crucially, too, the international community endorsed the poll.[52] After all, they reasoned, the court that disqualified Rajaonarivelo was merely upholding the law. Ravalomanana got his cake and ate it too: he rigged the election by excluding his most serious threat from the ballot and escaped international condemnation for a blatant manipulation of the contest.

There are dozens of other examples of electoral exclusion across the globe, from Iran's handpicked lists of 'approved' candidates,[53] to candidates in Côte d'Ivoire being disqualified on the basis of trumped-up charges that their parents have dubious birth certificates.[54] In all of these instances, the logic is the same: employ a targeted form of rigging to remove the candidate from the ballot and thereby eliminate the need to worry about their supporters. In the vast majority of cases where this practice has been identified, leaders have sought to use the courts to legitimize their actions, as in Madagascar. However, it is important to acknowledge that electoral exclusion, taken to extremes, may involve the deployment of the most intense forms of political violence, and in some cases death (chapter 3).

The broader impact of electoral exclusion

Electoral exclusion is profoundly damaging, because in addition to undermining the prospects for opposition parties it distorts the incentives that politicians have to be inclusive and to appeal to a broad base. To see why, let's perform a simple thought experiment: how would contemporary American politicians behave if we changed the level of political competition that they face?

Representatives contesting safe seats have little incentive to compromise with the other party. In fact, they have a strong disincentive to compromise. For example, in districts that are predominantly Republican, compromising with the Democrats is likely to increase the prospects that an incumbent will face a strong challenge from a more hardline Republican in the subsequent party primary contest. In other words, for a moderate Republican in a safe, uncompetitive district, the greatest electoral threat comes not from a Democratic challenger, who has no realistic chance of victory, but from a further-right challenger from within their own party. Of course, the inverse is also true in districts that are overwhelmingly filled with Democratic voters.

Under these conditions, the rational electoral strategy for leaders to pursue is to move away from the middle ground in order to protect themselves from being outflanked. Unsurprisingly, over time this basic logic makes it harder for moderates to get elected and hold their seats. This is a significant – though not necessarily the most important – source of the much-discussed process of political polarization in the United States.[55] For example, research conducted in 2014 found clear evidence that 'the more competitive the race, the more moderate is the voting record of the winning candidate in the next session of Congress'.[56] Similarly, a paper published in the *American Journal of Political Science* in 2009 concluded that levels of polarization were probably higher in gerrymandered districts than would be likely under 'neutral districting procedures'[57] – albeit not by that much. It therefore seems reasonable to conclude that politics is a little more likely to be consensus- and compromise-driven if districts are not distorted to guarantee that the incumbent can be re-elected like clockwork.

Worse, gerrymandering also alienates voters – which leads to decreased turnout and a sense of powerlessness. After all, if you live in a district where the result is a foregone conclusion in favour of the incumbent, why even bother voting? Many people do not, and this is part of the reason why the turnout in America's 2014 midterm congressional elections was so low.[58] No democracy can function properly if only a little over a third of eligible voters are casting ballots. The United States is no exception, and the sense of political alienation that presaged the rise of Donald Trump can certainly be partly traced to this sense of powerlessness in the democratic system.

If gerrymandering has this profound impact on the quality of the political process in the United States, the consequences can be even more severe in divided societies with a history of political violence and winner-takes-all politics. One of the problems in countries such as India, Kenya and Thailand is that all too often leaders explicitly promise to favour their own ethnic, religious or regional groups in the distribution of state resources.[59] What these countries need in order to build more-inclusive and stable political systems is leaders willing to compromise and listen to the needs and concerns of citizens from rival parties and communities.

It is for this reason that legal scholar and political scientist Donald Horowitz has proposed that countries with high levels of intercommunal tension should adopt a form of electoral system – the alternative vote (AV) – that provides leaders with incentives to attract a broader cross-section of support.[60] The AV system does this by allowing voters to rank candidates by preference, and redistributing their votes if their first-choice candidate comes last. In other words, candidates cannot simply rely on their own group to get elected – they have to try to position themselves as the second choice of other groups too. As a result, the cost of offending rival voters is considerably increased, providing a strong incentive – theoretically at least – for moderation.

Although not everyone agrees that Horowitz's model works in practice,[61] far fewer disagree with his assessment of the challenge. The problem with gerrymandering is that it tends to undermine precisely this kind of consensus-driven politics. By generating districts that are skewed towards a single partisan group, politicians have every incentive to ignore the will of other groups within the district. As a result, gerrymandering tends to encourage just the kind of winner-takes-all politics in divided societies that has been associated with political violence and ethnic conflict.[62]

Electoral exclusion can also be a driver of a broader range of social and political ills. As we shall see in chapter 3, the systematic exclusion of candidates and voters from certain backgrounds can undermine their confidence in the political system. In turn, this may lead disgruntled factions to disengage from the state or, worse still, to take up arms against it. This is a significant source of concern, because electoral exclusion is more common than you might think. Between 1989 and 2012, opposition candidates were excluded in 12 per cent of all elections.[63] Moreover, in specific regions the situation is much worse: electoral exclusion is a feature of one in three elections in the Middle East, one in four in post-Soviet states, and one in five in Asia.

Strengthening democracy by defeating 'invisible rigging'

Given the prevalence of 'invisible rigging', it is important to contest these forms of electoral manipulation. Of course, doing so is never simple. In the cat-and-mouse game between election watchers and election cheats, both the cats and the mice learn to adapt. Along with structural barriers to political reform, this can make it extremely difficult to improve the quality of the electoral process. Take the case of gerrymandering in the United States: this is difficult to protest because it is the result of redistricting processes which occur only once every ten years. For elections occurring in between these dates, there is no obvious flashpoint to protest, no obvious manipulation to try to defeat through democratic means. It is harder to take to the streets over the contours of district lines than it is to protest a specific policy under consideration. But even so, there are fixes to make the task more difficult for those who would rig elections well before polling stations open.

To avoid Russian name games such as the scheme used against Oleg Sergeyev, candidates should be listed on ballots along with their photographs and ideally their party affiliation, or if there is no party, their profession. Few people in St Petersburg would have accidentally voted for the guy who works at Tram Park Number Four if they were aware of that fact. But of course, entrenched authoritarians are unlikely to permit this change unless they face concerted international and domestic pressure to do so, and this is not always viable. It is therefore important to engage in voter education to level the playing field between election riggers and voters. Democracy requires not just institutions that prevent elites from manipulating the polls, but also citizens who are educated, engaged and vigilant.

When people are knowledgeable both about the candidates and the rules of the game, it makes it harder for politicians acting in bad faith to manipulate the process by finding similarly named candidate doubles. Significantly, while in most countries voter education is officially the preserve of the electoral commission, and is done poorly as a result, opposition parties can disseminate their own information through party structures and, in more-open authoritarian systems, social media. Especially where literacy rates and internet penetration are higher, this can liberate opposition leaders from having to be dependent on state structures to communicate key electoral rules.

Contesting gerrymandering is in many ways more problematic because it is dependent on the political will of the ruling party. Where political will does exist, though, there are solutions. In the United States, several states have taken the task of redrawing electoral districts out of the hands of politicians. California and Arizona, for example, have developed independent citizen redistricting commissions that feature a balance of partisan viewpoints. Iowa has turned the task over to a non-partisan state agency, aiming to separate district boundaries from partisanship completely.[64] But although recent academic research has shown that independent commissions generate the fairest districts, few states use them.[65]

Outside the United States, many countries have put measures in place to try to avoid or mitigate gerrymandering. The Australian Electoral Commission, for instance, is an independent federal agency charged with drawing district boundaries in Australia, thereby limiting partisan influence.[66] Similarly, in India, the world's largest democracy, albeit a fragile one, the rules of the Boundary Delimitation Commission prohibit anyone with political ties from serving on the commission and state that two of the three members must be judges.[67] Increasingly, international democracy promotion organizations are focusing attention on poorly drawn electoral boundaries and have been producing best-practice guidelines to try to minimize impropriety.

There are also a growing number of technological and mathematical innovations that can be used to combat gerrymandering with more objectivity. For example, a simple new analytical tool called the 'efficiency gap', which is based on counting the number of votes each party 'wastes' in an election to determine whether one party enjoyed a systematic advantage, has been used to determine whether gerrymandering generates an overall political bias.[68] In a similar rein, Moon Duchin, a mathematician at Tufts University, has used geometric mapping to identify and expose the inkblot-like districts that are drawn according to partisan lines rather than more natural ones. Duchin's Metric Geometry and Gerrymandering Group has trained countless mathematicians in civil rights law and relevant mapping, so that they can participate as expert witnesses in gerrymandering cases in the courts.[69]

However, in counterfeit democracies it is far harder to get agreement around genuinely independent boundary commissions or technical solutions, and so it often falls to the courts to challenge egregious electoral maps. For example, in Pakistan, a counterfeit democracy rated as 'partly free' by Freedom House, the High Court of Sindh referenced international best practices from pro-democracy NGOs in a 2014 ruling that invalidated a gerrymandered district.[70] In 2015, the same court found that the Election Commission of Pakistan had breached official guidelines on electoral delimitation, deliberately skirting the rules to 'facilitate gerrymandering'.[71] In response, the court ordered several districts to be rapidly redrawn prior to the elections, issuing a warning shot that could serve as a deterrent to future attempts at malapportionment. Thus, in competitive authoritarian states where ruling parties gerrymander but courts have a degree of independence, judges may be able to play a pivotal role in undermining gerrymandering – or at least in forcing politicians to engage in it less blatantly.

Thankfully, from the United States to Pakistan to Zimbabwe, greater awareness of gerrymandering means that it is increasingly being exposed as a threat to democratic elections. Moreover, the lessons from US states, Australia and Pakistan is that there are solutions to gerrymandering. Independent election commissions that take mathematical calculations of efficiency gaps and compactness into account are ideal for majoritarian first-past-the-post systems, while the courts can be useful, stepping in if an independent commission isn't up to the task; there are also possible changes that can be made to electoral systems. In this way, new democracies can learn from old ones in determining how to build a more democratic electoral district-drawing process.

Because leaders don't usually give up power without a fight, enforcing these measures is likely to be possible only if opposition parties can forge alliances with civil society groups and harness the support of the international community to force the ruling party's hand.[72] This is problematic because, as we have already noted, international election monitors rarely place a strong emphasis on pre-electoral manipulation, which occurs well before the full set of observers have been deployed.

Curtailing gerrymandering and political exclusion therefore requires monitors to be willing to cite the background conditions under which elections occur as a reason to question their outcome. Many groups, such as the European Union, have started to do this.[73] However, at present, the findings of long-term observation still tend to inform the background sections of observers' reports, not their conclusions.[74] This needs to change if pre-electoral manipulation is to be effectively tackled: as we discuss at greater length in chapter 6, doing so will require observation missions to be bolder as well as smarter.

As part of these efforts, it would help if election observation missions were willing to make stronger statements before the polls actually open. At present, elections are occasionally condemned, but almost always after the fact. In some instances, however, such as when it is clear that no fair election could possibly take place, monitors should be willing to speak out more clearly and forcefully before votes are cast. For example, when Madagascar's government excluded a major challenger, there was no way that such an election could be conducted in accordance with basic democratic principles. Stronger pressure applied *before* elections would push regimes to allow the opposition to compete on a level playing field. Once the polls open, it is often too late.

Of course, speaking out earlier will not work everywhere, and particularly recalcitrant governments may respond to such criticism by seeking to ban international observation teams. Although this would have the obvious downside of making it harder to track subsequent abuses, it would also have a major upside, namely that it would expose counterfeit democrats for what they are, and undermine their ability to profit from the façade of democracy. By contrast, if observers pull their punches and remain in the country, there is a serious risk that they will end up inadvertently legitimizing dubious processes by reporting that voting passed off without incident, when the only reason it did is that the government had fixed the outcome in advance.

Counterfeit democrats have figured out how to give themselves a massive head start before ballots are even cast. As we discuss in the chapters to come, this means that little will change unless opposition parties, observers and pro-democracy reformers also adapt.

Chapter 2

BUYING HEARTS AND MINDS

The art of electoral bribery

On 22 April 2013, President Yoweri Museveni of Uganda calmly walked onstage to address a crowd of thousands who had gathered in the Busoga region, in the southeast of the country near the source of the Nile. To audible gasps, he announced that he had come to make a donation of $100,000 to a local youth group.[1] As the crowd went wild, a member of the security forces came forward with a large white sack containing the cash, which Museveni proceeded to hand over to a member of the Busoga Youth Forum – who struggled under its weight as he carried it away.

Despite the clear impact of this gesture on his audience, Museveni was not finished. The same day, he handed over a minibus, a truck and fifteen motorcycles to local leaders and communities. That evening, he left Busoga fêted as a hero – a man willing not only to dedicate his life to public service but also to use his own resources to help his fellow countrymen. Museveni knew the feeling well: handing out gifts had become an established practice of his presidency, having previously given $58,000 to the Uganda Journalists Association and $20,000, again in cash, to Namirembe Cathedral for renovations.[2]

Of course, not everyone applauded Museveni's actions. The proceedings were broadcast on national television and immediately triggered a vigorous debate on social media. As #sackofmoney began to trend on Twitter, critics of the president accused him of bribery and misusing state resources.[3] Peter Magelah, a researcher at the ACODE think tank, told the BBC that 'This is just politicking by the president to gain popularity. . . . Do we know how the money will be spent? There's no system of accountability to make sure we get it back if the youth mismanage it. It's a loss for the country.'[4]

However, these allegations did not go uncontested. The president's supporters mounted a fierce rearguard action. Drawing on Museveni's comments on the day, some pointed out that he had made a personal donation and so claims about the misuse of state resources were unfair. Others argued that the fact that the donation was televised for all to see made it transparent, and pointed out that it was hugely popular with those on the round. Frank Tumwebaze, a government minister, even suggested that Museveni was engaged in rational development planning, arguing that 'The president is not taking the money to Las Vegas, he's supporting income-generating schemes.'[5]

While this defence was self-serving, it also tapped into long-standing public discourse in Uganda concerning the responsibilities of community and political leaders, and the purposes for which power can legitimately be used.[6] In countries where individuals are expected to have a primary loyalty to their ethnic group or region, an election often becomes a referendum on the ability of the incumbent to deliver development.[7] In other words, politicians who can dole out public funds to 'their' voters tend to be more successful. For example, the main thing that East African voters expect of their representatives is not to make good legislation but to network them into sources of government funding.[8] These expectations may be met by government service provision or by senior political figures donating their time and money to help build schools, hospitals and the like.

In this context, winning elections often requires giving handouts to voters. The distribution of largesse is doubly important because it both advertises a candidate's capacity to raise funds, and serves as a public demonstration of their willingness to channel resources back to the community. In other words, electoral bribery is typically just one component of a much larger system of clientelism, in which goods and services are exchanged for political support, often in a mixture of legal and illegal ways. Cash changes hands: votes are expected to follow.

Patronage politics generates both opportunities and challenges for aspiring leaders. A patron who fails to deliver on their campaign promises may find that voters are less willing to take their money – or will take it, but will not then feel bound to reciprocate with political support. Put simply, some voters may take the cash and then vote with their conscience regardless. As a result, vote buying is not as easy as it may sound. The same popular expectation of what it means to be a legitimate leader that encourages candidates to hand out money can also constrain them if they fail to deliver – acting like a straitjacket.

Indeed, popular expectations can be hard to manage: if you win by buying votes, you can lose if your opponent outbids you. Indeed, because voters cast secret ballots, supposed supporters can take the money offered to them and then secretly vote for someone else – or not vote at all. As a result, gift-giving can be a very inefficient way to win power, and many candidates have been left with 'buyer's remorse' after receiving considerably fewer votes than they believe they 'paid' for.

Even when an incumbent retains their seat, it can be hard to verify they got value for money. Recent analysis of the 2011 elections in Uganda, for example, has concluded that for all the money spent by the president, there is 'little evidence that Museveni benefited significantly from public goods outlays, district creation, and vote buying'. Instead, many people voted for the president as a result of a 'widespread satisfaction with macro-economic growth, and an improved security situation'.[9]

This may be a somewhat generous interpretation, overlooking as it does the general climate of intimidation and clientelism in which Ugandan elections are contested.[10] Nonetheless, it serves as an important reminder not to overestimate the impact of electoral bribery. Still, vote buying is prevalent; it occurs in nearly half of all elections. The limited punishment that is typically handed down to those accused of vote buying means that it is one of the most commonly used strategies in the authoritarian toolbox. But just because it is common does not mean it is always worthwhile. It doesn't always deliver, and requires leaders to develop ways to manage expectations and to monitor whether voters are fulfilling their side of the bargain.

Funding clientelism

In the vast majority of countries, it is against the electoral rules to 'bribe' voters by giving them gifts, or to 'treat' voters by handing out food and drink.[11] However, most countries – particularly authoritarian states and counterfeit democracies – do not enforce these basic electoral regulations. In turn, this creates an incentive for candidates from all parties to hand out small gifts to encourage voters to back their campaigns.[12]

Indeed, in many countries around the world, providing 'something small' to voters around election time has become an embedded ritual of democracy, to the extent that leaders who refuse to participate may jeopardize their chances of victory.[13] This reality is well understood by candidates, who save up money in between elections in order to develop war chests for upcoming polls. It is also understood by voters, who often view election periods as a time when they can extract resources from political systems that, all too often, are unresponsive to their needs.[14]

Vote buying tends to vary depending on two main factors: how strong political institutions are, and whether the political culture tends to be clientelistic or policy-driven. Variations in these two factors help explain why electoral bribery is more common in some places than in others.[15] As we saw in the introduction to this book, this form of manipulation is most prevalent in sub-Saharan Africa, where key democratic institutions are often particularly weak and compromised, and where neo-patrimonial ties facilitate and in some cases demand the giving of gifts (pp. 24–5). This helps to explain why 67 per cent of African elections held between 2012 and 2016 featured significant vote buying, as compared to 36 per cent in Latin America, where democratic institutions tend to be more robust (see appendix 14 for comparative data). However, it is important to note that while this practice is most common in Africa – hence why many of the examples in this chapter are drawn from the continent – it is far from an African problem. Instead, we see high levels of electoral bribery in Asia (45 per cent) and post-Soviet states (44 per cent), and significant challenges in the Middle East (29 per cent).

What is handed out also varies according to context. While it is often cold hard cash, as in the case of President Museveni's strategy described above, gifts do not always take monetary form. T-shirts bearing the logo of a candidate or party are extremely common, as is the distribution of food and drink – especially at campaign rallies where their provision helps to attract a crowd. There is also regional variation in the currency of clientelism. In Ghana, cutlasses – machete-like tools used in agriculture – are sometimes distributed.[16] In other countries, such as Malaysia, money is given out in ingenious ways designed to make it appear less like a bribe, such as 'lucky draw' raffles that offer cash prizes and are free to enter – so long as you are a party supporter.[17]

In Thailand, vote buying has been rampant throughout the country's electoral history. In rural areas like Chonburi Province, the going rate is reported to be around 300 baht ($9), but can rise as high as 3,000 baht ($90). The process is so ingrained in Thai politics that there is a specific term for the lucrative night before the election: *kheun maa hawn* ('the night of the howling dogs').[18]

The prevalence of vote buying in many new multiparty systems is one reason why the cost of election campaigns is so high and continues to rise. In Kenya, the total cost of the contest and campaigns for the six positions up for grabs on election day was estimated to be around $1 billion in 2017.[19] Even governors at the county level spend in excess of $6 million to win competitive seats.[20] In India, politicians spent an estimated $5 billion in campaigning for the 2014 elections, a figure second only to the exorbitant total cost of American elections.[21]

The costs are not only high for presidents. An aspiring female politician in Ghana told us that, along with her backers, she had invested over $300,000 just to 'establish' herself and win a parliamentary seat. This had stretched her to financial breaking point.[22] Had she lost the election, she was not sure she would have been able to sustain the interest payments on her debts. Similarly, while the cost of campaigning is significantly lower at the local level, candidates regularly spend between five times (Brazil) and ten times (Nigeria) their salary on campaigning.[23]

The high cost of elections has several important implications. In new democracies with low levels of development and where poverty is rife, parties cannot rely on financial contributions from their members. Although many parties boast of having hundreds of thousands of members – especially those in power who control access to jobs and economic opportunities – few actually charge a fee in return for membership. As a result, candidates are typically expected to personally fundraise for their campaigns.[24] This has two main components: first, personally footing the bill for basic expenses; second, persuading other wealthy individuals to back their campaigns. In turn, these requirements have had far-reaching consequences for the type of candidates who are likely to be successful, excluding those from poorer backgrounds. In places where votes are bought, wealth is a huge advantage.

The changing face of African legislatures demonstrates this point well. In the 1950s and 1960s most MPs were usually traditional leaders or teachers. These groups enjoyed high social status, and each benefited from a wellspring of legitimacy; advanced education in the case of teachers, and already being established community leaders in the case of chiefs. However, as the cost of campaigning began to rise, and voters increasingly began to demand that candidates link them into development resources, chiefs and teachers found that they could not compete with businessmen, who had their own sources of finance.[25] Consequently, multiparty politics in counterfeit democracies often resembles a competitive plutocracy, in which power is wielded by the wealthy, and poorer citizens rarely secure high political office.[26]

Of course, this is also true of many established democracies where the existence of weak or fragmented parties means that responsibility for campaign finance is decentralized and falls on candidates. For example, personal wealth is as important to political success in the United States as anywhere in the world. In 2012, Lieutenant Governor David Dewhurst of Texas spent $11 million of his own money trying to unseat the sitting Republican senator Ted Cruz. The money was wasted; Cruz won anyway, in part because he had even deeper pockets. Significantly, the incumbent's campaign was backed by the Club for Growth, a conservative lobby group that on its own spent $5.5 million on television ads. US senators are paid $174,000 per year: Dewhurst had spent the equivalent of sixty-three years' salary trying to get elected – and still lost.[27]

However, the consequences of this form of politics are particularly troubling in new democracies, because politicians are more vulnerable to the temptations of corruption when the rule of law is weak. In the United States, the need to raise funds forces candidates to enter into close relationships with the powerful donors that finance their campaigns, ensuring privileged access to power for wealthy companies and business leaders while undermining the spirit of democracy.[28] In places such as Armenia, Nigeria and Ukraine, the same pressures have similar consequences, but also lead to resources being illegitimately diverted from their intended purpose in order to cover election expenses.[29] In turn, this gives ruling parties a considerable advantage over the opposition. It's easier to be corrupt if you can sell power and your challengers have a harder time getting investors to finance their campaigns.

Government and opposition

It is important to note that vote buying is not simply the preserve of the ruling party. In many countries, opposition parties also invest heavily in vote-buying strategies, especially in their own heartlands. For example, in the 2017 elections in Armenia, election observers found that both the main parties handed out cash to their supporters.[30] These polls were the first elections held after the country had transitioned from a presidential to a parliamentary system – a change pushed by President Serzh Sargsyan so that he would not have to relinquish power when his two terms in office expired in 2018. By introducing a parliamentary system and taking up the position of prime minister, Sargsyan hoped to extend his control over the country.[31]

As this backdrop would suggest, Sargsyan was not a leader inclined to let the rules get in his way. In the election that followed, cash was handed out in a bid to secure enough seats to build an effective government under his Republican Party. Sisak Gabrielian, a reporter with RFE/RL's Armenian Service, found evidence that on the day of the elections people had been seen leaving a Republican Party office in Yerevan with cash in their hands. When he raised this issue with party officials, Gabrielian was attacked by ruling party loyalists.[32]

However, Sargsyan did not have things all his own way. A comparatively well-funded opposition coalition formed around Gagik Tsarukyan, a former arm-wrestler and one of the wealthiest men in the country, meaning that the opposition could also engage in vote buying.[33] Thus, while the main coalitions differed over a number of policy issues such as corruption, gas prices and national security, the campaigns focused heavily on the individual candidates and what they could do for their constituents, rather than political platforms or policies.[34] In total, observers noted ninety cases of vote buying, mostly perpetrated by the two main alliances, which is likely to be a significant underestimate given the small nature of the missions.[35]

However, while opposition groups such as Tsarukyan's alliance may engage in gift-giving, they typically face two disadvantages when compared with the government, which means that on average vote buying tends to help ruling parties stay in power. First, electoral commissions can be induced to selectively enforce the rules, punishing the opposition for its indiscretions but letting the government off the hook. In counterfeit democracies, the chairpersons of electoral commissions are typically selected by the president and the ruling party, contrary to international best practice.[36] Second, very few commissions enjoy a predetermined and ring-fenced budget, and are instead dependent on the minister of finance and the politicians in charge of electoral preparations for the funds that they receive. As a result, the government generally has several mechanisms through which it can exert influence on the commission to look the other way when its leaders are caught handing out cash.[37]

In Armenia, for example, the government faced no sanctions for the indiscretions described in this chapter. Initially there were hopes that some action might be taken when the working group created by the prosecutor general to investigate allegations of election-related offences identified 220 cases related to vote buying and obstruction of voting rights ahead of the elections. Of these, fifty-eight cases (including thirty-eight for vote buying) were referred to the police for investigation. Yet despite this relatively effective information-collection exercise, all the cases were ultimately dismissed.[38] The election cheats got away with it.[39]

Governments can also shape the economic environment in which they operate because they control the structure of financial markets and through this the availability of credit to opposition leaders. This is a critical point: a recent study has found that the success of opposition leaders in Africa is heavily shaped by access to resources.[40] If credit access is easy and open, opposition candidates have a low barrier to entry, and can easily challenge the incumbent. By contrast, if credit access is tightly regulated by the state, it can make it nearly impossible to raise the funds necessary to mount a credible bid for office. Without credit, it's far more difficult for prospective opposition candidates to co-opt other leaders, parties and supporters into their alliances.

The availability of finance is shaped by many factors, but one of the most important is the extent of banking liberalization. Although some of this variation can be explained by colonial institutional legacies, and whether the economy was export-orientated or not at the point of independence, it is also shaped by the decisions of sitting presidents and prime ministers. Where the banking system is more centralized and politicized, incumbents can use their influence to prevent their opponents getting loans. Thus,

> Africa's first post-independence leaders created financial reprisal regimes to control the business community in their countries. Financial reprisal regimes comprise a set of institutions and regulations – such as maintaining state ownership of banking, channeling credit to privileged sectors, and restricting access to foreign exchange – that enables leaders to exercise political discretion in determining who can access capital.[41]

Once this is done, dangerous political rivals can be starved of resources, putting them at a disadvantage when it comes to both coalition formation and vote buying. Such forms of rigging are difficult to detect and condemn. After all, it is easier to criticize an election that features blatant ballot-box stuffing than one that gives the incumbent an advantage through banking regulation.

Furthermore, governments typically have greater access to finance because they tend to secure more funding from business leaders and, where corruption is high, can redirect state resources to fund their electoral campaign. Indeed, one of the common features of election campaigns in authoritarian states is that they are preceded by large corruption scams that generate resources that can be used to run the campaign.[42] Perhaps most notoriously, the Malaysian prime minister, Najib Razak, allegedly transferred about $700 million from the Malaysian State Investment Fund to his own personal account so that he could use the money to win the 2013 elections – a story to which we will return later.[43]

In addition to straightforward financial malpractice, the corrupt sourcing of election finance often involves procurement scams in which the government purchases something it does not need at a vastly inflated price so that the excess money can be funnelled back into the pockets of party leaders, who can then treat it as their personal revenue. The link between campaigning and corruption is often obscured by the fact that such deals typically only come to light long after an election campaign has ended. By then, it's too late. But if you closely examine some of the highest-profile scandals of recent times, you will find that many of them were initiated in the run-up to an election.

As political scientist and democracy scholar Laurence Whitehead has noted, political corruption in Latin America often has more to do with political survival than personal enrichment.[44] In a number of different countries including Argentina,

Brazil, Colombia, Mexico and Peru, Whitehead demonstrates that governments deliberately and illegally acquired funds to win elections.

The case of Mexico under the Institutional Revolutionary Party (PRI) between 1929 and 2000 is particularly instructive in this regard.[45] Throughout this period, the PRI used bribery to maintain party unity and mobilize support, especially towards the end of its incumbency, when its popularity was declining and the 'options for manipulating election results were narrowed by sweeping reforms of the electoral law'.[46] According to political scientist Beatriz Magaloni, the ruling party 'enjoyed indiscriminate access to the government's revenue to run its campaigns'; it is alleged that 'the PRI governor of the state of Tabasco, Roberto Madrazo . . . spent between $40 and $80 million on his campaign for the 1994 gubernatorial election – at least twenty times the legally allowed amount'.[47] Along with the funnelling of government resources to its core constituencies, and a tightly controlled financial system that enabled the government to punish elites who defected by cutting them out of the distribution of spoils, this helped the ruling party retain power for seventy-one years.

However, this strategy did not always work. Although the PRI began life with considerable popular legitimacy, pledging to institutionalize the gains of the Mexican revolution of the early 1900s, it began to atrophy in the 1990s and was finally defeated in 2000. This transfer of power occurred not because the level of vote buying had fallen, but because it had become less effective in the context of an increasingly sceptical public.

Indeed, if anything, the PRI machine worked harder in the year it lost power than it had ever done. Ahead of the polls, the government generated a slush fund through a corrupt money-laundering scheme that came to be known as Pemexgate. Under the scheme, the trade union of the state-owned oil company, Pemex, applied to the company for a loan of $110 million, subsequently transferring $50 million to a bank account controlled by the PRI.[48] It was withdrawn by PRI officials the month before the 2000 election. Although the ruling party deliberately obscured where the money had come from, and how it had been spent, 'there were enough elements (the network organization, the time during which the bank account had been opened and the money had been withdrawn, and the identity of those involved with the money transfer) to assume that the PRI had received the money for campaign purposes'.[49] A subsequent investigation exposed a number of other illegal forms of party financing, including $25 million that was collected by two civil organizations headed by PRI leaders and a 'raffle' through which the government raised $15 million without actually selling any tickets.[50]

Despite all of this illicit activity, the PRI was defeated for the first time in its existence. After years of strengthening itself in incremental steps, first at the regional level and then at the national level, the National Action Party (PAN) was able to take advantage of a much strengthened electoral system and widespread popular dissatisfaction to win the election: the ruling party received just 36 per cent of the vote.[51]

Getting value for money

There's no question that distributing small gifts can help to build loyalty at the ballot box. But as the example of Mexico has demonstrated, it's not quite that simple. Buying votes on or just before election day can be a wasteful and ineffective strategy when done badly.[52] The first difficulty for politicians seeking to win elections in this way is that giving out a small amount of money once every four or five years may not be enough to capture voters' loyalty. Even in countries with low education levels, citizens know when they are being taken for granted. Indeed, the electorate is often deeply cynical about politicians.[53] For all of the capacity of presidents to build personality cults, citizens are generally sceptical about the motivations of political leaders and their ability and determination to deliver on their promises.[54]

In part, this scepticism stems from the fact that political candidates regularly break election promises made during campaigns. Pledges of schools, hospitals and roads rarely materialize; nor do commitments to listen to and act on the needs of voters. This point is well illustrated by the fate of members of parliament in first-past-the-post electoral systems, in which candidates compete to represent a specific geographical area or constituency. One common feature of these campaigns in countries in which party structures are weak and political competition is not structured around ideological differences is that they tend to focus on local issues as much as, if not more than, national ones.[55] As a result, the profile of a candidate and their record in representing the constituency is often what determines whether they will get elected or not.

Given the fact that many of the counterfeit democracies in sub-Saharan Africa and Latin America feature high levels of poverty and limited public services, voters typically scrutinize candidates for evidence that they have delivered the infrastructure and services that the community desires. Consequently, first-past-the-post elections often become referendums on the development performance of the incumbents.[56] They create parochial politics, as well as a focus on short-term projects rather than long-term solutions that may be more sustainable.

To ensure that voters take their promises seriously, elected politicians must avoid the perception that they will disappear to the capital city after the election, never to be seen again. Instead, to maintain local support, they must 'remember where they came from'.[57] That may mean travelling back for funerals, doling out money for local services through patronage, or even paying for school fees or hospital expenses. What is common to all of these strategies is the need for leaders to be visible and active in their constituencies throughout their parliamentary terms. If they are not, then when the next election rolls around vote buying is unlikely to prove effective. It is for this reason that smart members of parliament spend many hours and large sums on travelling back from parliament to their constituencies on weekends to meet with local power brokers.[58]

Failure to comply with these norms of political behaviour can be costly. Any politician who wins an election and is then perceived to have served themselves rather than their community – to have 'eaten alone', in East African parlance – can expect a frosty reception when they return home.[59] Worse still, they leave themselves open to challenge from rival candidates who can spend the parliamentary term building their own support base, taking advantage of the MP's absence to make the case that they would be a more effective and responsive community representative. In competitive constituencies, this threat often comes from opposition candidates. However, it also exists within safe seats in which the ruling party has a large majority, because unpopular leaders may be deselected or defeated in party primaries.[60]

In this context, handing out small gifts can be a valuable election strategy. As well as creating a personal bond between candidate and voter, the generous and public dispensing of gifts demonstrates that a candidate has the deep pockets and connections needed to deliver on their promises. However, vote buying cannot make up for years of neglect. A small handout in the weeks leading up to an election will not reverse a disliked or lazy candidate's fortunes. Indeed, the very impact of an election bribe depends on who gives it and how it is given.[61] If a locally popular MP who is seen to have devoted his life to the community distributes gifts such as T-shirts, cutlasses and food and drink, as we observed in Ghana, this is likely to be interpreted as a legitimate act – an appropriate aspect of the relationship between a community and its leader.[62] Under these circumstances, vote buying may serve to generate an effective patron–client contract and through it, political support.

By contrast, if the same action is done by a leader who is seen to have neglected the community, or who voters perceive to have been imposed from outside, it may have little or no effect. Indeed, there are plentiful examples of candidates whose wealth and gift-giving hurt them because it was seen to have been illegitimate – a way of pulling the wool over citizens' eyes, rather than genuinely empowering them. Because of this, successful leaders must recognize that there is a moral component to election campaigns. Gifts that are given in the wrong way can actually prove counterproductive, raising difficult questions about how the funds were obtained, and why, if a candidate has access to so much money, so little has previously been done to benefit the community.[63] Aspiring politicians who fail to recognize this are likely to end up doubly disappointed, finding themselves out of power with debts that they cannot repay. In other words, if you're going to buy votes, you have to do it the right way. This is one reason why around half of MPs lose their seats in many African legislative elections, despite enjoying the benefits of incumbency.[64]

Vote buying is therefore no panacea for neglect; politicians can only successfully buy hearts and minds if they have already laid the foundations by rewarding loyal communities with greater infrastructure in the form of roads and electricity, and preferential access to development expenditure. Thus, electoral bribery is most effective when it is part of a broader strategy to strengthen the ties between constituents and leaders – all the way up to the presidential level.

This point is well illustrated by the 2013 general election in Malaysia. In the run-up it was clear that the ruling party faced a serious challenge, with commentators describing it as the most hotly contested poll in the country's history.[65] Despite being in power since it was founded in 1973 as a coalition of two parties, the governing Barisan Nasional (BN) led by Prime Minister Najib Razak saw its fortunes wane in the late 2000s.

In the 2008 general election, the BN lost its two-thirds majority, meaning that it was no longer able to pass constitutional amendments. One reason for this was a growing urban–rural divide, and the emergence of a stronger opposition vote in multi-ethnic urban areas in which better access to information and education had led to growing criticism over issues such as corruption, human rights abuses, electoral fraud and poor economic governance.[66]

In a bid to head off the threat from the expanding urban middle class, the BN resorted to a form of ethnic politics, introducing policies that explicitly favoured the Malay majority. As a result, most of the Chinese minority, which had previously voted for the BN, switched sides – something described by Razak as the 'Chinese tsunami'.[67] Bolstered by this new support, it appeared that the main opposition coalition, Anwar Ibrahim's Pakatan Rakyat (PR), had a chance of victory.[68] Spurred into life by the intensity of the political competition, both sides embarked on widespread vote buying.

Although both 'treating' and 'bribing' are prohibited under Malaysian law, the election observers from the Merdeka Center for Opinion Research found that both sides held 'feasts', distributed gifts of travel vouchers, foodstuffs and appliances, and gave out clothing. As in Armenia and elsewhere, these practices tended to favour the ruling party: out of a recorded sixty-seven cases, forty-four involved the BN and only twenty-two the opposition. These subtler efforts to win voters' favour went hand in hand with the distribution of cold hard cash. The prime minister himself was reported to have handed out cash payments of RM50 (about US$11) for people to attend party meetings, as well as vouchers that enabled taxi drivers in the capital, Kuala Lumpur, to fit their vehicles with new tyres.[69]

The policies enacted by the BN over the previous five years strengthened the effectiveness of vote buying in some communities while undermining it in others. The credibility of promises of patronage and financial goodies to the Malay community were reinforced by Razak's implementation of preferential policies during his time in office and the fact that financially rewarding his supporters was, in effect, a non-stop activity.[70] In the previous five years alone, his administration had spent RM57.7 billion (about $13.6 billion) on providing 'election-related incentives', including a rice subsidy for the Orang Asli (a collective term for eighteen indigenous tribes), travel subsidies for students, and salary increases for public servants.[71] By contrast, members of the Chinese community, who had already seen the government's true colours in the discriminatory legislation that it had introduced, were unlikely to be persuaded by a last-minute handout.

Partly as a result, the outcome of the election was mixed.[72] While financial inducements enabled the BN to retain power, winning 133 seats to the PR's 89, the ruling party lost the popular vote for the first time. Indeed, the government only held on to its majority thanks to the use of two other strategies highlighted in this book – multiple voting (chapter 5) and gerrymandering (chapter 1). For example, East Malaysia represents a fifth of the country's total population but contributes a quarter of its parliamentary seats, and played a key role in returning the BN to power.[73] Razak's reliance on this broad range of strategies serves as an important reminder of the potential limitations of vote buying, and the fact that leaders often need to deploy a number of the tools at their disposal in order to retain political control.

Enforcing the deal

The second problem for political leaders who want to see a good return on their investment in electoral bribery is that it is often very difficult to tell if people have actually voted the 'right' way.[74] Where voting is conducted by secret ballot, it can be impossible for anyone other than the individual voter to know whether they have kept their promise or not. And if it is widely known that political leaders cannot work out who has reneged on their pledge, then those who break their promises cannot be punished, and so there is little reason for voters to keep the deals they have signed up to. The secret ballot means that there is no disincentive for citizens to take money from every candidate and then vote for the party of their choice.[75] Enforcement is therefore a key challenge.

This reality is not lost on opposition parties. Recognizing that vote-buying practices are so ingrained that it is unlikely to be possible to persuade people to reject the offer of gifts altogether, a number of opposition leaders around the world have encouraged voters to accept gifts but vote with their conscience. A very early manifestation of this strategy on the African continent came in Namibia in the elections in 1989 for a constituent assembly to usher in the country's independence. These polls, which in many ways heralded the onset of a new time of multiparty politics in Africa, marked the end of a long period of South African rule, characterized by the application of apartheid principles and the efforts of the South West Africa People's Organization (SWAPO) to liberate the country. Following the declaration of Namibian independence, which was formally set in motion in 1988 (though not fully implemented until 21 March 1990), SWAPO was widely expected to make a strong showing in the polls.[76] The South African government responded by funding the campaigns of at least seven rival political parties in a bid to deny SWAPO power. According to Pik Botha, then the South African foreign minister, the South African government transferred over £20 million to other parties on the basis that, despite having committed to Namibian independence, his government was still 'at war with SWAPO'.[77]

The most viable of these other parties was the Democratic Turnhalle Alliance (DTA), which had been formed as a coalition of eleven parties in 1977 in the wake of failed negotiations with the South African government over Namibia's future. The willingness of the DTA to work with the South African government in talks that excluded SWAPO and were based on a blueprint that would have left elements of the apartheid system intact undermined the party's legitimacy at home and abroad. In turn, this made it difficult to mobilize broad support on the basis of ideas, policies or track record.[78] As a result, the DTA's election campaign in 1989 focused on sustaining the support of the European-born and 'coloured' Namibians who had contributed the bulk of the party's members since its formation, while relying on anti-SWAPO messages and vote buying to build support within the black majority. Thus, small amounts of money, food and other gifts were regularly handed out to those who attended DTA rallies.[79]

Knowing that SWAPO could not hope to match the DTA's financial largesse, the liberation movement's leader, Sam Nujoma, did not try to compete in the field of vote buying. Instead, he encouraged his supporters to take whatever gifts were on offer but not be swayed by them. As one SWAPO leader memorably put it, 'Eat DTA, Vote SWAPO'.[80] This message proved to be highly effective, and this, along with popular scepticism towards the DTA, led to a landslide victory for Nujoma's party, which won 57 per cent of the vote, giving it a clear majority and a strong lead over the former ruling party, which only secured 29 per cent. SWAPO's advantage was further consolidated in the subsequent presidential elections of 1994, when Nujoma secured 75 per cent of the ballot.[81]

In the years that followed, similar slogans have become common features of election campaigns, demonstrating the vulnerability of vote-buying strategies. One of the most famous came in Zambia in the general election of 2011. In that contest, the opposition Patriotic Front (PF) had gained considerable momentum but risked being comprehensively outspent and outbribed by the ruling party. In addition to manipulating state machinery to support its efforts, the inaptly named Movement for Multiparty Democracy (MMD) engaged in a range of illegal activities including using state funds to pay for posters and, of course, vote buying.[82]

Unable to compete financially, PF leaders encouraged voters not to be swayed by offers of economic gain and threats of retribution. With this in mind, the party's deputy leader, Guy Scott, invoked the secret ballot to remind PF supporters that they could have their cake and eat it. A white Zambian of British descent, Scott could not recall all of the necessary words in Bemba, the language spoken by most of his audience, and so mixed Bemba with English, advising the crowd, 'Don't *kubeba*' ('Don't tell them').[83] The crowd instantly understood what Scott was trying to say: pretend that you support the ruling party, but vote for the opposition. The phrase instantly caught on, and was quickly picked up as one of the party's main slogans, daubed on walls and printed on T-shirts. Along with the populist rhetoric of PF leader Michael Sata, the 'Don't *kubeba*' message contributed to the defeat of the MMD, leading to only the second transfer of power through the ballot box in Zambia's history.[84]

The grass-roots resonance of 'Don't *kubeba*' is a perfect demonstration of the capacity of opposition parties to use the secrecy of the ballot box to stymie the effectiveness of vote-buying strategies and undermine ruling parties' hold on power. Given the potential for opposition parties to use these strategies, presidents may need to undermine the credibility of the secret ballot if they are to benefit from vote buying – and as a result many have set about developing new techniques for finding out how citizens vote.

There are three main strategies that can be used to achieve this. The first is to persuade voters that the ballot is not actually secret. This can be done by spreading rumours, posting security guards and government agents within polling stations, and removing screens that allow voters to cast their ballot away from public view. Such strategies are particularly feasible in countries where voting is often conducted outdoors. In many African states, for example, the uncertainty of electricity supplies and the need for greater space mean that polling stations in rural areas have historically been set up outside. In these contexts, people do not always cast their ballot behind a partition but in a shallow bucket, often in full view of those queuing to vote and the security forces. Significantly, this is not just a feature of counterfeit democracies: research in Ghana has found that a considerable number of voters worry that their vote may not be secret – challenging a core principle of electoral democracy.[85]

The second strategy that can be used to ensure that people vote as they have promised is to monitor voter behaviour at community level. Governments may not be able to tell how each individual votes, but they can use the turnout figures and results at a given polling station to assess how a particular area has performed. For example, if the ruling party knows that the vast majority of people who vote at a certain polling station attended rallies, received activists in their homes, and were given hand-outs, a low turnout and a disappointing vote share from that area for the incumbent president is clear evidence of political betrayal. Although the government cannot tell who failed to turn up to the polls on an individual basis, it can inflict a communal punishment such as cutting development expenditure or diverting much-needed food aid to other communities that demonstrated greater loyalty.[86] In turn, the knowledge that failing to give the ruling party sufficient support can harm a community's material interests often generates internal pressure on dissidents to toe the line.[87] As a result, those who don't head to the polls – readily identifiable by their lack of an inky finger – and those who are suspected of sympathizing with the opposition may face criticism, hostility and in some cases violence from their neighbours. In this way, community leaders and other notables can be turned into accomplices in the ruling party's efforts to get out the vote.[88]

The third strategy is to demand that voters publicly demonstrate that they have voted as promised, for example by photographic evidence. With the advent of camera-equipped smartphones, it is now feasible to tell voters that they must take a picture of their ballot papers. However, in most countries taking a photograph in a polling station is an electoral offence. Thus, a less problematic strategy is to ask voters to make a public statement of their voting intentions *as they vote*. In other words, voters are told to say out loud which candidate or party they are supporting as they cast their ballots. Of course, this tactic on its own is not a silver bullet for authoritarian vote buyers, because citizens can still lie about what they are doing. However, a specific feature of the electoral system can be manipulated to enable party activists to know for sure that a voter is telling the truth.

In the majority of countries around the world, the electoral rules allow voters to ask for help from polling station staff – and in some cases, from party agents or others present in the polling station. This is designed to enable illiterate, blind or disabled voters to secure the assistance they may need to vote as they intend. However, it creates a loophole that a number of ruling parties have exploited to keep tabs on the electorate, by turning the act of voting from a written into an oral process.

In both Kenya and Zimbabwe, for example, voters who do not appear to be blind, illiterate or disabled have been observed asking for assistance to vote, and then loudly stating how they would like their ballot to be filled out. Once this happens, the person helping them casts the ballot on their behalf on the basis of their verbal instruction. By loudly proclaiming their choice the individual effectively undermines the secrecy of their own vote. This information is then taken down by representatives of the candidate – either positioned within the station or standing nearby where they can clearly hear the proceedings – who record that the voter kept their promise.[89] It is thus even possible to buy votes and only pay up after proof of voting the 'right' way has been secured.

Alternative strategies have been used to similar effect in other regions. In Malaysia, the BN sought to ensure that the financial inducements it offered loyal voters would be effective by carefully tracking who had received handouts. According to Transparency International, those who accepted RM500 in 'aid' from the coalition were forced to register their names and then to collect the money from one of the alliance's political parties. In turn, the fact that the ruling party kept a record of who received election funds led to fears that it would track down those people who did not vote for it but who took the aid. Although the secret ballot should have made this impossible, the idea spread that the government had the capacity to check individual ballot papers, which caused considerable concern because 'so many people believe in rumours'.[90]

Through such mechanisms, parties can more effectively scrutinize how voters behave and enforce compliance, ensuring that they get value for money in return for the gifts that they have distributed throughout the course of the campaign. In this way, the challenges of enforcement posed by the secret ballot induce authoritarian leaders to adopt increasingly inventive strategies of manipulation and repression in order to retain control and ensure that deals made with voters are kept – a theme to which we will return in chapters 3 and 5.

The impact of vote buying

Before considering different mechanisms that could be used to try and reduce vote buying, it is worth noting that its consequences are not all bad – and so its removal may not be all good. Most notably, while curtailing vote buying is clearly a positive development for electoral fairness, it may produce unintended consequences that harm democracy in the short term. As the political scientist Frederick Schaffer has pointed out, if voters, accustomed to being 'thanked' for turning up to vote, find this reward removed, they might not bother going – causing a decline in voter turnout.[91] This may be problematic, as in the short run at least, low turnout can undermine government legitimacy, creating a series of problems later on.

Currently, many new, fragile democracies record higher voter-turnout levels than old, consolidated ones. This may in part reflect the impact of ballot-box stuffing (see chapter 5) and the fact that 'voting fatigue' has not yet set in, but it may also be related to the financial inducements that parties hand out to get voters to the polls. In Malaysia, for example, the combination of a close election and the vote-buying strategies described above pushed turnout up to 85 per cent, the highest in the country's history.[92] By comparison, as we have seen (p. 40), the United States' 2014 congressional elections featured a turnout of just 36 per cent.[93] Ending vote buying might be good for the opposition, but could also reduce public participation.

Readers may be thinking 'So what? Is there really any value in political participation that is driven by vote buying?' But such a response would be too hasty a dismissal of the importance of getting people to the polls. After all, one of the main arguments of this chapter has been that voters do not always fulfil their side of the bargain, and so their participation cannot be reduced to a mere economic transaction. In at least some cases, citizens drawn to the ballot box by handouts vote instead on the basis of their conscience, and otherwise might have stayed at home.

Moreover, recent research has found that the act of voting is habit-forming. Of those people who voted for the first time in South Africa following the reintroduction of multiparty politics in 1994, the vast majority voted again in the second election in 1999. By contrast, of those who were of voting age but did not go to the polls in 1994, very few did so four years later.[94]

Part of the explanation for this is that certain factors shape whether or not people are likely to vote, such as living with or near other voters, age and education, and so it makes sense that people would act consistently. But it is the case also partly because people are often put off from voting by a range of issues, such as not knowing exactly where their polling station is located, embarrassment that they don't understand the correct procedures, and worry that it might take a long time or that they will make a mistake.[95] In this context, voting for the first time is particularly significant, because it helps to overcome a number of these challenges and hence to make citizens feel more comfortable casting their ballots in future.[96]

One implication of this research is that even if a mechanism that gets citizens to the polls is problematic, it may have the valuable, long-lasting benefit of increasing long-term political engagement. Given this, it is important that efforts to curb vote buying go hand in hand with efforts to sustain voter turnout.

Strengthening democracy

The importance of enhancing political participation notwithstanding, it is clear that vote buying has a number of deeply problematic consequences, including that it enables ruling parties to win elections that they might otherwise lose. Moreover, it has a number of negative consequences for how politics operates. Most obviously, it drives up the cost of elections. This simultaneously incentivizes political corruption and threatens to turn politics into a plutocracy in which only the rich – or those well-enough connected to get rich – may wield power. Perhaps less obviously, vote buying constructs relationships between voters and political leaders that are based on a patron–client logic rather than an evaluation of leaders' ability to govern.[97] This threatens to undermine the very basis for holding elections, namely that they keep governments honest by enabling the electorate to reject incompetent or corrupt candidates.

For this reason, international donors such as the UK government's Department for International Development and the United States Agency for International Development have spent a considerable amount of money on trying to reduce vote buying.[98] Much of this has been directed towards voter education, on the basis that a better understanding of the electoral law will dissuade people from participating in transactions that break it.[99] There is much to be said for this approach, not least that it increases the prospects that those persuaded by the training might not only reject bribes but also report those who offer them. For example, a recent study in West Africa found that 'voter education campaigns may undermine the effects of vote buying on voting behaviour'.[100]

However, on its own, voter education tends to have a limited effect, and as we saw in the introduction to this book, the percentage of elections featuring vote buying actually increased between 2006 and 2010.[101] There are three main reasons for this. First, not all of the forms of 'treating' that take place around elections are formally against the rules, and even when they are, voters often see them as being legitimate. Established cultural practices are unlikely to be reformulated by a short training session on free and fair elections, no matter how well this is delivered by a Western-backed NGO. When offered a T-shirt, many newly 'educated' voters will still take it.

Second, in most of the countries discussed in this chapter, people are already aware that candidates are not supposed to hand over cash for votes – meaning that educating them about this fact is often redundant. They take the bribes not because they are ignorant of the law, but because local norms prevail over official rules, or the financial inducement is too tempting, or they feel coerced into doing so. In each of these situations, voter education is likely to have little impact. In other words, if there is a set of deeply entrenched local beliefs that favour accepting small gifts, reminding individual voters of the law is likely to have a minimal effect unless it is done intensively and over a sustained period of time, which is rarely the case. Similarly, if the gifts are sufficiently tempting, preaching about democratic virtues will probably fall on deaf ears. And if citizens are effectively coerced into taking bribes, as in countries like Zimbabwe, they may have little opportunity to 'do the right thing' even if they want to.

However, voter-education drives can still be valuable: they can help to highlight the negative consequences of vote buying, and lay a stronger foundation on which civil society groups and opposition parties can launch their own campaigns to persuade voters to take gifts yet vote for their chosen candidate.

International donors cannot condone citizens taking a bribe, because this transgresses the law. Media outlets critical of foreign aid, such as the UK's *Daily Mail*, would also have a field day if British taxpayers' money were to be used as part of a campaign that even came close to condoning vote buying. But international donors *can* support the principle of individuals voting with their conscience and, through anti-vote-buying messages, make it easier for domestic actors to persuade voters that taking money doesn't necessarily mean that they have to vote for the candidate who gives it to them.

Some readers are likely to be uncomfortable with the idea of opposition leaders and civil society groups engaging with the question of how individuals should act after having taken a bribe, rather than persuading them not to take the bribe in the first place. Of course, it would be purer, ethically speaking, simply to campaign against vote buying. But while condemning the giving of 'something small' around elections may be less morally problematic, throwing money and effort at strategies that have often proved to be ineffective has its own moral downsides – notably, that it fails to make the best use of scarce resources, and leaves a deeply problematic political landscape in place when something much better could be achieved. A two-track approach is therefore required: try to deter vote buying from happening, but also try to blunt its impact wherever it persists. Indeed, doing one is likely to make it easier to do the other, as ruling parties are unlikely to keep spending money on strategies that don't work.

Part of the solution, of course, lies in tightening up electoral regulations, and trying to get the police and judiciary to enforce them. Again, this is a worthy project, and improving the detection and prosecution of vote buying is the natural complement of efforts to change public attitudes. However, the challenge in most of the countries that we have discussed is not a lack of legal clarity or capacity but rather a lack of political will. When the ruling party controls a politicized judiciary or police force, enforcement will tend to happen on a purely selective basis, whereby opposition vote buying is prosecuted but ruling-party vote buying is not. Under these conditions, vote-buying legislation is unlikely to be comprehensively enforced.

Beyond political strategies, the long-term feasibility of vote buying depends on economic and demographic trends. Historical studies of vote buying explain the fall in voter bribery in Europe and North America as being predominantly driven by two main developments. First, the expansion of the franchise, to all adult men and then to all adult women, meant that aspiring politicians were faced with far more people to bribe in order to secure election, which increased the cost dramatically.[102] Second, the introduction of the secret ballot (in 1872 in the UK and in the 1880s in the US) made it harder for vote buyers to tell whether their clients had kept their side of the bargain.[103] Both of these changes were driven by broader socioeconomic developments, notably rising standards of living, the emergence of a more assertive middle class[104] and the expansion of education.[105]

The very same changes also led to a more aware citizenry, while the rise in wages, over a number of years, meant that voters expected greater financial compensation in return for their support. Taken together, these developments reduced the effectiveness and feasibility of vote buying, forcing candidates to look for other strategies to mobilize the electorate. One outcome of this transformation was that political leaders became more reliant on using government policy to reward their supporters, for example by increasing expenditure on certain areas, or by introducing targeted tax breaks.

While the mass franchise and the secret ballot are already in place in the world's new democracies, in many countries the processes that gave rise to them in the West – mass education, rising incomes and the growth of the middle class – are still ongoing. It is therefore possible that continued economic growth will undermine the viability of vote buying in the long run. This is not to say that economic expansion is a cure-all for electoral manipulation. Economic growth is unlikely to have these positive effects unless it is sustained and its benefits widely shared. Short-lived gains, or unequal growth that is monopolized by the wealthy – as the proceeds from oil and other natural resources often are – will not lift people out of poverty, and so may have a negligible impact on the feasibility of vote buying.[106] We must also keep in mind that many countries with high levels of poverty have managed to establish effective democratic systems, while some of the world's wealthiest states – such as the resource-rich countries of the Middle East – remain deeply authoritarian.[107]

Similar caveats need to be made about the significance of the middle class. It is easy to see why many journalists and a considerable number of academics have become excited about the role of the middle class in Asia and Africa.[108] Several classic theories of democratization have suggested that the emergence of an influential bourgeoisie is a critical step in the process of wresting power away from a small authoritarian elite and transferring it to the people.[109] When it comes to vote buying, it is often assumed that because the middle class are wealthier and more independent from the state they will be more willing to criticize breaches of the electoral laws. As a result, the expansion of the middle class – which is estimated to have tripled in Africa to 310 million in the thirty years to 2011 – has led to excitable headlines about how this group will simultaneously drive economic and democratic growth.[110]

However, while this may be true in some cases, it is important not to assume that the emergence of a middle class will be the silver bullet that stops vote buying. For one thing, many of the people who finance vote buying are themselves middle class.[111] It is also unclear what specific quality about being middle class is thought to make individuals behave differently. While it makes intuitive sense that richer citizens will feel less economic pressure to accept election bribes, recent research has found that where the middle class is more supportive of democratic norms and values this is typically a result of education rather than wealth.[112] Given this, we should be careful of assuming that a growing middle class will necessarily render vote buying a thing of the past.

These caveats notwithstanding, it is clear that socioeconomic development can facilitate an improvement in electoral quality and a reduction in vote buying. It is easy to forget that just 150 years ago the United Kingdom featured rampant voter bribery that matched – and in some cases exceeded – the examples provided here (see pp. 61–4). Improvements in the electoral law were critical to this process, but in most cases they followed or went hand in hand with an expansion of education and economic shifts that had the effect of giving citizens a greater degree of financial independence.[113] To the extent that fledgling democracies can sustain inclusive economic growth and use it to fund education, this is a reason for optimism.

This conclusion is an important reminder that efforts to strengthen democracy cannot be separated from other political and economic activities. As the significance of financial systems for the formation of opposition coalitions demonstrates, the prospects for transfers of power and democratic consolidation depend on a wide range of economic and political factors. One problematic aspect of most international and domestic efforts to strengthen democracy is that these projects typically occur in isolated ways that focus on political institutions but are disconnected from efforts to improve the economy.[114] As a result, the democratic impact of economic policy is not always fully understood, even within the ministries and development agencies of those Western governments that are still committed to promoting these goals around the world. More co-ordinated thinking that recognizes these connections – for example, through the formation of a joint taskforce that can bring together those working across these issues – is required if the manipulation of elections through vote buying is to be neutered.

Where vote buying is rendered less effective, either because opposition to the ruling regime is so intense that voters cannot be bribed, or because the government lacks the funds required to sway large numbers of people, incumbents must look for other strategies to retain power. Under these conditions, election rigging can quickly turn ugly, with violent repression and intimidation used in order to divide and rule – as we shall see in the next chapter.

Chapter 3

DIVIDE AND RULE

Violence as a political strategy

On 12 November 2005, Zamanbek Nurkadilov, the mayor of Almaty and one of the most prominent opposition leaders in Kazakhstan, was found dead in his house. An outspoken critic of the government and a member of the political council of the For a Just Kazakhstan reform movement, Nurkadilov had been shot twice in the chest and once in the head. According to the official investigation, his death was a suicide. Opposition leaders wondered how a man could manage to shoot himself three times in two different places. They also wondered about the timing – presidential elections were scheduled for 4 December, less than a month later – and declared Nurkadilov's death a political assassination.[1]

Although the government denied any involvement in the attack, it bore all the hallmarks of President Nursultan Nazarbayev's strategy to retain political control since coming to power in 1989 as the first secretary of the Communist Party of the Kazakh Soviet Socialist Republic (as it then was).[2] Although Nazarbayev likes to present himself as a liberal reformer, and has achieved considerable economic development, he is also a violent kleptocrat. Not only has the president put his daughters and son-in-law in charge of key parts of the economy, including construction, oil and gas, and the media, he also stands accused of personally profiting from the country's vast natural resources.[3] In 1999, Swiss banking officials discovered $8.5 billion in an account apparently belonging to Nazarbayev, which was allegedly a payment from the disgraced American businessman and trader James Giffen, made in order to secure contracts for the Tengiz oil fields for Western companies.[4] In short, Nazarbayev appears to have cashed in on his dictatorial powers.[5]

The president's strategy for protecting his regime against accusations of corruption and malpractice was a combination of co-optation and intimidation. When *Respublika*, an opposition newspaper, reported that Nazarbayev had effectively stolen over $1 billion of state oil revenue in the 1990s, a decapitated dog was strung up outside its headquarters, a screwdriver plunged into its body. The attached message read: 'There won't be a next time.' Meanwhile, the dog's head and a similar note were left outside the home of the paper's editor, Irina Petrushova. In case the message hadn't got through, three days later *Respublika*'s office was firebombed. Petrushova was not alone: as Nazarbayev tried to hide what he had done, opposition leaders were arrested, alternative media outlets were shut down, and critics of the government were beaten.[6]

That was in June 2002, and although the situation eased somewhat once the immediate threat of media exposure had passed, a similar wave of repression targeted opposition parties and civil society groups ahead of the 2005 polls. Incidents recorded by international human rights groups and election monitors included the assault of opposition candidates and supporters, the destruction of campaign material, and widespread intimidation of human rights activists by the police and security agencies.[7] Partly as a result, the main opposition candidate, Zharmakhan Tuyakbay, struggled to make inroads, despite considerable public dissatisfaction. Nazarbayev won a landslide victory, taking 91.15 per cent of the vote.[8]

The case of Kazakhstan demonstrates the capacity of governments to use violence to intimidate the opposition and maintain the ruling regime's dominance. As Paul Collier notes in *Wars, Guns and Votes*, 'elections should sound the death knell for political violence', but all too often this is not the case.[9] Moreover, 'enemies' in the opposition are only one target of state repression. Authoritarian regimes face two challenges: external opposition and internal betrayal. As a result, undemocratic governments also direct violence against individuals and factions who seek to defect and supposed allies who cannot be trusted. By attacking opposition supporters and elements within the ruling party who are seen as having not performed their duty to the appropriate standard, leaders can both disrupt the campaigns of their rivals and send a clear message to everyone else: opposing their rule comes at a high price.

As in Kazakhstan, where Nurkadilov had risen to prominence as minister of emergency situations within the Nazarbayev administration, the worst treatment is often reserved for former insiders perceived to have betrayed the cause. These kinds of attacks are particularly effective because the use of violence often serves to harden political identities, creating a stronger sense of 'us' and 'them' between the government and the opposition, which in turn makes it harder for moderates on both sides to find common ground.[10] Violence enables the executive to put into practice one of the most common elements of the despot's playbook: divide and rule.

The multifaceted impact of violence is what makes it so valuable to dictators, and explains why elections often go hand in hand with violence in counterfeit democracies, despite the considerable costs that this can generate. Between 2012 and 2016, almost a quarter of all elections held around the world featured significant state targeting of the opposition with violence, intimidation or harassment. However, as with many of the stories told in this book, average statistics mask significant regional variation. Such abuses were largely absent in Europe and limited in Latin America (18 per cent), but were a significant problem in Asia (39 per cent), the Middle East (38 per cent) and sub-Saharan Africa (38 per cent) – and were shockingly common in the former Soviet Union, where repression is a feature of almost half (47 per cent) of all elections (see appendices 11 and 12).

These variations reflect a number of different factors, including the legacy of closed political systems and states with relatively strong coercive power in the post-communist world;[11] the politicization and limited professionalization of the security apparatus in much of sub-Saharan Africa;[12] and greater progress towards democratization and the emergence of more independent judiciaries in Latin America.[13] They also reflect the willingness and ability of leaders to accept the cost of violence: once repression has become a part of a country's political culture, it's hard to stamp out.

But any ruling party that uses violence to win elections is inviting serious risks to itself too. Murders and assassinations conducted in capital cities draw international media attention and condemnation from watchdogs such as International Crisis Group, Amnesty International and Human Rights Watch.[14] They also risk alienating international partners, who may be prepared to tolerate electoral manipulation but not the pushback that can result from front-page coverage of human rights abuses. Overt violence is also likely to undermine the confidence of investors, and potentially to have a negative impact on economic growth – especially if it results in a period of economic inactivity.

The considerable risks of using force make it less common than other rigging tactics, such as vote buying (chapter 2). Recent research suggests that authoritarian leaders are most likely to employ electoral violence under two conditions. First, incumbents are far more likely to lash out when they operate in weak political systems and believe that they might actually lose.[15] Second, state repression is more likely when the government believes it can get away with it because it has a powerful illiberal international sponsor (think, for example, of the authoritarian allies of China or of the post-Soviet regimes that are still in the Kremlin's orbit).[16] This helps explain why state-led political violence is most common in the former Soviet countries: most are resource-rich states under Russian protection, and are far less dependent on Western financial and political support and so have less to fear from deploying repression.

In stark contrast to this situation, the potentially high cost of political violence presents those counterfeit democracies that are more susceptible to Western pressure with something of a dilemma. For repression to have its intended effect it must be public and high profile, otherwise it loses its deterrence value. If someone 'disappears' but nobody finds out, it doesn't create much of a deterrent effect. But there's a catch: if the voting public is aware of state brutality, so are investors, Western governments and human rights groups. The trade-offs are obvious.

Dictators, despots and counterfeit democrats have come up with solutions to this apparent catch-22. Sometimes they make use of shadowy militias and gangs in order for the government to generate 'plausible deniability'. By constructing a 'shadow state'[17] made up of groups that are widely known to be answerable to the ruling party but which cannot easily be identified as belonging to the police force or the security forces, authoritarian leaders can avoid international condemnation, and minimise the threat of prosecution by bodies such as the International Criminal Court.[18] When the shadow state strikes, the regime can pretend it was not involved – but opposition forces still get the message.

Other regimes respond to growing discontent by deploying an intense period of violence that is so visceral and painful that it remains in the public imagination long after it has taken place.

Once this has been done, beatings and murder may not be required on a regular basis, because people can easily be reminded of what happened in the past – and the potential for it to happen again. As they say in Zimbabwe, you do not always have to burn the house down – in some cases merely 'shaking the matchbox'[19] has the desired effect. In other words, once a pattern of repression has been established, it becomes possible to sustain it in a manner that is relatively low key – censoring the media, denying permits for opposition rallies, arresting potential 'troublemakers' – thus generating the benefits of violence without the associated costs. All it takes is a gentle reminder of the brutality that is possible. People who survive state violence tend to have long memories.

This kind of latent coercion is extremely valuable because it typically passes under the radar. It is hard to quantify and detect, and rarely makes international newspaper headlines. After all, how do you condemn the spectre of past violence being brought to voters' minds, when this can be sold as pre-election peacebuilding? As a result, counterfeit democracies that employ these strategies are often seen as being relatively respectable by the international community.[20] Once the initial condemnation of the use of extreme violence has died down – which, as we have discovered, can often happen after just six months – it becomes possible for the government to argue that 'lessons have been learnt' and that the country is on a stable and more peaceful footing. This is then the signal for international partners and companies sympathetic to the regime – or simply keen to exploit its resources and geostrategic potential – to re-engage, legitimizing the government and boosting its economic prospects (see chapter 6). In this way, clever authoritarians can use coercion without paying all of its costs.

Fighting elections

Electoral violence has become worryingly common in the world's new multiparty political systems. In many cases, these stories do not make the headlines because not enough people die to make it newsworthy for foreign audiences; but for those involved, elections are often moments of considerable stress and worry – and, for an unfortunate minority, trauma.

Consider the Sri Lankan elections of 26 January 2010. The polls were held nearly two years early because President Mahinda Rajapaksa wished to capitalize on the 2008 military defeat of the Liberation Tigers of Tamil Eelam (LTTE, often colloquially known as the Tamil Tigers), which had been operating in the eastern and northern part of the country for more than twenty-five years.[21] But instead of the elections ushering in a new era of peace and harmony, the polls generated violence on a remarkable scale. Although the country is small, with a population of just 21.2 million, the Centre for Monitoring Election Violence (CMEV) counted 860 incidents.[22] Some 386 of these were classified as 'major', meaning that they involved murder, attempted murder, hurt, grievous hurt, assault, threat and intimidation, misuse of state resources, robbery, arson or abduction. The vast majority of these incidents were carried out by Rajapaksa's coalition, the United People's Freedom Alliance (UPFA).[23]

In many cases, the violence followed the pattern of the civil war, with the use of indiscriminate attacks and explosives. In one of the most notorious incidents, gunmen opened fire on a bus near the town of Hungama, in the south of the island, killing a female supporter of opposition candidate Sarath Fonseka, and wounding at least four people.[24] In another high-profile attack, one of Fonseka's campaign managers narrowly escaped the bombing of his house on 22 January after he had received a series of warnings and death threats.[25] At the same time, the police were accused of intimidating opposition supporters through unnecessary searches and questioning,[26] while Nil Balakaya, the youth wing of Rajapaksa's party, was accused of threatening rival supporters.[27] A further 148 'major incidents' were reported on election day itself, and on 29 January, the day after the elections, Fonseka's party office in Colombo was raided by police.[28]

Against this backdrop it is hardly surprising that the opposition struggled to mobilize support. The risks were too high. The ruling party did not need to attack everyone; it just needed to make everyone understand that they could be next. The tactic worked: after the end of the conflict with the Tamil Tigers, comprehensive control over the political system and the excessive use of force saw Rajapaksa re-elected with 58 per cent of the vote.[29]

However, while election violence tends to favour the ruling party, it is important to note that, much like electoral bribery, it may also be deployed by opposition leaders seeking to make inroads and to defend their turf. Conflict also sometimes develops inadvertently, during spontaneous clashes between government and opposition supporters. In Sri Lanka, for example, there were twenty pre-election acts of violence that were attributed to the opposition United National Party, and a number of incidents were also recorded on polling day.[30] According to the most thorough academic study of this aspect of the election currently available, this strategy worked for both sides and as a result the two main candidates 'experienced declines in the percentage of votes in polling divisions where opponent party activists committed acts of violence or intimidation'.[31] In other words, both sides were guilty of violence, but the violence carried out by the ruling party was more effective.

In some cases, all three dynamics – government-led, opposition-led and spontaneous outbreaks of violence – come into play at the same time. When this happens, physical attacks may be widespread at both the national and the local levels. The Brazilian local elections of October 2012 demonstrate this point well. Despite the fact that Brazil was widely seen to have consolidated an impressively stable democratic political system, and the elections were for local positions (where typically less is at stake), 5 per cent of all candidates reported being the target of attacks or the threat of attack. Worse still, twenty-two people were murdered in the run-up to the polls, leading 410 towns to request additional security from the police.[32] In the Brazilian context, political murders are driven by the complex interaction of political competition, the battle for control over political and economic resources, and personal feuds in a country in which the rule of law is often weak.[33] Against this backdrop, elections do not cause violence so much as bring it to the fore. Still, such widespread abuses damage the integrity of the democratic process.

A similar story emerges from elections in Guatemala, where presidential polls in 2007 and 2011 were marked by widespread clashes that, in the latter year, resulted in the death of at least thirty-six candidates and activists. Elections did not simply generate this conflict; rather, they played into and exacerbated an already dysfunctional political context.[34] Despite Guatemala only having 14 million inhabitants, roughly 5,500 are murdered each year, making it one of the most dangerous countries in the world. One of the reasons for this is the existence of the drug cartels that have become embedded within the political landscape, some of which have migrated there from Mexico to escape that country's 'War on Drugs'.[35]

Growing competition between the cartels, and the refusal of Guatemala-based Mexican groups to buy into a tacit agreement between their Guatemalan counterparts and the country's government to avoid using violence against civilians, help explain the high murder rate.[36] This also accounts for a considerable portion of the spike in violence in 2011, as rival cartels sought to make sure that sympathetic or corrupt politicians who could be bought off would end up winning.[37] In turn, the failure of the state to effectively investigate these abuses – just 2 per cent of the violent incidents have been successfully prosecuted[38] – contributed to the rise of a culture of impunity that has in turn encouraged the further use of violence.

Violence as a tool of electoral manipulation

Authoritarian governments use a vast array of different methods for inflicting violence around elections. Indeed, the range of strategies available to counterfeit democrats is frightening. These efforts can be broken down into three broad and overlapping categories: assassination, intimidation and detention of opposition leaders; harassment of opposition supporters, civil society representatives and the media to generate a culture of fear and intimidation in order to reduce turnout and criticism of the regime; and the use of violence to displace voters, and thereby disenfranchise them.

Removing rivals

In the first chapter, we discussed how authoritarian regimes that act early are able to prevent opposition candidates from even making it onto the ballot. But many authoritarian regimes act too late or fail to prevent opposition figures from standing because they enjoy too much public support or international backing. Under these circumstances, authoritarian states may simply remove rivals by throwing them in jail.

In Russia, opposition leaders and civil society activists are frequently arrested for doing little more than arranging public meetings and speaking their mind. Notably, in August 2016 one of the most prominent opposition figures to hold public office, Yevgeny Urlashov, was sentenced to twelve and a half years in prison.[39] The former mayor of Yaroslavl and anti-corruption campaigner had built a reputation for being an outspoken critic of the Kremlin. His allies believe that the charges were politically motivated, designed to prevent him from building an opposition stronghold in a city that sits 250 kilometres north-east of Moscow.

Just one year before his arrest in 2013, Urlashov had been elected mayor of Yaroslavl in a landslide, taking 70 per cent of the vote.[40] A member of Civic Platform, the opposition party founded by Russian billionaire Mikhail Prokhorov, Urlashov's rise to prominence hinted that anti-government sentiment was not confined only to Moscow, but had spread to regional towns. Indeed, just before he was detained Urlashov had spoken about his intention to run for a more powerful position – that of governor of Yaroslavl Oblast. This represented a significant threat to United Russia, the ruling party of Vladimir Putin. An opposition supporter even went so far as to argue that 'the road to the Kremlin is through Yaroslavl'.[41] In this way, Urlashov's independent power base had the potential to challenge Putin's political dominance.

Targeting Urlashov thus served two purposes for the government. Once a district court had found him guilty of extorting one bribe and receiving a second of 17 million rubles, a potential opposition figurehead was removed from the political stage. At the same time, the former mayor's fall from grace served as an important lesson to other opposition leaders not to get ideas above their 'correct' station in Russia's politics. Far from keeping the arrest under wraps, a video of Urlashov being arrested by masked members of the security forces was broadcast on state television to ensure that the lesson hit home.[42] The message was clear: behave like Urlashov and you will meet the same fate, or worse.

In other cases, opposition leaders have been forced to leave the political arena under the weight of the repression they face. This has frequently been the case in Tajikistan, where President Emomali Rahmon has won three elections in a row, none of which have been free and fair.[43] Although his political movement – the ironically named People's Democratic Party of Tajikistan – has secured more than 70 per cent of the seats in every election since 2000, Rahmon remains concerned that the latent opposition to his rule will one day coalesce around an opposition leader.[44]

To prevent the rise of such a rival, he has adopted strong-arm tactics. For example, in the run-up to the 2013 presidential elections, the regime reacted to the decision of two opposition parties to nominate the well-known civil society leader Oinihol Bobonazarova as their candidate by threatening three of her family members with job losses and prosecution.[45] She later dropped out of the race, citing the pressure from the authorities.[46]

Creating a culture of fear

As is often the case, the government's intimidation of Bobonazarova in Tajikistan was part of a much broader strategy designed to scare ordinary voters into either supporting the ruling party or staying home on election day. This included a number of attacks on Rahmon's critics that were so frequent it created the sense that regime outsiders were collectively under attack. In May 2013, Zaid Saidov, the minister of industry who had recently established an opposition party, New Tajikistan, was detained at Dushanbe airport. He was later charged and found guilty of corruption, embezzlement, polygamy and rape. Other leaders from his party subsequently called a press conference to allege that he had received death threats warning him to 'stay away from politics' before his arrest. Around Saidov's trial, the offices of New Tajikistan were sealed and protests in favour of his release were violently dispersed.[47] As in the case of Urlashov in Russia, the message to the Tajik opposition was received loud and clear.

The same month, Sherik Karamkhudoev, a prominent figure in the Islamic Renaissance Party of Tajikistan, was sent to jail for fourteen years in a trial conducted behind closed doors for 'participating in mass disorders'. Karamkhudoev's family have stated that he was tortured by security services from the time he went missing in April 2012 until his trial.[48]

It was not only individuals who were targeted. The Association of Young Lawyers (Amparo) was shut down on charges that it claims were trumped up by the courts because its work had exposed corruption and the use of torture within the Tajik army.[49] In other areas, the law did not have to be manipulated because it was written to entrench authoritarian control. Notably, Tajiks do not enjoy freedom of speech and can be prosecuted for insulting the president or any government representative.[50] Unsurprisingly, in this climate of violent repression and political fear, President Rahmon won the 2013 elections in a landslide.[51]

Moving the masses

The benefits to incumbent leaders of generating a climate of fear are also clear from the case of Kenya, where political violence around elections has taken a particularly brutal and effective form. In the late 1980s, the government of President Daniel arap Moi's Kenya African National Union (KANU) came under increasing pressure to end the country's single-party status by legalizing opposition political parties. Moi initially sought to resist calls for reform, but, following the decision of international donors to withhold financial assistance until the government had embarked on 'good governance' reforms, he relented.[52]

Ahead of the transition to multiparty politics, Moi had argued that the one-party state should be maintained because unchecked political competition would result in rising ethnic tensions and violence.[53] Once his one-party state had collapsed, he set about ensuring that his prophecy came true. In particular, the president's political machine deployed violence to displace and disenfranchise suspected opposition supporters. More specifically, in the run-up to the elections in 1992 and 1997, the government plotted to create 'KANU only' zones in the regime's heartlands of the Rift Valley.[54] To do this, the ruling party sponsored ethnic clashes in the area, in which militia groups aligned with the regime were encouraged to intimidate and attack ethnic communities such as the Kikuyu, who were assumed to support rival candidates.[55] This strategy was particularly effective for two reasons. First, Moi's own Kalenjin community had an established rite of passage that created tightly bound groups of men in generational cohorts and taught them how to fight.[56] Second, some KANU supporters stood to gain greater political power and control over land and other resources by chasing away minority communities. In other words, they had both a motive and an opportunity to deploy political violence.[57]

By orchestrating the clashes, KANU was able to achieve two goals simultaneously: intimidating critics into staying quiet while keeping opposition voters away from the polls. In the run-up to the two elections held in the 1990s, clashes between rival communities led to over 2,000 deaths and the displacement of over 500,000 people.[58] Because many of those fleeing were not able to take their identification documents with them, and because Kenya had a rule that citizens could only vote where they had registered, the displacement of opposition supporters effectively disenfranchised them.[59]

However, even with rampant corruption and the targeted use of violence, Moi remained politically vulnerable. The Forum for the Restoration of Democracy (FORD) that had been set up to campaign for multiparty politics brought together a strong coalition of leaders from a range of different communities. Kenneth Matiba represented the powerful Kikuyu ethnic group while Oginga Odinga could deliver the support of most voters from his own Luo community. Other leaders commanded significant influence with the country's smaller ethnic groups. Given Kenya's strongly ethnic voting patterns, the array of forces lining up against Moi signalled that he might actually lose. Consequently, KANU responded to the launch of FORD by violently repressing the new movement, banning its rallies and detaining and beating Matiba, who never fully recovered from the torture that he experienced at the hands of state security officials.[60]

But FORD had too much momentum to be derailed by repression alone – and international criticism of repressive strategies hurt the reputation of the regime. As a result, Moi embarked on a different approach, buttressing the intimidation of opposition supporters with a form of divide-and-rule politics delivered with Machiavellian skill.[61] One of the main elements of this programme was to have government-funded operatives infiltrate FORD by passing themselves off as opposition activists and, once on the inside, encouraging rifts between different factions of the pro-democracy movement.[62]

Setting FORD's leaders against one another was a fairly easy task given the size of their egos, their personal ambitions and the tensions between the ethnic groups they represented.[63] Odinga, who took over the leadership of FORD following Matiba's detention, had long dreamed of occupying State House, and – as one of the only FORD leaders not to have recently served under the KANU government – saw himself as the country's most credible opposition leader. For his part, Matiba expected that his bravery in launching the campaign for multiparty politics, and his suffering in detention, would be rewarded with the FORD ticket for the presidential election.[64]

Armed with this information, government agents carefully drove a wedge into the heart of the opposition. When Matiba arrived back in Nairobi following hospital treatment in London, KANU paid for people to bolster his welcome party, cheering him home.[65] The more confident Matiba became about his chances, the less willing he was to play second fiddle to Odinga. Over the weeks that followed, FORD began to split in two, effectively becoming two parties in one, FORD–Asili under Matiba, and FORD–Kenya under Odinga. Having deliberately placed barriers in the way of new parties officially registering to contest the elections ever since the constitution had been changed to legalize opposition parties, the Registrar of Parties approved both applications to ensure that FORD would appear twice on the ballot paper – therefore dividing the vote between them.[66]

Along with the corruption perpetrated by the regime, and some targeted ballot-box stuffing, the splitting of the opposition enabled Moi to retain power with just 31 per cent of the vote. Had Matiba and Odinga remained united, they would probably have won; on their own, they both fell way short of Moi's total, but between them they secured 36 per cent of the vote.[67] Moi's strategy had worked. Divide and rule had become divide and win.

The multiple uses of political violence

This combination of violence and divide-and-rule politics is not unique to Kenya. It is particularly common in regimes that face the threat of both external opposition and internal fragmentation. Countries typically transition to multiparty politics from personal dictatorships, one-party states or military regimes. In all three cases, the executive has typically benefited from the fact that opposition to its rule has been illegal. Most analysis of this kind of pure authoritarianism focused on the most obvious aspect of this form of political control: the capacity to prohibit rival political movements and detain rival leaders. After all, if you could manage to jail a rival or ban their party outright, not much else was needed to win an election. But the ability to ban opposition forces was important in a second way, because it also helped leaders maintain internal discipline.

To see why, it is worth looking back to the 1960s, shortly after African states won independence from their colonial masters. Having secured political autonomy, the continent's 'founding fathers' faced two main challenges: first, to develop economies that had been set up to serve the colonial metropole rather than their own people; and second, to manage their broad coalitions. These tasks proved to be equally difficult. During colonial rule, groups with completely different agendas were able to unify in opposition to their common enemy: the colonial power.[68] But once independence was achieved, and the common enemy removed, their vast differences were laid bare. Infighting began almost immediately.

As a result, hope and expectation quickly turned to frustration and distrust. One consequence of this was that the continent's presidents and prime ministers started to receive threats that unless they were more generous in the distribution of jobs and resources, disgruntled leaders and factions would leave their coalitions. In Zambia, for example, President Kenneth Kaunda railed against the members of his own party who had been 'blackmailing' him into making unaffordable concessions.[69] It was against this backdrop that leaders in countries such as Kenya, Senegal, Tanzania and Zambia established one-party states.[70] By prohibiting opposition, the likes of Kaunda simultaneously removed the threat of rival parties gaining ground and the possibility of defection, strengthening their hand against internal opposition. In the years to come, it would be easier – though far from straightforward – to manage their own coalitions.

The legalization of opposition parties in Latin America, post-communist Europe and sub-Saharan Africa during the last three decades of the twentieth century once again exposed leaders to forces that threatened the cohesion of their ruling coalition. With the possibility of forming a new party or joining an opposition coalition, defection was put back on the table, and with it the ability to 'blackmail' the executive. Moreover, as in post-independence Africa, many of the dominant political parties that we see around the world today are effectively broad coalitions. With a small number of important exceptions, these alliances lack a coherent ideological underpinning, and are largely kept together by personal networks, clientelism and patronage. But if such coalitions are held together by the doling out of slices of the government pie, then such governments are liable to fragment dangerously when there are only crumbs left.

This dynamic places particularly strong pressure on the executive in cases where elections have been close, because under these conditions the defection of a section of the ruling alliance can be the difference between winning and losing. It is in situations like this, when leaders face strong opposition from within and from without, that the most extreme forms of political violence become likely.

For example, it was precisely this consideration that made ethnic cleansing such an attractive proposition to Hutu elites in Rwanda after plans were put in place to reintroduce multiparty elections in the early 1990s.[71] Having come to power in a coup in 1973, Juvénal Habyarimana constructed a single-party state under the National Revolutionary Movement for Development (MRND). However, in the late 1980s the MRND's political control was undermined by economic difficulties and the invasion of the Rwandan Patriotic Front (RPF), a force of mostly Tutsi refugees who had been living in exile in Uganda, which enjoyed the support of the government of the Ugandan president, Yoweri Museveni. At the same time, Habyarimana also faced sources of opposition closer to home. In particular, the president's willingness to favour his own northern base when giving out state jobs and resources sparked criticism from disgruntled Hutus in the south and centre of the country.

International actors responded by supporting a dual strategy of simultaneous peace negotiations and political liberalization, hoping that a process of conflict resolution would culminate in elections. Over the next two years Habyarimana legalized political parties, and entered into talks to end the war. However, neither Habyarimana nor the hardline figures around him were committed to democratic reform.[72] One of their greatest worries was that although it appeared to be powerful, the MRND would not hold together when the opportunity for defection presented itself.[73] Instead, shorn of the legal protection of a ban on opposition parties, the government was vulnerable to fragmentation, raising the prospect that it could be outmanoeuvred by a new alliance of Tutsi and moderate Hutu forces.[74]

In response, Hutu extremists began articulating a hardline pro-Hutu agenda and planning an unprecedented programme of political violence. The central component of this strategy was the demonization of Tutsis. Through this process, Rwandan Tutsis came to be identified with the RPF, even if they had little to do with the rebellion; the Rwandan army even staged fake attacks on Kigali that they blamed on Rwandan Tutsis in order to bring this particular scapegoat to life.[75] In the background, armed militias, notably the infamous Interahamwe, were trained, to enable the regime to make good on its threats.

While this strategy served to entrench political and ethnic cleavages, it had disastrous consequences for political stability and national identity. In contrast to many of the other cases discussed here, violence went from being a strategy for retaining political control to an end in itself. In the process, radical Hutu elites ceased to be concerned by the need to hide their activities in order to maintain the regime's reputation. While this may have been partly because they retained the support of the French government – which had helped to arm the regime – and so believed they could get away with the atrocities that they were committing,[76] it also serves as a visceral reminder that political violence does not always follow a rational logic, and risks spinning out of control.

In the Rwandan context, the impact of the hardliners' strategy was to polarize the political system into 'Hutu' and 'Tutsi' blocs in which individuals were placed under great pressure to defend and support their own community. As a result, hardline Hutu leaders were empowered to depict dissenting individuals as 'traitors', and hence to impose intra-group discipline.[77]

At the same time, many ordinary Hutu citizens who had been sold the story of a Tutsi plot against the nation demanded that their government act against the political and economic 'threat' represented by 'outsiders'.[78] Taken together, these two developments enabled Hutu leaders to escape sanction for violent acts – and made it harder for more moderate leaders to succeed. Thus, by increasing the tension between the two communities, the MRND reduced the threat that moderate Hutus and Tutsis would join forces.

As the use of divide-and-rule strategies became more pronounced, the political system became increasingly divided between a cluster of more extreme parties such as the MRND and the Coalition for the Defence of the Republic (CDR), collectively known as Hutu Power, and a range of moderate and increasingly fearful opposition parties.[79] When the president's plane was shot down in controversial circumstances,[80] Hutu Power extremists used his death as a pretext for the onset of genocide. Subsequently, the presidential guard and Interahamwe instigated a wave of killing that was taken up – often under duress – by ordinary Hutus.[81] The resulting tsunami of violence claimed the lives of over 800,000 Tutsis, along with many Hutus who bravely refused to participate.

Although political violence is most shocking when it involves genocide, it has not always been expressed in ethnic terms. Rather, in countries such as Zimbabwe, the divide between 'us' and 'them' has been defined on a partisan or economic basis. The strategies employed by Robert Mugabe to retain power demonstrate this point well.[82] As we saw in chapter 2, by the early 2000s, the ZANU–PF government had come under mounting pressure both inside the party, from a new generation of leaders, and outside it, from a fast-growing opposition.[83]

As in Rwanda, this combination encouraged the ruling party to deploy violence as a political strategy. Fearing that ZANU–PF might eventually lose power, Mugabe moved to turn one of his weaknesses into a strength, and formed an alliance with the war veterans. To do so, he reversed his previous stance on agricultural policy and encouraged the invasion of white-owned farms in order to meet the demands of his new constituency.[84] This change of strategy ushered in a period of intense political repression that had two goals: to make it near impossible for the opposition MDC to function, and to frighten those within ZANU–PF into staying loyal.

Of course, the violence utilized in Zimbabwe did not approach the scale of the genocidal acts committed in Rwanda, but Mugabe nonetheless proved to be one of Africa's most adept practitioners of repression. However, although earlier violence against the president's political opponents in Matabeleland featured a clear ethnic dimension,[85] the attacks on the MDC were not defined in ethnic terms. Instead, the government fostered a sense of 'us' versus 'them' that did not map onto ethnic divisions. The party's intellectuals had long been engaged in the process of reinterpreting Zimbabwean history, playing on the country's multifaceted liberation struggle to construct a narrative in which ZANU–PF were national saviours, their actions necessary to defend the country's sovereignty against foreign aggressors.[86]

Within official 'patriotic history', opponents were demonized as 'sell-outs' and thus legitimate targets of state violence.[87] Following the rise of the MDC and the growing support for the opposition, the focus of patriotic history was tweaked. By aligning ZANU–PF with an influential group of war veterans, Mugabe reaffirmed his 'revolutionary' credentials, heading off internal criticism.[88]

At the same time, ZANU–PF exploited some white farmers' support for the MDC to depict the opposition party as a tool of Zimbabwe's white minority and, by extension, as a representative of foreign colonial powers. But although Mugabe played heavily on race, the regime hit out against black communities of varying ethnicities that were known to have either voted MDC or to have failed to provide sufficient support for ZANU–PF. Consequently, violence followed lines of party allegiance that cut across communal identities. In turn, the effectiveness of Mugabe's strategy demonstrates the capacity of counterfeit democracies to shape and reshape political cleavages to their own advantage.[89]

As we saw in chapter 1, the significance of violence to electoral outcomes in Zimbabwe is best demonstrated by the fraught contest of 2008. In the first round of voting, the momentum behind the MDC enabled its leader, Morgan Tsvangirai, to push Mugabe into second place (the first time this had happened), but neither candidate got enough votes to win outright. Facing likely electoral defeat, the wave of violence that ZANU–PF unleashed in response was so ferocious that Tsvangirai felt that he had no option but to pull out of the second-round run-off, which in turn meant that Mugabe was returned to office.[90] Thereafter, the constant threat of violence served as an ever-present deterrent against anyone else crossing Mugabe – inside the party or outside it.

Reducing the cost of violence

One of the major risks of deploying violence is detection and prosecution, as the case of Kenya makes clear. Following a flawed election in 2007/8 in which President Mwai Kibaki was declared the winner, ethnic clashes erupted on an unprecedented geographical scale, leading to over 1,000 deaths and the displacement of 600,000 people. After militias supportive of the opposition Orange Democratic Movement (ODM) targeted communities assumed to have voted for the president's Party of National Unity (PNU), similar groups allied to the government committed 'revenge attacks'.[91] The clashes made headlines around the world, and a combination of domestic and international pressure led to a government investigation that found evidence that a number of political leaders had played a central role in organizing the violence.

Following the failure of the Kenyan government to establish a domestic tribunal to try those named in the report, the International Criminal Court (ICC), an intergovernmental organization that sits in The Hague in the Netherlands, launched prosecutions against a number of prominent figures, including opposition leader William Ruto and establishment leader Uhuru Kenyatta.[92] Although these prosecutions ultimately collapsed, they caused major embarrassment and annoyance to Ruto and Kenyatta, who had to travel to The Hague to defend themselves.

Indeed, it seems likely that the court proceedings, and the knowledge that the world was watching, temporarily made political leaders and journalists more cautious of the use of hate speech and political violence at the next election in 2013.[93] In that contest, the combination of the ICC process, a strong domestic and international campaign for peace, and the heavy deployment of state security forces in potential hot spots resulted in a much smaller number of deaths around polling day, despite the disputed outcome.[94] The fallout from the Kenya crisis highlights the potential risk to political leaders of deploying violence in an era in which regional and international courts such as the ICC can bring cases against those seen to have undermined human rights.

However, there are strategies that clever authoritarians can use to hide their tracks. One of the factors that made it hard to prosecute Ruto and Kenyatta was that the two leaders were alleged to have helped fund and deploy violence through loosely organized militias. This made it more difficult to prove their guilt, because doing so typically requires demonstrating that the accused had effective control of a coherent organization. Unless this can be shown, leaders can claim that they did not know what was happening, or that their orders were not followed or were misunderstood.[95]

In Kenya, in order to make an effective case against William Ruto prosecutors argued that he was in control of an organized and hierarchical 'Kalenjin network'.[96] This was a problematic claim: even some of Ruto's critics, who believed that he was guilty, would not have characterized these militias in quite this manner. As a result of the way that prosecutors were forced to make their case, and the controversy and intimidation surrounding the process, many academics and experts were unwilling to testify.[97] In turn, this significantly weakened the case of the prosecution.

Thus, operating outside formal structures can enable leaders to escape censure for their actions by making it harder for human rights organizations to lay the blame for election violence at their door. While the police and security forces are often involved in political intimidation, leaders can use unidentified groups or individuals who cannot be easily traced back to them for the worst violence. Doing so creates an aura of plausible deniability that can prove politically convenient.

A second strategy that can reduce the cost of violence for incumbents is to create a political landscape whereby intimidation and fear are part of everyday life, to the extent that overt force rarely has to be used. This is a strategy that has been effectively deployed in Zimbabwe by ZANU–PF. Following the explicit state-led violence of 2008, President Robert Mugabe was obliged to form a power-sharing government with the MDC, creating the post of prime minister for Morgan Tsvangirai. Although the MDC lacked real power within this forced marriage, ZANU–PF was keen not to repeat the experience. Consequently, for the subsequent 2013 elections, the ruling party reined in physical attacks, not because its underlying instincts had changed, but because they were no longer needed.[98]

Once the coercive capacity of the government had been demonstrated, intimidation could be achieved through implied threats ('shaking the matchbox'), brought to life by more sporadic beatings and arson. As part of this strategy, the government even established the Zimbabwe Human Rights Commission (ZHRC) in a bid to appear serious about investigating and preventing human rights abuses. In reality, this was a PR strategy with little substance; the commission was so starved of resources and inhibited by the country's legal framework that the first chairman, Reginald Austin, resigned in protest. And as the polls neared, ZANU–PF militants set up bases in disputed rural voting districts to intimidate any more independent-minded voters.[99]

Along with a number of difficulties that beset the opposition, including internal splits and public disappointment at the limitations of the power-sharing government, this enabled Mugabe to have his cake and eat it. On the one hand, the government won the election with a comfortable majority. On the other, observers were forced to admit that the environment surrounding the polls was a significant improvement on 2008, creating the impression that ZANU–PF was engaged in a process of reform.

Indeed, things seemed so calm on the surface that African Union observers, who rarely look too closely at how ruling parties retain power,[100] could report that 'Voting was conducted in an atmosphere devoid of violence, harassment and disturbances.'[101]

The consequences of violence

Political violence is a particularly effective strategy of electoral manipulation. Evidence from countries as diverse as Nigeria and Mexico shows that individuals who suffer, or who live in areas blighted by, violence are less likely to go to the polls, making repression an effective way for ruling parties to depress the opposition vote.[102] As a result, cross-national studies have found that the deployment of violence increases both a government's prospects of victory and its likely victory margin.[103] Moreover, by deploying violence against both internal and external enemies, leaders can help to prevent defections while suppressing the opposition vote. However, while the deployment of political violence helps incumbents retain power in the short term, it can create long-term division and political volatility – in some cases undermining the very fabric of national identity.[104]

This is clear from the Rwandan case (pp. 110–12), but it is also true of countries that do not deteriorate into such extremes: even when violence is deployed in a more targeted and careful way, it can still throw off the fragile political and cultural balance needed to maintain stability and peace. By playing divide-and-rule politics, leaders harden identities that exacerbate social tensions. By boosting the capacity and importance of the police and the security forces, an emphasis on coercion enables 'securocrats' to exert greater influence over broader policy issues.[105] And by arming and funding gangs and militias, regimes risk undermining the capacity of the state to maintain political order in the long run.

The danger posed by political violence is particularly high in post-conflict contexts. Although international actors often see the holding of an election as the successful culmination of a peace process,[106] such polls can have deleterious consequences if safeguards are not put in place.

The dangers of post-conflict elections are well illustrated by the case of Cambodia. Following the fall of the brutal and genocidal Khmer Rouge regime in 1979, and the end of the subsequent Vietnamese occupation, the country held elections in 1993. In part because these elections were tightly policed by the international community and held under the supervision of the United Nations Transitional Authority in Cambodia (UNTAC), they were relatively successful. Although Norodom Ranariddh and his royalist FUNCIPEC (United National Front for an Independent, Neutral, Peaceful, and Co-operative Cambodia) won a majority of the vote, he formed a coalition government with the Cambodian People's Party, whose leader, Hun Sen, became second prime minister.

However, Hun Sen, a former prime minister and member of the Khmer Rouge, was not willing to play second fiddle. Following clashes between the two factions that killed dozens of people, Hun Sen moved to topple Ranariddh and seize power for himself in a coup. According to the UN Centre for Human Rights in Cambodia, this period saw over 100 political killings,[107] described as 'a systematic campaign of intimidation, torture, and summary executions'.[108]

Once Hun Sen had established control of the military and the government, he was persuaded to hold elections in 1998 as had been scheduled. However, the campaign occurred under the most difficult of conditions, as 'Voters were forced by CPP [Cambodian People's Party] officials to swear oaths to vote for their party, sometimes in the presence of Buddhist monks. In some cases, villagers were even asked to drink from a glass with a bullet resting on the bottom to demonstrate their commitment to vote for the CPP.'[109] In total, the UN Centre for Human Rights investigated 140 reports of political violence between 20 May and 27 June 1998, including twelve deaths.[110]

Against this backdrop, the result of the election was hardly surprising. Hun Sen was elected prime minister after his party won a majority of seats in the National Assembly. The CPP has remained in power ever since.

As the Cambodian experience demonstrates all too clearly, holding elections in challenging contexts may generate significant difficulties for both national unity and long-term democratization. Deterring the use of violence around elections is therefore an essential, but extremely difficult, task. None of the cases discussed in this chapter has seen the successful prosecution of the main perpetrators. There are obvious reasons for this. When violence is deployed by the ruling party, the government has a vested interest in covering it up. Given the limited independence of the police, media and courts in most counterfeit democracies, this means that prosecutions for election-related violence are unlikely to advance unless they are of the opposition or figures who have fallen out of favour.

Indeed, in some cases the previous use of violence becomes a fresh barrier to political reform, because those who have perpetrated it – militias, state security agents, political leaders – fight harder against losing power to opposition parties who may seek to prosecute them for past abuses. As we noted in the introduction to this book, when faced with the threat of prosecution, incumbent leaders have an additional incentive to rig elections so that they can protect their immunity.

Strengthening democracy and deterring political violence

This raises the question of whether there is anything the international community can do to prevent the worst excesses of political violence. Western powers have long asserted a right of intervention in cases of severe human rights violations.[111] The contemporary version of this argument came to the fore in April 2017, after President Bashar al-Assad of Syria launched a sarin nerve gas attack on his own people in the town of Khan Shaykhun.[112] Even in the context of a prolonged civil war noted for its brutality, the indiscriminate use of gas made headlines around the world.

In turn, photographs of young children foaming at the mouth had a 'big impact' on US President Donald Trump, who suggested that Assad had crossed a red line and that the decent nations of the world were duty-bound to act.[113] Shortly after, Trump moved to launch fifty-nine missiles against a Syrian airbase, in an attack that was designed to hurt the regime's ability to deploy chemical weapons, and to demonstrate the high cost of its doing so.

Trump's response itself turned out to be highly controversial and sparked a heated international debate. While Assad's allies claimed that there was no evidence that he was responsible for the use of the gas, a number of critical newspapers speculated as to whether the United Kingdom, which had spoken out against Assad,[114] had in fact sold his regime the chemicals in the first place. Others suggested that the use of force might prove unproductive.[115] However, what was less controversial was the idea that certain types of government abuses, if proven, should not be overlooked. Indeed, in the late 1990s, the belief that there are certain human rights violations so bad that the international community cannot allow them to pass unchallenged led 139 states to support the formation of an international court with the capacity to try leaders for major crimes such as genocide, crimes against humanity and war crimes: the International Criminal Court, already briefly introduced above (pp. 110–12).[116]

In principle, the formation of the ICC represented a decisive blow against authoritarian excess. Although only 118 of the 139 countries that signed the Rome Statute ultimately ratified the document – meaning that they were willing to use the ICC in their own state – this represented a wide range of countries, including a large number outside the classic club of Western liberal democracies. Moreover, the court's decision to launch prosecutions in Kenya, discussed in the previous section (pp. 115–17), highlights its potential to punish the perpetrators of electoral violence and so dissuade against its political use. But as we have seen, the ICC faces a number of major challenges when it comes to effectively addressing government-led abuses. The first of these has already been addressed: by using non-state structures, leaders can make it difficult for international prosecutors to build their cases.

Two more structural challenges compound this problem. First, the ICC lacks the capacity to collect evidence and is therefore dependent on the co-operation of the countries in which it works. This is akin to the prosecution or the police asking the accused criminal for help in gathering and providing evidence about the crime being investigated. The problems with that arrangement are obvious. Second, the ICC has no formal witness protection programme, which leaves those who give evidence to the court particularly vulnerable.[117] These two weaknesses contributed to Ruto's and Kenyatta's ability to defeat the charges laid against them. A remarkable number of key witnesses died, disappeared or changed their minds during the course of the trial, undermining the prosecutors' evidence base.[118] Furthermore, the Kenyan government unsurprisingly failed to offer its full support, especially once Kenyatta and Ruto formed an 'anti-prosecution' alliance and won power as president and deputy president in 2013. The Kenyan case thus demonstrates why the ICC is usually only effective when the accused has lost power and the new regime wants to punish the old one.

Although the failure of the ICC in the case of Kenya has been particularly glaring, it is only one in a series of examples in which the court has been left with egg on its face. Prosecutions in the Democratic Republic of Congo, Sudan and Uganda have been no less controversial, and rarely successful.[119]

The difficulties experienced by the ICC suggests that other non-judicial strategies might be more effective in combating the use of electoral violence. The United Kingdom and the United States have, for example, been willing to use sanctions to target those who fund and organize violence, for example by freezing their assets or by denying them the right to travel. These strategies have the clear advantage that they can be implemented quickly and on the basis of less evidence. They can also be put in place before and during violent episodes, and have a more immediate deterrent effect.

However, such efforts have three significant limitations. The first is that while these punishments represent annoyances, they are rarely applied widely enough to undermine a regime's hold on power.[120] The second is that they are subject to the foreign-policy interests of Western states. The United States isn't about to freeze the assets of a geopolitical ally, such as the Saudi monarchy, over ongoing political repression and brutality. As we shall see in chapter 6, the enforcement of democratic norms varies in part in accordance with the vested interests of global powers. Finally, direct Western intervention is problematic because it is often perceived as neo-colonial meddling.[121] Indeed, the inconsistent application of human rights principles is one of the main factors that empowers many authoritarian leaders to depict the treatment they receive as being arbitrary and unfair.

This has also been a significant problem for the ICC. A series of prosecutions of African leaders in the 2000s left the court vulnerable to the accusation that it was carrying out the agenda of Western powers, targeting weaker African states while ignoring comparable crimes committed by European or North American leaders.[122] Although many African countries played an active role in the formation of the ICC, campaigns led by African leaders prosecuted by the court in recent years have resulted in the emergence of an anti-colonial critique that has proved to have considerable resonance with leaders and ordinary people alike.[123] This has allowed war criminals to deflect blame by painting themselves as victims of an imperialist and even racist system.

The limited legitimacy of the ICC raises the question of whether interventions designed and implemented through more-inclusive international forums, such as the United Nations and regional bodies such as the African Union (AU), could provide a more legitimate and therefore more effective route to counter electoral violence around the world – a question that we take up in the conclusion.

Violence comes with serious risks, which is why many leaders avoid it. Repression is often highly visible, and many savvy autocrats know that if they play their cards right and use alternative forms of electoral manipulation they can rig elections while securing international endorsement for their regimes. In the twenty-first century, such 'clever' election rigging is increasingly taking place in cyberspace – the Wild West of election rigging, its rules often unwritten and almost never enforced.

Chapter 4

HACK THE ELECTION

Fake news and the digital frontier

Andrés Sepúlveda sleeps under a bulletproof blanket, behind bombproof doors in a maximum-security prison in central Bogotá, Colombia. When he travels to judicial hearings or to meet with prosecutors, he is accompanied by a caravan of motorcycles and armed guards with serious firepower. As they move at high speed through the Colombian capital, the motorcade uses sophisticated equipment to jam mobile phones, in order to lower the risk of a co-ordinated assassination attempt.

Sepúlveda is one of the world's most effective digital election-rigging specialists. Now that he has been caught and put in jail, he is helping to atone for his crimes by pulling the digital curtain back. What he is exposing is not pretty and the people he used to work with want him dead.

Sepúlveda started small. In 2005, he began hacking into the files of opponents' campaigns, stealing their databases of voters and donors, and occasionally defacing a website with digital graffiti. It was small-time digital harassment, but he began to understand how information could be the most powerful weapon in a democracy. After all, political competition is a battle to shape the opinions of the electorate. If you manipulate the information available to voters, you can manipulate the election too.

Within a few years, Sepúlveda was running a team of hackers that offered an array of services in the shadows of the internet that could take down Latin America's most powerful politicians. For $20,000 a month, Sepúlveda would provide prospective campaigns with a menu of digital manipulation – from hacking smartphones and email servers to sending out mass texts or emails laced with perfectly timed misinformation. This was a pittance for campaigns that sought to secure re-election to the highest echelons of power in Latin America. As a result, business was brisk. Sepúlveda and his hacker squad worked for campaigns in Guatemala, Venezuela, Mexico, Honduras, El Salvador, Panama, Nicaragua and Costa Rica. Across the region, he knocked down left-wing rivals and helped his chosen right-wing candidates. While he could not guarantee a win, his team was able to confer a considerable advantage on its clients, and appears to have been responsible for several narrow victories.

Unsurprisingly, Sepúlveda was always careful to keep his work in the shadows. When anyone met with him in a hotel, he would not even allow a smartphone to enter the room. That meticulous attention to secrecy helped him net prominent clients in Latin American politics; he allegedly masterminded a digital effort to secure a big electoral win for Mexico's current president Enrique Peña Nieto in 2012. Sepúlveda told law enforcement officers and a Bloomberg investigative team that he had been given a budget of $600,000 by the Peña Nieto campaign.[1] With that money, according to Sepúlveda, they hacked into opposition networks, stole files, tapped into private email accounts and used an enormous army of fake social media accounts to control the digital debate.

Whenever Sepúlveda chose to, he could make certain topics trend on Twitter, or use hundreds of rapid-response bots to shape a narrative in a more favourable direction for the campaign.

After all, he realized, voters tended to respond and engage more with bots designed to look like real people than with slick elite pundits analysing the campaign on television. Through this process, Sepúlveda accurately discerned the potency of fake authenticity. Or, as he put it from prison: 'When I realized that people believe what the Internet says more than reality, I discovered that I had the power to make people believe almost anything.'[2]

Partly thanks to Sepúlveda's alleged work in the digital shadows, Peña Nieto narrowly won. As Sepúlveda watched these returns alone in Colombia, he cracked open a beer, and then started getting rid of the evidence – drilling holes through hard drives, smashing phones and, for good measure, shredding all sensitive documents and flushing them down the toilet.

Sepúlveda was eventually caught after operating more publicly as he tried to help the right-wing opposition candidate Óscar Iván Zuluaga in Colombia in 2014. For his efforts to support Zuluaga's campaign against peace talks with the Revolutionary Armed Forces of Colombia (FARC) rebels, he was arrested. During the trial, thugs representing powerful bosses held up photos of his family members, making clear that if he talked their lives would be at risk. Sepúlveda eventually entered a guilty plea, confessing to crimes ranging from hacking to espionage. He is currently serving a ten-year prison sentence.[3]

This high-stakes political intrigue is not unique to Latin America. Sepúlveda is not the only person to have figured out that information is the most important weapon in democracies, particularly during election campaigns. In fact, some of what Sepúlveda was doing echoes the infamous Watergate scandal surrounding US President Richard Nixon, which was fundamentally perpetrated in pursuit of the same goal: to steal damaging or valuable information from his political rivals. But the new digital tools of hacking, spreading misinformation online and social media manipulation have all presented fresh opportunities to play dirty in ways that Nixon could never have dreamed of, with worrying implications for the quality of democracy.

The advantages of this kind of rigging are clear. Because it is often difficult to track the source of hacking and misinformation disseminated anonymously online, this is a strategy that ruling parties can set in motion and then disown. The same is true of spreading fake news generated in troll factories abroad, as it's difficult to trace the origin and easy to deny involvement. The key is plausible deniability, which is far easier to establish when lies and misinformation are being spread through official propaganda channels. This is the same logic that explains why incumbent autocrats turn to militias that they can disown rather than using state security forces (chapter 3). Hacking from the shadows makes it easier for authoritarian leaders to orchestrate rigging and then wash their hands of it and point the finger elsewhere.

Beyond helping leaders escape censure, digital disinformation and misinformation tactics can influence the way that both domestic and international audiences perceive a wide range of issues, from the record of the incumbent to the reputation of the opposition and the quality of the election itself. By throwing mud at the opposition, governments can create the impression that both sides are equally bad – regardless of whether that's true or not. By spreading fake polling data and boosting the profile of regime insiders on social media, counterfeit democrats can create the impression that they are destined for victory. In turn, setting up the expectation of a good performance means that an overwhelming victory does not come as a surprise, and is less likely to arouse suspicion. In this sense, hacking and fake news may become a central element in the construction of a rigged election that is designed to secure international praise (as discussed in detail in chapter 6).

However, these strategies are different from most of the others discussed in this book in one respect: they can be deployed by both the government and the opposition. In most cases, manipulation strategies clearly favour the ruling party. When it comes to gerrymandering, the ruling party has the power to set constituency boundaries (chapter 1). If we look at vote buying, it is clear that governments can generally outspend opposition parties (chapter 2). The same pattern holds for electoral violence, where incumbents can abuse their control of state security forces (chapter 3), and fraud, which requires control of the electoral commission if it is to be done successfully (chapter 5). But when it comes to hacking, ruling parties or candidates can be victims just as much as perpetrators.

This is because opposition movements don't need much money or infrastructure in order to hack. It's cheap and can be done by a small number of people sitting in a room with an internet connection. Moreover, globalized information flows have internationalized this form of rigging in a way that is impossible to imagine with ballot-box stuffing or physical repression. The Russian government, for example, can now meddle with elections abroad without even having an agent leave Moscow or St Petersburg. One important implication of this shift is that foreign governments and networks have a new route through which to interfere in the electoral process in countries of interest to them. In this sense, the electoral chess-board has expanded considerably, as candidates and parties become the digital pawns of a geopolitical rivalry.

These trends have come to the fore in the United States, where digital operatives working from Russia sought – at the very least – to collude with American supporters of Donald Trump to tilt the 2016 election in favour of the candidate of the opposition party. The strategies used during this period included the creation of fake news disparaging Trump's main rival, Hillary Clinton, and efforts to amplify the reach and impact of pro-Trump messages. Russian troll farms were so successful that top-level Trump campaign officials even shared Kremlin propaganda on social media days before the election. In fact, Trump's own son shared a tweet from a Kremlin-operated account on election day itself.[4] In at least one instance, Russian government accounts organized a series of pro-Trump rallies that Americans subsequently attended – all without leaving Russia.[5] While there is no clear-cut evidence to suggest that these tactics affected the outcome of the election, it is certainly possible, given that the result was decided by roughly 80,000 votes spread across three crucial swing states.

However, even though opposition figures can engage in digital hacking and fake news campaigns, incumbents still typically have the upper hand. In a liberalized media environment such as the United States, it is feasible for the opposition to effectively get its message across using mainstream and social media. This is less likely to happen in authoritarian states in which the government retains tight control of the information landscape. For example, autocrats who do not face a strong civil society and powerful business lobby can simply turn off access to the internet, undermining the kinds of strategies employed in the United States; counterfeit democrats may suffer embarrassing hacks but still be able to block their people from finding out about it.[6]

Moreover, the capacity of the opposition to effectively deploy these strategies depends, in part, on the proportion of the population with access to a mobile phone and the rate of internet penetration. In the United States, you would have had to be living under a rock not to know about the hacking of Hillary Clinton's emails and campaign documents. It spread like wildfire across social media platforms, which most Americans use, and then on even further, reaching the mainstream airwaves. But in places where social media penetration is limited, it is likely to be less important than traditional media such as radio and television. This is the case in much of sub-Saharan Africa, where only 31 per cent of the population is estimated to be connected to the internet – although this figure is increasing every year. Elsewhere, penetration rates tend to be higher: 47 per cent in Asia, 59 per cent in the Middle East, 62 per cent in Latin America, and over 80 per cent in Europe and North America.[7] In those countries where fewer people have access to news and information through Facebook, Twitter and WhatsApp, the role of traditional and state media is typically more significant, which plays to the strengths of the ruling party.

For example, in Ukraine's 2014 elections, a Russian outfit known as CyberBerkut hacked into the Ukrainian Central Election Commission and changed the result to show that the winner was the far-right candidate, Dmytro Yarosh.[8] The commission noticed the attack just before the results went live, and managed to reverse it, avoiding the chaos that might have ensued from releasing the wrong winner's name, and demonstrating the benefits that incumbents have when it comes to limiting the damage from an unfavourable hack. In Russia, the Kremlin-controlled state media operation broadcast the false result – suggesting a co-ordinated strategy to sow confusion and turmoil in Ukraine.[9]

More recently, the suggestion that activists working to secure Donald Trump's victory tried to hack election machines in the United States has focused attention on the fact that relatively few governments that use election technology have taken the necessary steps to protect digital information. This is clearly problematic, especially since some election machinery has no paper trail: sophisticated efforts to digitally stuff the ballot box or switch votes undetected pose a severe challenge to electoral integrity across the world. However, while it is true that in democracies the most significant risk may be that electoral data are hacked by radical opposition groups or external enemies, things look very different in the authoritarian world.

Under counterfeit democrats, the use of electronic processes creates a new avenue through which leaders can push home their advantage. Most obviously, through their control of the electoral commission and, in some cases, the procurement of election technology, governments know which weaknesses in the digital election infrastructure to exploit. In some cases, this may mean simply being handed the necessary log-in details and passwords, removing the need for any actual hacking. Under these circumstances, it can be relatively easy to manipulate a digital register of eligible voters, and even the vote itself, to the incumbent's advantage.

Given this, the spread of digital election technology over the past ten years – which has often been celebrated as a potential saviour of democracy – is also a cause for concern. This is because its growing use has rendered the electoral process increasingly vulnerable to digital manipulation. Increasingly, the administration of elections – from voter registration databases to the tallying process – is being managed on digital servers. And a number of countries have also introduced electronic voting, including Brazil (general elections), Namibia (general elections), Norway (being piloted for local and parliamentary polls), Switzerland (used in parts of the country for municipal and cantonal polls) and the United States (used in parts of the country for general elections – for full details see appendix 16). That shift, aimed to make election administration more efficient and resilient, has also made it more vulnerable to new forms of interference.

As a result, the digital manipulation of data and information is one of the newer strategies in the authoritarian toolbox. Moreover, it is likely to become more common as autocrats around the world come to appreciate its particular advantages. In addition to being hard to trace, some forms of digital manipulation are not illegal and do not necessarily even represent election rigging in a strict sense. This is clearly not the case when it comes to the fixing of election results, but it is true of the manipulation of news and information.

Consider the efforts of companies such as Cambridge Analytica, a private political consultancy that is partly owned by Robert Mercer, an American hedge-fund manager known for supporting conservative causes. In the past few years, the company is believed to have worked on the campaigns of Donald Trump, the 'Leave' team in the United Kingdom's Brexit referendum, and President Uhuru Kenyatta in Kenya, among others. Cambridge Analytica promises to 'use data to change audience behavior'.[10] In the electoral context, it does this by mining data about voters through online sites such as Facebook, and using this information to encourage its clients' supporters to vote and their opponents to stay at home. Its platform is bespoke; it targets specific messages at each individual according to a sophisticated profile of their likely attitudes and beliefs based on their internet activity.

While using 'attack ads' to demobilize opposition supporters and scare tactics to keep rival voters away from the polls clearly contravenes the spirit of democracy, it typically doesn't break any laws. And while such activities may violate electoral regulations if they include clauses designed to ensure equal media access to different candidates, such provisions are rare and weakly enforced. Moreover, in counterfeit democracies, they are also likely to be treated as minor infractions by election monitors, and so are unlikely to be cited as evidence of a rigged election.

Thus, by operating in this legal grey area, ruling parties can give themselves a significant electoral advantage while claiming to be merely following the example of campaigns in established democracies.

The digital revolution

Given the vulnerabilities exposed by digital innovation in elections, it is sobering to reflect that the digital revolution was initially widely hailed as the great democratizing force – a game-changer that would put citizens on an equal footing with despots. Digital information flows, it was often argued, would be harder to control. To some, that meant that autocrats would have to be on the defensive, as pundits predicted that tyrants would be toppled by tweets and the abuses of autocrats would be exposed on Facebook.[11]

This optimism was not completely misplaced, but enthusiasm for democracy's digital revolution failed to accurately anticipate that digital platforms would simply become a new battleground, rather than a weapon to be wielded exclusively against counterfeit democrats. Indeed, despots have proved remarkably adept at using cyberspace to their advantage, finding new ways to use digital tools to rig elections.[12]

Unfortunately, the rise of fake news typically also undermines public confidence in key institutions, including both the traditional media and elements of the state itself. When it becomes difficult to discern what is true and what is false, citizens begin to place less trust in official institutions. While it is clear that the public is capable of disaggregating more and less reliable sources of information, there is also evidence that, overall, fake news has had the effect of increasing public scepticism and eroding the capacity of specific institutions to serve as accepted authorities.

Significantly, this is a problem in both democratic and authoritarian contexts. According to a survey of 1,000 respondents conducted in Britain in 2017, just 20 per cent of people said that they were confident that the news they were reading was real.[13] If autocrats can achieve the same outcome, it will give them an enormous edge, because counterfeit democrats find it easier to hold onto power when they can rubbish and undermine independent sources of information that challenge the official state narrative.

If they want to see how it's done, the 2016 presidential election in the United States provides, as we have seen, some valuable lessons: the digital manipulation of information flows – both real and fake – were used to enrich the prospects for Donald Trump. Furthermore, that campaign also revealed the vulnerability of

American election infrastructure to digital hacking, even if there is currently no evidence that any votes were actually changed in the process. While the United States is not an autocracy, and Trump was not the incumbent, it is worth reflecting on this experience because it provides one of the most far-reaching and best-documented cases of digital manipulation available. As a result, the American case reveals insights into the ways in which authoritarian leaders can and will deploy these techniques, often hidden by censorship and a lack of investigative journalism in undemocratic contexts.

According to the unanimous findings of the United States intelligence community, most of the election interference during the campaign was directed by Russia's government, likely at the behest of the Russian president Vladimir Putin.[14] However, there were also other influencers – even including some teenagers who were just out to make some money.

To get a sense of how this works, let us travel to Veles, a small Macedonian town of 40,000 people, nestled amid green hills on the banks of the Vardar river. The odds are very high that you have never heard of Veles (or of the Vardar) and do not know that much about Macedonia. However, the odds are even higher that you have read articles produced in Veles, a fake news factory that may have given the presidential candidate Donald Trump a decisive push towards the White House. Of course, some of the phoney stories churned out of Veles hurt Trump too. In the fake news factories of the world, what matters is not who wins or who loses but how many clicks can be generated for their hastily created sites.

In February 2016, a young Macedonian teenager posted a false story on his website. Its premise was salacious, its 'facts' completely wrong. The story claimed that Donald Trump had accosted someone in the audience at a campaign rally and slapped him. This was not true. But the story took off on social media, and the young teenager made $150 in ad revenues from all the clicks he was generating. In that instant, he decided to quit high school and become a full-time producer and distributor of fake news on America's elections.[15] Soon, he was raking in large sums of money by generating made-up viral stories.

By October, Veles was home to more than 100 pro-Trump websites. They ran stories such as 'Pope Francis forbids Catholics from voting for Hillary' and 'Proof surfaces that Obama was born in Kenya – Trump was right all along!'[16] One seventeen-year-old involved in the fake news factories of Veles told BuzzFeed News that he did not care about Trump, Clinton or politics in general. Instead, he wanted to buy music equipment. Duping voters in America made that possible: 'I started the site for an easy way to make money. In Macedonia the economy is very weak and teenagers are not allowed to work, so we need to find creative ways to make some money. I'm a musician but I can't afford music gear. Here in Macedonia the revenue from a small site is enough to afford many things.'[17] It is impossible to say precisely how many people read the fake stories that may have been penned by a Macedonian teen in order to finance his desire for musical instruments, but the number is said to be enormous – as high as 126 million on Facebook alone.[18]

Of course, not all the fabricated stories were being produced by youths in Macedonia. Some were written by men in their twenties in Romania. Others by young students in Georgia (the country, not the US state) like Beqa Latsabidze. One of his articles, claiming that Mexico would close its border to Americans if Trump won the election, went viral and earned him some much-needed money to help fund his studies.[19] And, of course, not all the fake stories were coming from outside the United States. One American media company called Disinfomedia, for example, registered domain names like washingtonpost.com.co and usatoday.com.co, in order to try to masquerade as the legitimate news outlets.[20] They published debunked stories too, although some of these American efforts were ideologically rather than financially driven. But wherever the stories came from, the conveyor belt of disinformation likely had a significant impact on voter perceptions of the election campaign and the candidates contesting it.[21]

Sixty-two per cent of American adults reported getting at least some of their news from social media in 2016.[22] That is not necessarily worrying. After all, new media replace old media in cycles, in the same way that mass printing in the nineteenth century drove citizens towards newspapers, and would later face new competition from radio and then television and now the internet. But social media present a new and much more uncontrollable challenge. In 2016, the most viral *fake* stories were shared more times than the most viral *real* stories.[23] Furthermore, the sheer scale of the spread of misinformation is astonishing. One 2017 study examined 115 fabricated stories that were pro-Trump and 41 fabricated stories that were pro-Clinton. They found that those 156 stories were shared on Facebook a combined total of 37.6 million times. Each of those shares would be visible to the user's network of Facebook friends, greatly amplifying its potential reach.[24] A thorough BuzzFeed analysis of social media during the campaign found that several fake news stories eclipsed the social media impact of many genuine news scoops, such as when the *New York Times* revealed that Donald Trump had actually declared the loss of nearly $1 billion in an unreleased tax return.[25]

All this raises the question of whether the fake ads benefited one side or the other, or cancelled themselves out. Of the twenty most shared fake news articles during the final stages of the presidential campaign, seventeen were explicitly pro-Trump or anti-Clinton. As multiple investigations after the election documented, pro-Trump messages were most effective – partly because of the demographics of Trump voters and partly because they had help from Russia to spread the news (of which more shortly). Topping the list of pro-Trump fake news was an absurd story claiming that

Pope Francis had endorsed him, followed closely by another fabricated tale suggesting that Hillary Clinton sold weapons to ISIS.[26] Both stories had nearly a million engagements on Facebook, and both were completely made up. Of course, many people would have known that these articles were not to be trusted, but some did not, and many equally false stories were more believable in tone.

Despite appearances, the viral nature of these fake stories was not really organic. Instead, the incentives of impoverished teenagers in Macedonia aligned with the geopolitical machinations of the Kremlin. Fake news factories were the unwitting accomplices of the most high-profile digital election interference campaign by a major state power in modern history. If the analysis of the United States intelligence community is correct, Vladimir Putin sought to influence the election to help elect Donald Trump. This verdict was reached despite Trump's nonsensical reaction that it 'could have been anybody', even, as he suggested, an obese man lying in bed in New Jersey.[27] In the midst of the campaign, inadvertent digital bedfellows ended up forming a potent team against Hillary Clinton.[28]

Whilst some of the false stories are crude, the way in which they are shared is not. Computer algorithms can be used to identify which messages would be most powerful to which users. If you search the internet daily for a job, you are more likely to get economic messages. If your profiles indicate a greater cultural malaise, you might get messages about immigration or ISIS. What you clicked on in the past dictates how digital manipulators may try to influence you in the future.

These efforts are so specific and individual as to seem beyond the realms of plausibility. In fact, they are very real. In one case documented by *Time* last year, a Russian soldier based in Ukraine posed as a forty-two-year-old American housewife in a Facebook group and interacted with members following on from specifically tailored messages.[29] And in many instances, Russian operatives working for various wings of the GRU (Russia's largest foreign intelligence directorate) crafted messages tailored to specific groups, which would then be propagated throughout social media by botnets. In fact, researchers from the University of Southern California estimate that one in five politically orientated tweets in the final two months of the US presidential campaign were generated not by humans, but by algorithm-driven bots.[30]

Away from the United States, the implications of fake news and digitally manipulated information may be even more severe. Some commentators have suggested that the plethora of conflicting information now available to citizens has led to the emergence of a 'post-truth' world in which 'facts' are disputed to the point where they lose the power to convince, with voters acting more on the basis of emotional responses to particular issues and leaders. The term 'post-truth' was first used by the playwright Steve Tesich in 1992 in a piece on the Iran–Contra scandal and the Persian Gulf War, in which he worried that 'we, as a free people, have freely decided that we want to live in some post-truth world'.[31] However, it did not enter common usage until Trump's victory in the Republican primary election, after which it became so ubiquitous that it was selected as the Oxford Dictionaries Word of the Year in 2016.[32]

The emergence of post-truth politics in some countries – or at least the emergence of elements of such a form of political discourse – is problematic because it plays into the hands of authoritarian leaders. A world in which all information can be contested is a world in which it is easier to dispute accusations of electoral manipulation, and hence to hold rigged elections that are passed off as legitimate ones. Remarkably, Tesich recognized this in the article in which he coined the phrase over twenty-five years ago. Writing about the American people, he concluded that 'We are rapidly becoming prototypes of a people that totalitarian monsters could only drool about in their dreams. All the dictators up to now have had to work hard at suppressing the truth. We, by our actions, are saying that this is no longer necessary, that we have acquired a spiritual mechanism that can denude truth of any significance.'[33] This is not a new idea. George Orwell's prophetic novel *Nineteen Eighty-Four* imagined a world in which totalitarian power is secured because the government has complete control over what is true and what is false – and can even change those facts at will by forcing citizens to accept obviously untrue statements. In authoritarian governments, this often manifests itself in the form of outlandish cults of personality around despots. That is precisely the reason why North Koreans are told that Kim Jong-il invented hamburgers and that his son, Kim Jong-un, started driving a car when he was three years old.[34] When facts can be invented or discarded at will, it makes it easier to subject a population to authoritarian rule.

In Syria, for example, Hafez al-Assad built an extreme cult of personality that has been inherited by his son, Bashar. The police state is extensive, and questioning any aspect of the official version of events can end in torture.[35] In such an environment, where the only truth that matters is the one dictated by the Assad family, it's not hard to see how most sham presidential elections in Syria ended with Bashar al-Assad winning 99.7 per cent (in 2000), 99.8 per cent (in 2007) and, in the positively nail-biting 2014 election, only 88.7 per cent of the vote – while Syria was embroiled in one of the bloodiest civil wars in modern history.

The 2014 election was notable in that it was used as a prop to try to legitimize the Assad regime while its leader was butchering his own people with chemical weapons and indiscriminate barrel bombing. This hints at a post-war future in which the Syrian regime will seek to set itself up as a counterfeit democracy, once again manipulating elections in order to paper over the authoritarian reality. An 88.7 per cent victory replacing a 99.8 per cent victory suggests that the government has learnt that there is an upside to allowing a slightly more credible result (as explored in more depth in chapter 5). When authoritarian leaders operating in a post-truth context can control the flow of information in this way, they may not even need to do much rigging of the actual ballot. Instead, they can allow indoctrination and fear to do their work for them.

Furthermore, digital tools can be used to chill dissent, making sure that people self-censor and do not speak out against the ruling regime. In China, for example, one of the few countries that does not hold national-level elections, the government is developing a 'social credit' score.[36] This rating, which is largely based on online activity, drops when people associate with dissidents or make anti-government comments on social media. China has, for now, delayed implementation of the social credit score.[37] But it is highly likely that such tactics will become more common in the dictator's toolbox of the future, not least because governments around the world have been following China's example when it comes to cyber censorship and the introduction of punitive social media legislation.[38] According to recent research coming out of Stanford University, a process of authoritarian learning across borders has led to a small number of companies providing a wide array of counterfeit democracies with the capacity to monitor and censor online activities. As a result, Jaclyn Kerr has predicted the rise of 'digital dictators'.[39]

Hacking and harvesting

These days, though, post-truth politics has spread even into consolidated democracies that feature free flows of information. The disinformation and misinformation campaigns promulgated by the Russians around the US elections were not limited to the realm of social media. Instead, the orchestrated hack against Hillary Clinton's campaign may not only have influenced the outcome of the election, but continues to overshadow Donald Trump's presidency. It changed perceptions in an important way, and not just for Facebook or Twitter users.

The dramatic saga began with a simple typo. On 19 March 2016, John Podesta, Hillary Clinton's campaign chairman, received an email purporting to be from Google about his Gmail account, which instructed him, apparently for security reasons, to click on a link and reset his password. Podesta's chief of staff, Sara Latham, was suspicious of the email and forwarded it to Clinton's technology adviser, Charles Delavan.[40] To his credit, Delavan understood that the email was likely a spear-phishing attack – an effort to get a user to click on a fake link dressed up as a real one. When a user clicks on such a link, they are prompted to enter their password. Once they do so, the hacker has it and can easily access the account. It is a simple form of attack that relies on human fallibility rather than any sort of tech wizardry. Recognizing the seriousness of the email, Delavan shot back a quick reply, urging Podesta to change his password immediately. However, Delavan's reply read: 'This is a legitimate' – rather than illegitimate – 'email.'[41] This was a tiny error, but massive damage was done. Podesta clicked the link. He entered his password. And just like that, the hackers had access to the private emails of Hillary Clinton's campaign chairman.[42]

Once the hackers gained access, they quickly grabbed all the data on the account. Subsequent analysis by the United States intelligence community demonstrated that Russia's government – likely at the personal direction of Vladimir Putin – was behind the attack.[43]

The Podesta emails were just one part of a sustained effort to undermine Clinton's campaign. Nearly a year earlier, in July 2015, the Democratic National Committee's servers had been breached by the Russian government. A Russian intelligence directorate called Cozy Bear is widely believed to have orchestrated that attack. This was followed up by an assault on the DNC servers by a GRU-affiliated unit known as Fancy Bear in March 2016, at the same time as Podesta's personal email was hacked.[44]

But information is only powerful if you can use it to sway opinions. The Russian government had private and potentially embarrassing emails from a top official in the Clinton campaign. What they needed was a way to weaponize them to do the greatest possible damage at the right moment. Over the following months, the DNC and Podesta emails were made public. Some were published directly by front groups that aimed to obscure the identity of Russian intelligence agents, most notably DCLeaks.com and Guccifer 2.0. These audiences, however, were too small for maximum effect. To achieve that, messages were sent to WikiLeaks, and from there the information was available to the world.[45]

The emails were released in batches aimed at maximizing political impact. At times, they were strategically released to distract attention from damaging stories about Donald Trump. For example, Podesta's emails were posted online just an hour after the story broke about Donald Trump boasting on the set of *Access Hollywood* that he had groped a series of women, saying, 'When you're a star, they let you do it.'[46] The damage from that story was blunted, at least partially, because the pro-Trump contingent could point to fresh embarrassing revelations from the newly released Podesta messages. The timing was probably deliberate, intended to stanch the political bleeding.

This raises a critical question: was Donald Trump's campaign involved in colluding with the Russian government or with WikiLeaks to co-ordinate the most damaging impact of the hacks and subsequent revelations? At the time of writing, the American government is in the midst of an ongoing series of investigations in Congress involving a special counsel who is reportedly investigating the president himself for criminal wrongdoing.[47]

There is already considerable circumstantial evidence to suggest that elements of Trump's team did collude with the Russian government, such as the fact that Roger Stone, a close

Trump confidant, repeatedly discussed his backchannel communications with Julian Assange of WikiLeaks and boasted that he knew when the next data dump would occur before it happened.[48] Stone also told a Republican group in Florida that he had communicated directly with Julian Assange.[49] Moreover, we also know that on 14 August 2016, Stone directly communicated with Guccifer 2.0, the alter ego of Russian intelligence officers involved in the campaign hacking. And weeks before Podesta's emails were released by WikiLeaks, Stone – who denies any wrongdoing – tweeted that 'it will soon [be] the Podesta's time in the barrel'.[50]

However, the most damning evidence so far has been produced by Donald Trump's own son, Donald Trump Jr. In mid-July 2017, media reports began to circulate that top Trump campaign officials, including the campaign's chairman Paul Manafort, Trump's son-in-law Jared Kushner and Donald Trump Jr had secretly met with several key Russians – with ties to the Russian government – in Trump Tower a year previously, in the midst of the presidential campaign. When that news broke in the summer of 2017, President Trump dictated a statement denying that the meeting was of any consequence, claiming it had been exclusively about adoption.[51] In the next days, though, that lie fell apart.

When it became clear that the media had received copies of the email correspondence related to the mystery meeting, Donald Trump Jr released the email thread himself on his personal Twitter page. In clear language, the exchange – between Donald Trump Jr and the British publicist Rob Goldstone, who was brokering the meeting – reveals two smoking guns. First, the email from Goldstone explicitly says that the meeting is intended to provide 'very high-level, sensitive information' that would comprise 'part of Russia and it's [*sic*] government's support for Mr. Trump'.[52] This seemed to support the intelligence community's assessment that Russia's government was deliberately interfering in the American election process.

Second, the email thread contained Donald Trump Jr's response to the promise of espionage-related dirt on an American from a foreign power: 'I love it.' As a result, Trump Jr rushed to set up the meeting; and three hours after it was confirmed, Donald Trump made remarks regarding new information on Hillary Clinton's 'crimes', including some supposedly related to Russia – something that the meeting promised.[53] When the discussion took place, it involved a Russian lawyer who had previously represented the FSB, the reincarnated version of the KGB; a suspected money launderer; and an alleged Russian hacker who had been implicated in corporate espionage lawsuits.[54] It's hard to believe this was a meeting about adoptions when the initial topic under discussion was clearly something more sinister.

At the time of writing, it is impossible to know what will come of the investigations surrounding President Trump and his campaign's potential collusion with the Russian government. But whether or not a direct relationship existed, it is clear that the Republican candidate used the Russian government's hacking efforts to his advantage. In the final month of the campaign, Trump mentioned WikiLeaks 164 times – averaging more than five per day.[55] With renewed fervour, the Trump campaign used the fresh ammunition available to undermine what looked for all the world like a sure-fire Clinton victory.

The WikiLeaks documents also provided fresh grist for the fake news factories' mill. With this new information, teenagers in Macedonia could mix genuine leaked emails with falsehoods, adding sentences that were not there in the originals, or taking emails out of context to make them seem salacious or improper in some way. The real email threads provided a flimsy veneer of plausibility to some of the more outlandish stories being churned out by the fake news websites – and they stuck.

At this point, a certain segment of voters – we do not know exactly how many – began to believe completely bogus lies about the candidates. The story that Hillary Clinton murdered a Democratic Party staffer took hold, and high-profile media figures such as Sean Hannity of Fox News were still pushing it through the summer of 2017 – even though it had already been repeatedly debunked.[56] Similarly, many people falsely believed that Hillary Clinton was running a child sex-ring out of a Washington, DC pizza parlour called Comet Ping Pong. A disgruntled man even drove to the pizzeria and shot his gun into the ceiling in protest.[57] Thus, although these stories were completely absurd digital fantasies, they appear to have affected real-world behaviour.

Considering these tactics – from Kremlin agents getting access to the private correspondence of foreign campaign officials from thousands of miles away, to young teenagers in post-communist Europe convincing farmers in Wisconsin that an American presidential candidate has committed murder – it is quickly apparent that none of them would have been possible on this scale before the digital revolution. And in a system of government where information flows indirectly determine which person runs the country, these new vulnerabilities are enormous challenges to the integrity of elections and democracy everywhere.

Profiling the people

In addition to this kind of high-profile hacking, there is also a new frontier of election manipulation that does not rely on state-sponsored foreign-policy goals. Instead, it relies on capitalism.

In relation to politics and elections, the most prominent firm at the centre of this new frontier of targeted messaging is Cambridge Analytica (mentioned briefly above), which boasts that it can use big data to sway opinions and influence behaviour. The firm worked for the Trump campaign,[58] but was most recently at the centre of a firestorm surrounding the June 2016

British referendum on membership of the European Union, popularly known as Brexit.

There is an ongoing legal battle related to reporting over Cambridge Analytica's involvement (or non-involvement) in the Brexit referendum. An exposé in the *Observer* newspaper alleged that Cambridge Analytica was part of a shadowy network – funded by Robert Mercer – which used underhand means to persuade voters to support leaving the European Union.[59] One of the key players in the Leave.eu campaign told the *Observer*'s investigative reporter that Mercer's friendship with UK Independence Party (UKIP) leader Nigel Farage prompted Cambridge Analytica to assist the Leave campaign. Cambridge Analytica at one point also boasted that it was helping the campaign to gain traction on social media,[60] but now denies that it had anything to do with Farage's efforts.[61]

The strategy employed by Cambridge Analytica combines military tactics known as psy-ops (psychological operations) with big-data analysis. That potent cocktail can prove influential. By looking at internet activity, such as which articles and pages a user 'likes' on Facebook, the company creates a unique profile of a user's presumed demographic background, political attitudes, religion and even sexual orientation. The company then purchases existing databases that contain information about users' magazine subscriptions, airline travel and other consumer habits. It merges those consumer-driven databases with its own analyses of online activity from social media and other metadata.

In combination, analysis of this information gives Cambridge Analytica a way of surveying the landscape of the electorate and the tools to figure out which types of messages are most likely to sway, for example, a forty-one-year-old white single mother who votes Labour, subscribes to *The Economist*, and travels regularly to the south of France. These tactics have created a new grey area for elections. To many people, there is something insidious about the use of personal profiling to persuade people to vote for a certain candidate or issue. It can feel like an intrusion of privacy to know that a nameless, faceless database contains all that personal information in one place.

The story here, however, is not just about Cambridge Analytica. Rather, it is about the increasingly sophisticated ways in which campaigns working with a number of different companies can engineer victories using information to their advantage. Defenders of these new tactics point out that targeting simply makes campaign messaging most relevant to each voter. Why, they argue, would you waste a Facebook ad about climate change on someone who does not believe it exists? Isn't this the same as traditional media advertising, which uses surveys and focus groups to identify the best way to pitch newspaper and TV adverts to voters?

Perhaps on one level. But there is also a disturbing endpoint to this continuum, and a clear risk that we are heading towards a future, previously imagined only in science fiction movies, in which our actions and beliefs are recorded and manipulated at a level of detail that was hitherto unthinkable. And whether we like it or not, such methods are being increasingly deployed in an ever-larger number of elections, with important consequences. When elections are decided by small margins, big data can be decisive.

This is particularly problematic in the counterfeit democracies described in this book. While big-data profiling has been used by both governments and opposition parties in the world's democratic states, in authoritarian contexts it tends to benefit the ruling party. This is both because the incumbent has greater campaign funds and because they can deny visas to companies coming to the country to work for the opposition. As a result, Western consultants are frequently used to generate legitimacy for shady regimes. This is particularly problematic because messages can be designed either to get voters to the polls or to prevent rival supporters from turning up. These negative adverts are particularly controversial because in divided societies in which political violence is a significant threat, attack ads may serve to raise the political temperature to boiling point.

For example, during Cambridge Analytica's engagement in Kenya in support of the campaign of the Jubilee Party government in 2017, it was accused of producing videos that purported to show the terrible things that would happen to Kenya were the opposition candidate, Raila Odinga, to be elected. A report by Privacy International subsequently found that some of the most troubling adverts, which depicted Kenya as a dystopia beset by ethnic violence, had actually been produced by a different American company, Harris Media – a 'far-right' organization that had previously worked for Trump and a number of right-wing European parties.[62] Kenyan civil society groups pointed out the dangers of employing such a strategy in a politically charged environment. As John Githongo, the country's former anti-corruption tsar and a pro-democracy campaigner, put it: 'Here it can lead to war ... The wrong video, the wrong information, it can go out of control.'[63]

However, the limited internet penetration in some parts of the world undermines the kind of individual profiling advertised by companies like Cambridge Analytica. Big-data analysis only works where big data exist, as it requires companies to be able to track individuals through social media.

In less developed countries where comparatively fewer people use social media or the internet, foreign firms are more often employed to assist counterfeit democrats in other, more conventional ways, such as managing communications and delivering slicker ad campaigns. Azerbaijan's dictator, Ilham Aliyev, who launched the iPhone app discussed in the introduction, employed a consultant who had also worked for David Cameron in the British government to generate a favourable opinion poll that would make the government look good.[64] In 1,000 in-person interviews, the firm, Populus, recorded a 96 per cent approval rating for Aliyev.

Of course, opinion polls are a normal part of electoral activity. But this one was a little different: participants would most likely have been afraid that any statements they made might be seen by the government, and would therefore have censored their answers to protect themselves. As a result, they probably felt compelled to give positive answers despite the fact that many of those participating had good reasons to be critical of the government: some 32 per cent of the respondents were unemployed, and about one-quarter reported that they had trouble affording basic items like clothes.[65] If this is indeed what happened, a foreign company has helped an authoritarian regime to whitewash its failures, painting it with the brush of seemingly objective data that were, in reality, engineered to depict a dictator positively. This is a phenomenon that is on the rise, and will be increasingly common – and increasingly difficult to combat – in the future.

The vulnerabilities of new technology

As we have already set out, the new digital election battleground is not just about information. There is also a much more direct way to rig elections with computer technology: hacking vital election infrastructure that is housed in servers rather than in ballot boxes. This vulnerability is of more and more concern as digital technology is increasingly integrated into electoral systems and some countries start to use voting machines rather than paper ballots.

Technology generates vulnerabilities within election infrastructure that are not present in more traditional forms of election administration. Most obviously, you can stuff ballot boxes but you cannot hack them. Once upon a time, to do the dirty work of changing votes you had to be present in the actual polling location (see chapters 3 and 5). That is no longer true. This is a serious concern, because even in a technologically savvy country such as the United States, election technology is poorly protected from manipulation.

In 2012, researchers from the University of Michigan urged the government to address critical gaps in election infrastructure. To prove their point, they hacked into voting machines and changed ballots at will. Then, they changed the software on each voting machine so that every time a ballot was cast, the machine would play the University of Michigan's fight song in celebration of a successful vote. Another team of researchers tampered with a device so that it became a Pac-Man game – and did so without breaking the supposedly tamper-proof seal on the machine.[66]

In the process, researchers have found that a stunning array of American voting machines are still running Windows XP software that has not been updated with essential security patches.[67] In other words, the devices have not even been updated to address threats that are already known to security experts. And, of course, there are always unknown threats and emerging ones in the cat-and-mouse game between hackers and those who seek to defend machines from hacking. During the 2016 American presidential election, Russian hackers probed voting databases and machines in at least twenty-one US states.[68] The threat is real.

It is important to realize that this is not just an American issue. In democratic Estonia, a leading adopter of computerized voting, nearly a quarter of votes are cast online – making it uniquely vulnerable to attacks. In Mexico, 90 million voter records kept in a government database have been breached.[69] These problems are sure to become more widespread in the future.

In 'Making Democracy Harder to Hack', a team of researchers from Harvard and Indiana University have identified three key elements of election infrastructure that are vulnerable to manipulation, attack and rigging: voter rolls (who can vote); voting machines (who you vote for); and tabulation (the government's count of how many votes each candidate received).[70]

In many American states, voter rolls are housed electronically. In some states, there is no paper trail. Given this, all it would take to seriously skew an election would be to hack into these records and to delete the entries for people who are either known to be supporters of a particular party, or are suspected to vote a certain way based on demographic information. Deleted voters would arrive at polling locations and be turned away – likely with no possibility of being put back on the voter roll until after the ballots had been counted. Thankfully, this strategy can be easily addressed by ensuring that there are multiple copies of the database, including on offline servers and in paper records, and by having a mechanism in place to record any alterations to the database so that any deletions are immediately flagged.

As for the hacking of voting machines themselves, it depends on what kind of equipment is being used. There are two main types of device – one that produces a paper trail and one that does not. Those that produce a paper trail record the initial vote electronically, but the tally can be cross-verified against actual paper ballots that are produced in real time with each vote. This system therefore makes re-counts possible. For those voting machines that do not produce a paper trail, this cannot be done. Thus, if a hacker managed to gain access to those types of device without detection, they could change votes at will. So long as the total number of votes cast matches the total number of voters who were marked down as having cast their ballots by precinct staff, this kind of manipulation would be impossible to detect.

Unfortunately, both types of machine have key vulnerabilities that can be exploited for nefarious purposes. For example, some have wireless internet connections to communicate with servers or to obtain software updates. The convenience of that connectivity provides a huge vulnerability, and the Harvard researchers have demonstrated that many of the machines do not have strong encryption on their internet networks; some do not have any encryption whatsoever and are completely open – the electronic equivalent of an open door with a sign reading 'Hackers welcome!'

Others can be infiltrated physically, for example by simply sticking a USB stick loaded with malicious code or software into the machine. But despite a series of teams exposing these vulnerabilities, they persist. And while there is no clear evidence to date of this type of manipulation having taken place in American elections, unless the problem is urgently addressed it is only a matter of time. This is only the tip of the iceberg: keep in mind that countries with far fewer resources than the United States or India are even more vulnerable to voting machines being manipulated.

Moreover, the risks come not only from the outside. In counterfeit democracies, governments may tamper with machines directly, using their control of electoral commissions to gain access. As we discuss at greater length in the conclusion to this book, such strategies have the double advantage of allowing the regime to appear to use electronic systems to demonstrate their commitment to cutting-edge technology, while simultaneously using them to make it easier to manipulate the ballot.

Strengthening democracy on the digital frontier

The vulnerability of digital election equipment to manipulation raises the question of what can be done to protect essential democratic systems. In January 2017, Secretary Jeh Johnson of the US Department of Homeland Security classified election-related machinery and databases as 'critical infrastructure', essential to the national security of the United States.[71] It may sound odd to place voting machines in the same category as nuclear power plants, but in genuine democracies, elections determine how all other decisions are made. As a result, they are a meta-vulnerability, an area in which rigging or interference can completely tilt the policy direction of the entire country.

It is therefore striking that the Trump administration, either through negligence or worse, has not made addressing this vulnerability a top priority – something that Jeff Sessions, Trump's own attorney general, admitted during Senate testimony in October 2017.[72] That seeming indifference, combined with the fact that election security is often left up to states, which approach it with varying degrees of seriousness, means that the 2018 midterm elections and 2020 federal elections (including the presidential contest) could be vulnerable to hacking.

This is particularly frustrating because there are some straightforward strategies that can be put in place. A world away, India has boasted that it has produced a tamper-proof voting machine. The design of the machine is impressive: it compartmentalizes each vote on an individual microchip, which means that tampering would require physically replacing one of the chips. That is difficult to do, and the Indian authorities have candidates or their representatives secure the equipment with wax and a seal, making it easier to detect if any machine has been tampered with. However, University of Michigan researchers built a custom-made device that used Bluetooth technology to steal votes without tampering with the physical device.[73] Thus, even with ingeniously designed systems, hackers may still find a way to gain access.

To cope with this challenge, governments need to make electoral cybersecurity a top priority. Working with researchers, like those at Harvard's Belfer Center or the University of Michigan, election administration officials can identify a set of best practices that can be uniformly applied internationally. Doing so would provide a layer of checks to deter and detect possible attacks on election infrastructure.

Moreover, every part of the electoral process must be subject to routine audits – not just in situations where the result is close. For example, many American states only conduct re-counts if the result is within a certain percentage point, 0.1 or 0.5 per cent for example. Should hackers be aware of this, they could guarantee that their manipulations are not detected simply by ensuring that the margin of victory falls outside that range – at 0.15 or 0.55 per cent, for example. To combat this, election officials will have to consider sometimes auditing all results, from voter registration databases to tabulation and everything in between. Doing so will add cost. But without these measures, countries may pay the price of losing their democracy. Surely audits represent good value for money if they bring the peace of mind of knowing that elections are fair.

More fundamentally, this raises the question of whether digital elections – and associated forms of digital election technology – are more trouble than they are worth, a question to which we turn in the conclusion. Already, three of the fourteen countries that have to date experimented with electronic voting have discontinued it (see appendix 16).

The situation is also very challenging when it comes to countering fake news. Civil society groups have begun to respond with the formation of a number of fact-checking websites and groups designed to expose fake news. For example, Africa Check operates across the continent both to verify the content of news and political statements and to encourage accurate reporting.[74] It is part of a broader International Fact-Checking Network that has affiliates in a number of authoritarian and democratic regimes worldwide.[75]

All of these initiatives are to be welcomed, and have clearly gone a long way towards creating a better-informed and more careful public. However, the sad reality is that these fact-checking sites receive far fewer hits and retweets than the stories that they are trying to debunk. Moreover, in more-authoritarian contexts in which the government tightly controls the information environment, corrections are unlikely to be carried on state media, and so may only reach a limited segment of the population.

This suggests that the problem needs to be tackled at source, and social media sites have responded by experimenting with a range of different strategies designed to expose biased information and to prevent it from being circulated. Facebook has been trialling including information about the publishers of news reports to give readers more context about the links that they see,[76] while Google has introduced tools that allow users to report misleading content and to integrate fact-checking software so that more-reliable sites appear first.[77] These initiatives promise to re-weight the balance in favour of factually accurate stories. However, there is still a long way to go. A recent investigation by the *New York Times* found that as recently as October 2017 Google was placing adverts for fake news sites on, of all things, fact-checking websites.[78]

But the creation of fake news, and efforts at rigging through the control of information, are not always successful. Where they fail, or simply cannot make up for a government's low popularity, other strategies must be employed. We now turn to what is perhaps the best-known form of electoral manipulation: ballot-box stuffing.

Chapter 5

BALLOT-BOX STUFFING

The last resort

Ballot-box stuffing is one of the most effective strategies available to counterfeit democrats, but also one of the most risky. To see why, it is useful to briefly return to the Kenyan election of 2007 to explore what triggered the outbreak of political violence. As we saw in chapter 3, the race for the presidency that year was particularly close. While the incumbent, Mwai Kibaki, enjoyed many of the advantages described in this book – more funding, an ability to control the state and electoral system, and so on – a wave of popular frustration with his government enabled his main challenger, Raila Odinga, to move ahead in some opinion polls.[1] When voting got under way on 27 December, many experts concluded that the election was too close to call, but opposition leaders were confident of success.[2]

The sense of excitement and anticipation in Odinga's strongholds continued to build as the early results began to come in. Because many of the constituencies that declared quickly were in Odinga strongholds, the opposition quickly built up a healthy lead. By the end of the first day of counting, some opposition supporters were preparing to celebrate.

But that night and in the days to come, the atmosphere shifted markedly. First, the flow of results began to slow. Second, the chair of the Electoral Commission of Kenya (ECK), Samuel Kivuitu, publicly admitted that he did not know where many of his returning officers were, and that he was worried that they might be 'cooking' (as in 'cooking the books').[3] As the process of counting and releasing the results was delayed, accusations of vote rigging began to increase. Ahead of the polls, the opposition had alleged that key democratic institutions were being stacked with Kibaki loyalists, and implied that the government was planning to steal the elections if it could not win them fairly.[4]

Events on 29 and 30 December appeared to confirm this interpretation. Having trailed for almost all of the vote count, a sudden flurry of results boosted Kibaki's total.[5] As tensions peaked, domestic election monitors – including Nic, who was researching the election[6] – were forcibly removed from the counting centre. Meanwhile, Kivuitu was rushed upstairs to announce that the incumbent had won the election – a declaration that private and international media were not allowed to film.

The result, and the way in which it was handled, sent shockwaves through the country. The perception that Odinga's historically marginalized communities had been cheated was compounded when European Union observers reported that the official declaration of the total votes cast for Kibaki by the ECK was in some cases considerably higher than the figure that its officials had recorded at the constituency level, implying that the president's tally had been artificially inflated to get him over the line.[7] In turn, the combination of disappointment, frustration and ethnic tensions led to the ethnic clashes discussed in chapter 3 (pp. 105–7), in which over 1,000 people lost their lives.[8]

The Kenyan example demonstrates two very important points about ballot-box stuffing. On the one hand, it is a dangerous way to win an election because it is vulnerable to detection and high profile, and therefore risky. It is also far from certain to guarantee victory. Leaders do not always know how many votes they need to 'stuff' in order to win in advance, so they may fail to add enough. Furthermore, getting caught in the act can result in international embarrassment and domestic conflict. For these reasons, the most effective authoritarian governments do not rely on this strategy; in countries such as Kazakhstan and Rwanda, the election is rigged well before polling day (see appendix 13 for figures on election-day irregularities).

However, on the other hand, the Kenyan case also shows that it is possible to get away with manipulating an election at the last minute, even if this is identified by election monitors. In Kenya, as in many other countries, the logistical challenges of re-counting the 9.8 million votes cast in the presidential election after electoral officials had returned home and ballot boxes had been left unattended meant that this was never going to be a feasible way to resolve the impasse.[9] Consequently, we will never know the real result of the poll, and controversy continues to this day about which candidate actually won the most votes.

What we do know is that Kenya's period of political instability in early 2008 led to international mediation and the formation of a power-sharing agreement that allowed President Kibaki to retain his position and control the most important cabinet positions.[10] Odinga was forced to make do with the lesser role of prime minister, which proved to be chronically weak: it was created by an act of parliament and lacked constitutional foundations. When the next elections were held in 2013, it was the opposition that suffered, securing a lower percentage of the poll than in 2007.[11] Thus, Kibaki and his allies largely escaped punishment for the subversion of the electoral process in full view of international observers and the media.

Given the electoral outcome in Kenya, it is unsurprising that a number of different governments have deployed this tool over the years. However, managing this process is not always straightforward. Seeking to avoid making the same mistakes as Kibaki, many authoritarian leaders around the world want to rig so as to ensure victory, yet to win modestly enough for the result to be plausible. While a comfortable win is desirable – it can demoralize political challengers[12] while also persuading election monitors that there is nothing worth investigating – a landslide victory often arouses suspicion. As President Alexander Lukashenko put it when speaking about the 2006 presidential election in Belarus (which we will hear more about in chapter 6): 'I admitted . . . that we rigged the election . . . I gave the order to change it from 93% to around 80% . . . because more than 90, just psychologically, that is not well received.'[13]

But getting the amount of ballot-box stuffing right has not always proved straightforward. This is because in most cases ballot fraud is not simply a decision made by one individual who can calculate exactly how many votes to add. Instead, leaders have to rely on the 'collaboration of a large number of local agents'[14] who operate under conditions of considerable uncertainty. As a result, a combination of paranoid leaders and overzealous officials has at times resulted in the phenomenon of over-rigging. Here, the efforts of apparatchiks to please their leader – and the candidate's fear that they might lose if they are not careful – can result in a final election outcome that is so one-sided as to beggar belief, exposing the ruling party to ridicule.

Compromising the commission

By the time election day arrives, there are four main rigging options available, two that can be deployed while voting occurs, and two after. During voting, candidates can employ multiple voting (getting their supporters to vote more than once) and illegitimate voting (having underage citizens or non-citizens illegally cast ballots). The other two strategies come into play once voting has taken place, and are to stuff ballot boxes with fake votes, or to make sure that the final result doesn't reflect the actual ballots cast by tampering with the counting process. As this chapter will demonstrate, these strategies have different strengths and weaknesses, which are shaped by several factors including demography and the distribution of party support. However, they all have one thing in common, namely that they can only work if the electoral commission is involved in – or at least is willing to turn a blind eye to – the rigging.

Electoral commissions are critical to the quality of elections, but although they have overall responsibility for implementing electoral regulations and organizing the poll, they typically have a relatively low profile until the election campaign moves towards polling day. This is because, in many countries, offences committed during the campaign, such as the use of violence, are dealt with by the police rather than by the electoral commission itself, which typically lacks the capacity to collect evidence and carry out prosecutions.[15] Indeed, between elections, most commissions only maintain a skeleton staff.

More often than not, the work of an electoral commission is divided between a small technical staff or secretariat, who are actually responsible for the day-to-day running of an election, and a set of political appointees who assume overall responsibility for making key decisions about the interpretation and implementation of the electoral rules, and are usually called commissioners. While a subset of the secretariat is employed full time, commissioners – including the chairperson, who will ultimately declare the election result – may be part time and are often appointed relatively close to the election itself. In Zimbabwe, for example, the chair of the Zimbabwean Electoral Commission (ZEC), Rita Makarau, is also the executive secretary of the Judicial Service Commission, and has to divide her time accordingly.

The difficulty that some electoral commissions face as a result of their limited capacity is compounded by the fact that many electoral commission chairs and commissioners serve at the pleasure of the government. Given their limited security of tenure and the high stakes of many electoral contests, taking on such positions can be a poisoned chalice. This is particularly the case where the election management body is officially under state control. Between 2012 and 2016, 27 per cent of all elections held took place in countries in which this was the case, rising from 0 per cent in Europe to 34 per cent in sub-Saharan Africa, 43 per cent in the Middle East, 48 per cent in Asia and 56 per cent in post-Soviet Europe (see appendix 9). These figures are significant, because the likelihood of a credible election is inversely proportional to the degree to which the ruling regime directly controls the election management body.

Even in some of the cases in which electoral commissions are nominally independent, commissioners seeking to improve the quality of elections have been intimidated and threatened by supporters of the ruling party, or simply moved away from their posts. In Madagascar's 2013 elections, for example, the election commission president Béatrice Atallah told Brian that she received an envelope filled with bullets as a warning during the campaign.[16] In Zambia, the highly respected jurist Irene Mambilima was brave enough to run a credible election in 2011 and then announce that the opposition Patriotic Front (PF) and its leader Michael Sata had won, defeating the ruling Movement for Multiparty Democracy (MMD).[17] However, when in office, the PF became increasingly focused on the task of retaining power, especially after Sata died in office and the opposition United Party for National Development (UPND) began to expand its support base. Against this backdrop, Sata's successor, Edgar Lungu, came to see Mambilima's integrity and reputation as a threat to his ability to control the 2016 polls.[18]

In response, Lungu followed a tried and tested bureaucratic solution for getting rid of problematic figures without being accused of attacking them: he promoted her. Come the next election, Mambilima had been moved to the post of chief justice and the chair of the electoral commission was handed to Esau Chulu.[19] Although opposition leaders accused Chulu of having close ties to the president, their criticism fell on deaf ears. Against this backdrop, it is perhaps unsurprising that Lungu's narrow victory in the 2016 election inspired significant controversy and acrimony. Although international observers identified no major instances of electoral manipulation, the UPND has continued to reject the election result, claiming that the electoral commission colluded with the ruling party to rig the vote.[20]

In more extreme cases, the electoral commission is not insulated from political pressure at all and is better thought of as an appendage of the ruling party. This is effectively the case in Zimbabwe, where the opposition has alleged that the ZEC is effectively under the control of ZANU–PF and the security forces. Although the ZEC does feature some civilians and officials who are less partisan, many senior figures are known to be closely networked into the ruling party and the security services.[21] Moreover, ZANU–PF's refusal to relinquish power means that the ZEC's actions are tightly constrained. Not only do more significant decisions have to be approved by the Ministry of Justice, but the commission also lacks ultimate authority over the voters' register, which is presided over by the registrar general, Tobaiwa Mudede, a ZANU–PF hardliner who has been described as 'ZANU–PF's election-fixer-in-chief'.[22]

It is easy to see how under these conditions electoral commissioners can be intimidated and bullied into perpetrating – or simply ignoring – electoral manipulation. As a result, in many counterfeit democracies, opposition parties, donors and international observers spend much of their time keeping tabs on the activities of the electoral commission itself.

Fiddling the figures

Once a candidate is sure of the complicity of the electoral commission, they can implement the various strategies outlined above. Perhaps the most notorious of these is multiple voting. Indeed, the phrase 'Vote early, vote often' has been used – often in a tongue-in-cheek fashion – by election candidates and commentators around the world. Like a number of the other terms used in this book, it appears to originate in the United States. As early as 1859, Richard Henry Dana Jr wrote a letter to his friend, Lord Radstock, in which he highlighted some of the common mechanisms of manipulation used in American elections:

> Our experience has shown us that in the excitement of great popular elections, deciding the policy of the country, and its vast patronage, frauds will be committed, if a chance is given for them. If these frauds are allowed, the result is not only that the popular will may be defeated, and the result falsified, but that the worst side will prevail. The side which has the greater number of dishonest men will poll the most votes. The war cry, 'Vote early and vote often!' and the familiar problem of 'how to cast the greatest number of votes with the smallest number of voters', indicate the direction in which the dangers lie.[23]

This kind of strategy was used to great effect by the Tammany Hall political machine that controlled politics in New York City around this time. Under that system, multiple voters, called 'repeaters', were given small amounts of money and gifts of alcohol to traipse back and forth to the polling station. In Martin Scorsese's depiction of this process in the film *Gangs of New York*, based on stories from that era, drunkards who had voted once were then forced to shave so that they could go back a second time with a different appearance.

Such schemes are made possible by the fact that some people don't turn up to vote and dead voters often remain on the electoral roll long after their passing. This allows the supporters of candidates to vote in the names of the deceased and those who fail to show up, without the risk of ending up with more ballots being cast than there are voters – which is clear evidence of fraud. Of course, if the register of voters is reliable and up to date, the effectiveness of multiple voting is constrained. Dead voters and voter fraud are now minuscule problems in the United States (despite false claims to the contrary by Donald Trump).[24] But in authoritarian electoral contexts, this is rarely the case, because governments deliberately prevent the voting rolls from being brought up to date and checked for accuracy.

The advantage of using real people to cast fake ballots is that voter-turnout figures match footfall in polling stations, and there are long queues for monitors to observe. However, real people are not necessary, because the dead themselves can be made to vote. This can be achieved by simply pre-marking ballot papers and stuffing them into the box before the votes are counted. Given the number of spare ballots, having party agents or electoral officials fill some out is easy to accomplish in party strongholds or remote areas where there are no election monitors, and where rival party agents are either absent or pressurized into keeping quiet.

Both forms of ballot-box stuffing were a significant problem in Nigeria under the government of the People's Democratic Party (PDP). A classic counterfeit democratic regime, the PDP presided over some of the most dubious elections held in Africa over the past twenty years. The 2007 general election, in particular, was so flawed that international observers joked that their report on its failings was so long that it broke the printer.[25] Some years later, a senior US official who had been serving in Nigeria at the time commented to Nic that the process had been so bad that it had not really been an election at all, and should rather be referred to as an 'election-type event'.[26]

One of the main problems in that poll was a bloated electoral register that permitted both 'ghost voting' and ballot-box stuffing. The problem was not simply that the existing register was not effectively cleared to remove dead voters; parties also engaged in new efforts to flood the roll with further false registrants. Most notoriously, one report alleged that six registration machines were found at the home of a politician, who was using them to conduct his own 'registration drive'.[27] As so often, attempts to subvert the electoral process were facilitated by the electoral commission, which 'admitted that it would not be able to remove duplications from the voter register'.[28] As a result, it is estimated that around 4 million dead people made it onto the list – and many of them 'voted'.[29]

In the Nigerian context, the term 'ghost voters' is also understood to cover a variety of electoral sins, including efforts to register underage voters and those who live over the border in neighbouring countries such as Niger and Cameroon, so that they can later be mobilized for one party or another. A BBC investigation into the previous election revealed how this was done. In Plateau State, officials were unwilling to require Muslim women to remove their veils, and so said they could not tell whether they were under age. Meanwhile a businessman in Kano said that he had witnessed newly registered voters 'wiping the ink from their fingers' so that they could go and register again. Not to be outdone, a registration centre in Abeokuta in southwestern Nigeria registered a boy called Dele Ogulowo who, according to the Associated Press, looked no more than ten years old. Such events were not rare, and did not only happen in places that were out of the way. Just an hour before Ogulowo was added to the voter list, the outgoing president, Olusegun Obasanjo, had 'visited the centre to check on the registration'.[30]

Although leaders from a number of parties engaged in similar tactics, the ruling party benefited most because it controlled the electoral commission. Moreover, the influential regional electoral commissioners were appointed not by the chair of the commission but by the president. It was therefore unsurprising when it was announced that Umaru Yar'Adua, the PDP's presidential candidate who was handpicked by Obasanjo to be his successor, had 'won' the election with a commanding 70 per cent of the vote.[31]

Whilst the inflation of a candidate's vote is a familiar story, what is less well known is that it is also possible to make opposition votes disappear. This form of electoral magic is less common, but a number of recorded cases exist. One occurred during the Ukrainian presidential election of late 2004. That contest pitted the incumbent prime minister, Viktor Yanukovych, against a strong independent leader, Viktor Yushchenko. While Yanukovych was an establishment figure and had strong backing from Leonid Kuchma, the outgoing president, Yushchenko – who had held the post of prime minister between 1991 and 2001 – presented himself as a more credible candidate on the basis of his experience as head of the National Bank of Ukraine from 1993 to 1999.

Underneath the surface, however, the campaign was less about credibility and policy concerns and more about ethnolinguistic politics and the dominant question of whether the country should develop deeper links with the European Union or with Russia.[32] Yanukovych's strong ties to Moscow, along with support from the Russian president Vladimir Putin, went down well in the Russian-speaking parts of eastern Ukraine. By contrast, Yushchenko's support was strongest in the Ukrainian-speaking parts of the country such as western Ukraine and the capital, Kiev, where most people feel stronger religious and cultural ties to central Europe, and fear Russian domination.[33]

As no candidate secured the 50 per cent + 1 of the vote needed to win in the first round, the election went to a run-off. Yanukovych was declared to have won by 880,000 – a margin of only 3 per cent. However, almost immediately rumours began to emerge of widespread manipulation in his favour. In the days that followed, a remarkable litany of ballot-box stuffing and ballot deletion was revealed. To start with, the voter register was packed with the names of dead people and duplicate registrations, enabling multiple voting.[34] This was topped up by ballot-box stuffing, which resulted in an unbelievable turnout of 98.5 per cent in Yanukovych's stronghold of Donetsk – including turnout exceeding 127 per cent in some precincts.[35] But although these abuses were well documented, the form of rigging that stole the headlines was the use of 'invisible' ink.[36]

According to Stephen Sestanovich, a US observer from the New York-based Council on Foreign Relations, his delegation witnessed the use of ink that was designed to fade four minutes after application in pro-opposition areas. Those unfortunate voters who used these pens left polling stations believing that they had done their bit to support Yushchenko. In reality, after the ink later disappeared, electoral officials would have little option but to set aside their ballot paper as invalid.[37]

Although ingenious, this strategy has an obvious problem, namely the surprisingly high number of blank ballot papers found during the counting process. As in Kenya, the clear evidence of an attempt to manipulate the election led to widespread criticism, with serious consequences for the regime. But in contrast to what happened in Kenya, mass civil society protests known as the Orange Revolution focused the world's attention on Ukraine, and the Supreme Court annulled the result of the run-off.[38] When the second round of voting was held again a month after the first vote, Yushchenko won, paving the way for a transfer of power and demonstrating the danger of leaving rigging to the last minute.

A second way to manipulate the result late on is to allow the process of voting to pass off normally and then to fraudulently add votes to one candidate's total during the tallying phase. This is possible because the tallying process is often quite complicated, with the votes from tens of thousands of polling stations being aggregated at constituency, regional and then finally at national levels. Each of these stages provides a possible opportunity for the regime to fudge the numbers. Significantly, if lower-level results do not have to be made public, it becomes much easier to change some of the figures without the opposition realizing.

This form of rigging often, though not always, goes hand in hand with a degree of ballot-box stuffing. This was the case, for example, in the Turkish constitutional referendum of 2017. The election was particularly controversial because a 'Yes' vote would introduce a raft of constitutional amendments, effectively turning the country's parliamentary system into an executive presidency, significantly strengthening the powers of President Recep Tayyip Erdoğan. A classic counterfeit democrat, Erdoğan was desperate for the legitimacy that a credible referendum would bring to his power grab, but unwilling to listen to the voice of the people.[39] As a result, his Justice and Development Party (AKP), backed by the far-right Nationalist Movement Party (MHP), set out to control the process from start to finish. On the opposition side, the centre-left Republican People's Party (CHP) and the pro-Kurdish People's Democratic Party (HDP) campaigned against the proposal, claiming that it would mean an end to the separation of powers and amounted to 'democide' (democratic suicide).[40]

In order to ensure victory, the government engaged in a systematic process of ballot-box stuffing in AKP strongholds, combined with simply adding numbers to increase the 'Yes' vote in parts of the country where opposition parties were stronger. These strategies were supplemented by a deliberate strategy of deleting 'No' votes, although instead of the disappearing ink used in Ukraine, AKP leaders appear to have opted for the more straightforward strategy of dumping unfavourable ballots in bins and on building sites.[41] The cumulative effect of these abuses was staggering: according to one observer group,

2.5 million votes may have been fraudulent, although it admitted that the magnitude of the malpractice meant that it was hard to be sure.[42] What is clear is that Erdoğan would not have got his way without electoral fraud: the 'Yes' vote won out against the 'No' vote by 51 per cent to 49 per cent, and this margin of victory was half the size of the number of votes that observers believe were manipulated.[43]

Selecting a strategy

Although often used together, it is important to distinguish between ballot-box stuffing and fraudulent counting, because they have different strengths and weaknesses. Fudging the numbers during counting is usually easier. Instead of mobilizing underage voters or filling out thousands of ballots, it simply requires a small number of people to be willing to change the numbers at a given stage in the process. As a former election observer told us, 'You just have to take out your pen and add a zero to the total, or change a one to a nine. It is as simple as that.'[44] This saves the need for developing and paying for a large, complex, organized operation. Fudging the numbers is perhaps the most efficient of all forms of election rigging.

However, this pro comes with a con: fixing the poll by inaccurately adding up the tallies from different polling stations is vulnerable to detection. Opposition candidates might notice large discrepancies between the tallies, especially if they are able to mobilize party agents to record polling station results and then generate an alternative count. Similarly, international observers and academics have developed new techniques to detect whether a set of results has been manipulated. One of these relies on the fact that while the final digits of a set of figures that come about by chance are likely to be equally distributed, the human brain tends to opt for some numbers more than others, resulting in a distinctive pattern.[45] As a result, by entering a full set of results into a computer program, analysts can determine whether or not they are likely to have been manipulated. These forms of detection are particularly problematic where tallying fraud is concerned, because if the election is sufficiently dubious to inspire a re-count, there will not be sufficient votes in the actual ballot boxes for the ruling party to substantiate the official result.

By contrast, stuffing the ballot box with fraudulent votes suffers from no such drawback, because it generates a paper trail that can subsequently be invoked as an example of electoral quality. Once a candidate's total has been topped up by adding illegitimate votes, the process of counting and tallying can be allowed to take place transparently, with the candidate safe in the knowledge that the required votes have already been secured. This means that the rigging process is better insulated against a forensic audit of the result. For example, if there is a re-count, observers and monitors will find the 'correct' number of votes in each ballot box. Everything will therefore appear to be above board, so long as the total number of votes in a precinct does not exceed the number of voters registered in that area.

However, while ballot-box stuffing is less vulnerable to exposure after the fact, it suffers from other drawbacks. Most obviously, it requires considerable effort and planning. For example, if underage party supporters are to be used they need to be identified and mobilized in the same way as any other voter, and this comes at a cost. Moreover, while ballot-box stuffing is hard to trace after the event, it is more vulnerable to detection on polling day itself. Long lines of young voters, or piles of pre-marked ballots, may be noticed by election observers and the media, while pre-stuffed ballot boxes can be exposed if opposition leaders demand that they are inspected prior to polling stations opening to the public.

In many ways, the ideal strategy for a counterfeit democrat is to use both strategies in unison. Moderate levels of ballot-box stuffing are less likely to be detected, and can still give a leader a high degree of security if they are accompanied by moderate levels of tallying fraud to secure the preferred outcome. Employing both tactics together also gives incumbents greater insurance against either strategy failing.

However, in practice it is not always possible to take this approach. Instead, which strategy is most effective is shaped by the context of the election and the distribution of party support. Imagine two fictional countries, the Competitive Kingdom and Strongholdland, each with three political parties. In the Competitive Kingdom, the three parties are all equally competitive across the whole territory, i.e. they all expect to win roughly one-third of the vote in each area. In Strongholdland, each party dominates one-third of the territory but has almost no support in the other areas.

Because parties in the Competitive Kingdom know that supporters from rival parties are likely to be present in the vast majority of polling stations, they have a strong disincentive to attempt ballot-box stuffing because it is liable to be detected and resisted. Instead, they are more likely to try and rig an election by manipulating the tallying process. In contrast, parties in Strongholdland have a facilitative environment for ballot-box stuffing in their home areas because they enjoy a political monopoly, and so such manipulation is less likely to be exposed. Under these conditions, there is a risk that elections become an arms race, with each party seeking to artificially increase turnout in the area that it controls, in the knowledge that other parties are doing the same elsewhere.

Of course, the Competitive Kingdom and Strongholdland do not really exist – in reality, no country features parties that can compete so effectively in every region, or voting patterns that are quite so Balkanized. But a number of states do approximate one or the other of these ideal types. Most obviously, countries in which ethnic or regional identity shapes voting behaviour, as in much (though by no means all) of sub-Saharan Africa, share the core characteristics of Strongholdland. Partly as a result, we often see remarkably high turnout levels in parties' home areas due to a combination of political fervour, ballot-box stuffing and intense social pressure to vote with the community and get an 'inky finger'.

In Uganda, for example, forty-three polling stations in Kiruhura District in the heartland of President Museveni's National Resistance Movement (NRM) recorded a remarkable feat in 2016.[46] Not only did every single voter turn out to vote, but they all voted for President Museveni. What is more, in a country with pockets of illiteracy, which records thousands of spoilt ballots every election, not a single person had their vote rejected.[47] The perfect turnout and vote in Kiruhura District were, of course, most probably a lie. Although there was no an electoral offence, as the number of voters did not exceed the number on the electoral roll, securing the support of the entire voter register is practically impossible because at least a handful of voters are likely to die between elections, or to be unable to vote, for example as a result of sickness. A turnout of 100 per cent is therefore indicative of a government stuffing the ballot box beyond the bounds of credibility, if not legality.

Under Strongholdland-type conditions, it may also be possible for opposition parties to engage in similar strategies (although they rarely benefit from these to the same extent as the ruling party). This is because, in areas where opposition parties can impose a degree of control over the electoral officials, they can act like the government. In Kenya, for example, opposition leaders have long been able to establish their own political fiefdoms within which they can exert great influence. Because the vast majority of people come from the same community and vote the same way, it can be very hard for election officials – who often work in areas close to where they live – to resist the pressure to allow the locally dominant party to gain an advantage. This does not mean that the opposition competes on a level playing field with the ruling party, but it does mean that they have some opportunities to close the gap. In the 1992 elections, it is estimated that the 250,000 ballots that were artificially added in areas supportive of President Daniel arap Moi were partly offset by the tens of thousands added in the heartlands of his rivals, Kenneth Matiba and Oginga Odinga.[48]

Things look very different in countries that come closer to the Competitive Kingdom model, as do some Latin American countries where ethnicity is less central to political behaviour. In Venezuela, for example, the government of President Maduro had clear strongholds in the country, but when it tried to hold a controversial vote to select a new constituent assembly to redesign the political system it faced two major challenges. First, opposition voters boycotted the poll, arguing that the creation of the assembly was designed purely to enable the ruling party to circumvent checks and balances by creating a new body with supremacy over the legislature.[49] In turn, this threatened to reduce the level of turnout, undermining the credibility of the exercise. In seeking to boost the rate of participation in the elections, President Maduro also faced a second challenge, namely that his government would encounter ridicule were it to be exposed; and opposition supporters and civil society groups were fairly evenly spread across the country – particularly in larger cities where protests against the government had been the most pronounced.

The government's solution to this conundrum was simply to inflate the turnout to its desired figure. When the official results were announced, Venezuelans were falsely told that 41.5 per cent of registered voters – more than 8 million people – had gone to the polls. Given the chaos surrounding the election this duplicity might not have been detected, were it not for the fact that Antonio Mugica, the head of Smartmatic, the company that had designed the election technology, recorded the vote results as they came out, and publicly challenged the government's figures. According to Mugica, 'the turnout numbers on Sunday 30th July for the Constituent Assembly in Venezuela were tampered with' – to the tune of at least a million votes.[50]

Mugica's claims were backed up by an investigation by Reuters that found that by 5.30 p.m. – one and a half hours before the end of regular voting – only 3.7 million people had cast their ballots.[51] Even if there had been a massive late surge of voters to the polls, it is logistically infeasible that 4.3 million people voted in just ninety minutes, especially as this would have amounted to more people than had voted during the whole of the rest of the day. These revelations were embarrassing to Maduro, and further undermined his domestic and international credibility. They did not prove fatal, though – once the constituent assembly had been sworn in on 4 August, he could change the law to suit his needs, including defending himself against electoral complaints.[52]

One challenge of ballot-box stuffing that Maduro did not face was the risk of over-rigging. Especially when leaders set up structures in which the grassroots units of a decentralized political system are encouraged to demonstrate their value to the leader, ballot-box stuffing can get out of hand, generating a result that is not plausible. In turn, this can undermine the credibility of the broader process, and hence the capacity of leaders to retain legitimacy.

As a result, leaders who typically rig often try not to rig too much. If a seemingly competitive contest ends up with a final tally of 95 per cent for the incumbent, the opposition, monitors and foreign governments are likely to raise a few eyebrows. The sweet spot of ballot-box stuffing is probably something in the vicinity of a 5 to 15 per cent margin of victory, as that is still believable, but also has the virtue of showing that the election wasn't really that close. The vast majority of politicians we have talked to about elections over the last few years identified a vote share within this spread as being ideal. Interestingly, a research project on presidential coalitions in Africa, Latin America and post-communist Europe that interviewed 350 members of parliament in a number of young democracies and competitive authoritarian states found that, if they were to rise to the presidency, the average legislator would like to hold 60 per cent of the seats in parliament. This figure was selected for a number of reasons, including signalling strength, ease of coalition management, and the fact that it makes it feasible to change the constitution – which often requires a majority of around two-thirds.[53]

In the electoral arena, a healthy winning margin is also important because it sends a signal to opposition parties and election observers alike. Rival leaders are likely to be disheartened if they lose heavily, and this may even compromise their ability to raise funds for future campaigns. At the same time, size really does matter when it comes to the attitude of international donors and observers. If an election is decided by, say, just 1 per cent, then monitors are far more likely to be detail-orientated, knowing that any abnormality may have swayed the final outcome. With margins of 15 to 20 per cent, observers sometimes end up overlooking what are often described as 'discrepancies', because they reason that these weren't decisive and that it is therefore not worth rocking the boat by raising concerns. In contrast, if an incumbent wins by 1 per cent, observers are more likely to investigate every possible suggestion of fraud or rigging. This creates a strong incentive to ensure that the election isn't too close.

Strengthening democracy and protecting the ballot

As we have seen, ballot-box stuffing and tallying fraud can be highly effective, but are also particularly risky strategies. They are more likely to be detected than many of the other forms of election rigging identified in this book, and leaders never know quite how much rigging they need to do in order to win. Despite this, counterfeit democrats tend to second-guess the strength of their own position, and often pursue these strategies despite the costs. There are good reasons for this – lacking independent media and surrounded by 'yes men', autocrats have relatively few ways to ascertain the true beliefs and opinions of their supporters. In place of reliable news and opinion polls, rumours and speculation gain ground. And when leaders feel unsure of their position, and are subject to few checks and balances, they often become willing to take additional measures to be extra sure that they will win. As the study of presidential coalitions cited earlier demonstrates, most politicians prefer to minimize political risk by giving themselves a greater cushion than they strictly need. Consequently, the situation facing opposition parties and candidates becomes even more difficult.

So, what is to be done? One option that has become increasingly popular over the years is for domestic observation groups – usually managed by a coalition of civil society organizations – to conduct a parallel vote tabulation (PVT), which typically involves collecting results from a sample of polling stations in order to deter rigging during the counting process. If an independent tally is carried out then it becomes far harder simply to change the numbers without anyone noticing. The second option is to introduce new biometric technology into the process in order to reduce the scope for multiple voting and the like,[54] while the third option combines elements of the first two with a more old-fashioned approach: election observation and the deployment of party agents.[55] All these options have strengths and weaknesses, meaning that only a combination of the three is likely to reduce the tendency towards ballot-box stuffing.

The main attraction of a PVT is that if it is conducted by an independent organization, it can serve as an effective check on the tally carried out by the electoral commission. In contexts in which the credibility of the commission itself is at stake, this can be extremely valuable. As a result, PVTs have become increasingly popular in recent years. The American NGO the National Democratic Institute has helped civic groups in 52 countries perform over 200 parallel counts.[56] In almost all cases, this does not mean counting up the vote from every single polling station, which would be too costly and logistically demanding. Instead, observers are deployed to a nationally representative sample of stations to record the results and feed them into a central system that generates a projected outcome.

However, while such a check may serve to keep an electoral commission honest, it is important to note that a PVT has three main weaknesses. The first is that because it is based on a subset of results, a PVT does not tell you exactly what percentage of the vote each candidate received, but rather forecasts a figure around which the election outcome can be considered to be plausible. Moreover, because they are typically conducted on the basis of limited samples, PVTs usually suffer a high margin of error.

Much like an opinion poll, the smaller a sample is, the less certain we can be about the findings. For example, a PVT conducted on the basis of 1,000 polling stations will have a margin of error of 3 per cent. This means that the result can plausibly fall anywhere within a 6 per cent spread of votes without being considered problematic. Consider a case in which a PVT projects that two candidates will each secure 48 per cent of the vote. Given a 3 per cent margin of error on the figure for each candidate, the PVT can be interpreted as confirming the plausibility of every possible election outcome. This is because this margin of error is large enough to cover one candidate winning with 51 per cent of the vote, the other candidate winning with 51 per cent of the vote, and a situation in which there is a dead heat between the two, requiring a run-off. As a result, a PVT may not be much use when an election is close.

The second limitation of PVTs is that, like any analysis based on a sample, they are only reliable if the polling stations that they include are truly representative of the whole country. Where census data are contested – as it often is because faulty census data can be used to justify gerrymandering (chapter 1, pp. 35–43) – the question of whether a given set of polling stations is nationally representative may be extremely controversial, undermining the credibility of the PVT's findings.

The third weakness of parallel counts is less technical, but in some ways more profound than the first two. Recording votes at polling station level and comparing them to the official outcome once these results have been added up by the electoral commission can reveal tallying fraud, but tells us nothing about whether the results recorded at polling station level were themselves legitimate. And as we have seen, in many cases tallying fraud, ballot-box stuffing and multiple voting go hand in hand. Indeed, because they take polling station results at face value, PVTs may actually incorporate the outcome of these abuses into the very mechanism that is supposed to expose manipulation.

PVTs may thus expose one form of rigging but mask another – and can even lend independent legitimization to a rigged election. For this reason, it is critical that PVTs are only conducted in polling stations that have been thoroughly monitored throughout the day of voting and counting – something that is now becoming standard practice for groups like the National Democratic Institute, but which is not always the case when opposition parties and media houses employ this strategy. PVTs are therefore a valuable tool in the fight against election rigging, but they are no silver bullet.

Given the limitations of some of the strategies currently being used to enhance electoral quality, it is easy to see why the introduction of new technology has won so many adherents when it comes to registering citizens, verifying voters and transmitting results. By capturing voters' fingerprints and tying them to their voter identification, biometric voter-registration processes can help to make sure that each voter only appears on the roll once. Moreover, by holding a fresh registration process and ceasing to use old rolls, dead voters can be removed. If the new roll is then subject to an independent audit so that any errors and duplicate registrations can be detected and removed, it may then be possible to generate a much more credible electoral register that accurately reflects the voting age population. In turn, this would reduce the scope for multiple voting and for ballot-box stuffing, because there would be fewer false entries on the register for those set on rigging the election to exploit.

Of course, this is easier said than done because incumbents understand the danger that it would pose to their electoral dominance. But recent experience demonstrates that it is not impossible. For example, in Nigeria a growing consensus on the need to strengthen and relegitimize the electoral process led to gradual improvements under a new and highly respected chair of the electoral commission, Attahiru Jega. Notably, the introduction of biometric voter registration, complete with biometric permanent voter cards, is credited with removing as many as 10 million illegitimate registrations from the electoral roll, paving the way for better-quality elections and, ultimately, facilitating a transfer of power in 2015. According to the Commonwealth Observer Group, 'the introduction of biometric Permanent Voter Cards is, in our view, a major factor in enhancing the integrity of the electoral process by ensuring that only eligible voters could cast ballots on polling day'.[57]

These kinds of victories for electoral integrity have generated great excitement about the potential for the digital revolution to protect elections and strengthen democracy.[58] New election technology makes it possible not only to register voters electronically but also to verify them before they cast their ballots using fingerprint recognition software. If this were to be effectively implemented, it would have the potential to take multiple-voting fraud permanently off the table. Moreover, digital vote-tallying processes promise to create new checks on tallying fraud, for example by instantly transmitting polling station results to a live online tally, cutting out the middle man.

However, as we saw in the previous chapter, it is important not to place too much faith in digital technology: it can be used for good or for ill. In addition to logistical challenges, digital processes are typically managed by the electoral commission and so are themselves susceptible to manipulation. And the more elections are digitized, the more vulnerable they become to hacking.

Thus, as we argue at much greater length in the conclusion to this book, making the most of new technology will require it to be transferred into the hands of independent civil society groups and opposition parties. With this done, the prospects for detecting ballot-box stuffing become much better, leading to a damaging loss of legitimacy for election cheats.

This leads us to the final rigging strategy open to counterfeit democrats – one that supersedes all others, because it promises to generate a free pass for regimes that commit a wide range of abuses. In the next chapter, we turn to look at how regimes either dupe or co-opt Western governments into rubber-stamping rigged 'Potemkin elections', shrouding even the worst elections in the guise of legitimate, free and fair contests.

Chapter 6

POTEMKIN ELECTIONS

How to fool the West

In 1787, Catherine the Great set out for New Russia (modern-day Crimea). A dizzying array of Western dignitaries accompanied her on the tour, as she sought to show off the new jewel of Russia's empire. She was eager for their approval, hoping to be seen in the eyes of the West as a legitimate power rather than a pariah.

The governor of the region, Grigory Potemkin, was one of Catherine's favourite lovers. As a reward for his relationship with her, he was tasked with cleaning up and rebuilding New Russia in the wake of a destructive war and subsequent annexation. Catherine believed that a dazzling show of opulence and modernity would sway European diplomats to take her side in an impending conflict with the Ottoman Empire.

Legend has it that Potemkin sought to amaze the visiting dignitaries with a series of pristine villages. There was just one problem: the villages were not really that pristine. So, according to popular myth, Potemkin simply constructed façades of glittering new villages along the river route. In the distance, they were awe-inspiring. Up close, they were flimsy fakes. The story goes that he would construct a signature village in advance of

Catherine's arrival and deconstruct it shortly after she left, repeating the same charade over and over. Whilst historians dispute whether this ever actually happened, the term stuck. A 'Potemkin village' now refers to a façade – whether literal or figurative – constructed to conceal an underlying shabbiness. They are meant to look good to outsiders who will only gaze in their direction for a short period of time. And when the observers leave, the façade collapses and the rot is revealed.[1]

Today, there are 'Potemkin elections'. The pageantry of campaigning, the parade of voting, the charade of counting, all are engineered with one simple goal – to fool the West into believing that all was conducted fairly in a shining model of democracy. But behind the façade, the actual democratic scaffolding is often rotten – if it exists at all.

Azerbaijan's 2013 election, which was mentioned in chapter 4 (pp. 149–50), was a perfect example of a Potemkin election. Except in this case, it was as if the façade of the village fell over just as the audience showed up, exposing the whole thing as a farce. That year, Azerbaijan was ranked as the eleventh most authoritarian country in the world.[2] President Ilham Aliyev, like his father, is the very caricature of a despot. He runs the country like a personal fiefdom all the while trying to maintain the mirage of democracy and good governance. He insists that he is not enriching himself, and points to his reasonable $250,000 salary as his primary source of income. Yet in 2010 investigative reporters found that his son, then eleven years old, had allegedly purchased Dubai real estate worth $44 million, so it is not hard to see through that lie.[3]

Like many despots, though, Aliyev held elections because he saw them as a tool to bolster his claim to national and international legitimacy. The government set everything up for an election to be held on 9 October 2013. The ballots were printed. The polls were ready. Observers from around the world arrived – including a congressional delegation from the United States, along with representatives of the Parliamentary Assembly of the Council of Europe and the European Parliament.

The government boasted of its transparency, showcasing the new iPhone app (discussed in the introduction to this book), which magically disseminated the result a day before voting was due to take place.[4] Although the government played down the incident as a 'test run',[5] it soon became clear that the whole process had been rigged well before that gaffe. Aliyev was no amateur and was not about to leave anything to chance – or to the will of the electorate. In the run-up to the polls he had reportedly excluded a major opponent from the election, denied rival candidates media time, and ensured that the public only received cheerleading messages from state media (chapter 4, pp. 149–50). At the same time, reporting also showed that the regime embarked on a process of systematic harassment of both candidates and voters. As a result, the opposition did not stand a chance.

Despite the repressive atmosphere and the iPhone app, voting went ahead as planned. To the untrained eye – or those only looking from a distance – it was a normal election. Voters went to the polls and cast ballots. Everything was peaceful. Fortunately, though, trained eyes *were* watching more closely: election monitors were present to document abuses and personally witnessed the polls at close hand. Surely, then, the Western reaction to Azerbaijan's 2013 election must have been universal condemnation of a rigged vote?

Unfortunately, where election rigging is concerned, things are rarely so straightforward. Although there are some groups that are more committed to democratic values, such as the Carter Center – an independent monitoring group founded by the former American president Jimmy Carter – and although the individuals who make up observation teams are typically hardworking and conscientious, the leadership of most missions either contains a political component or has to take into account political considerations. And this is where the problems can come in.

In Azerbaijan, a congressional delegation from the United States dispatched to watch the polls ignored the seemingly glaring red flags all around them and endorsed the election. Congressman Michael McMahon, a New York Democrat, called the election 'honest, fair, and really efficient'. There were no queues at polling stations, he pointed out, a sign of bureaucratic efficiency.[6] The real reason was probably that people did not bother to show up because they knew the outcome was predetermined.

It is tempting to interpret the comments of Congressman McMahon as an example of the naïvety of a single deluded Western official. Sadly, it was not the exception. Both the Parliamentary Assembly of the Council of Europe and the European Parliament also fawned over an election that appeared to be blatantly rigged. Their statement suggested that Azerbaijan's dictator had presided over a clean poll: 'Overall around Election Day we have observed a free, fair and transparent electoral process ... From what we have seen, electoral procedures on the eve and on Election Day have been carried out in a professional and peaceful way.'[7] It was as if Potemkin himself had given the visiting dignitaries a tour of the flimsy façades passed off as the real thing, and the dignitaries had simply applauded the workmanship from outside before moving on.

Aliyev's attempt to deliver a respectable-looking election demonstrates an important point about the costs and benefits that an incumbent faces when deciding to rig an election. It is tempting to think that when it comes to electoral manipulation leaders face a set menu of options, all with clear and predetermined prices, with those who choose a free and fair poll gaining legitimacy but risking defeat, and those who select election rigging all but guaranteeing victory while exposing themselves to international criticism and a loss of legitimacy.

In reality, however, these costs are not fixed, but are shaped by the ability of a government to hide its electoral manipulation and hence to rig cost-free. In the case of Azerbaijan, the use of digital technology to confer a sense of modernity and due process on the election failed, but nonetheless reveals the way in which leaders can try and dress up even the most problematic of elections so that they appear good enough to get a pass mark from the international community.

Moreover, this is only one tactic among many available to autocrats. In addition to employing modern technology – a theme explored in chapter 4 – and making use of other subtle rigging techniques, counterfeit democrats can also try to fix the game by picking their own audience. By investing in loyalist civil society groups and setting up state-friendly monitors primed to approve the result, autocrats can create Potemkin observers to oversee their Potemkin elections. In other words, despots and counterfeit democrats can establish their own monitors, who will *always* praise elections no matter how rotten they are.[8]

Through this process, leaders can ensure that they receive supportive evaluations of their electoral victories that can be invoked as they take office. In the best-case scenario, positive pronouncements from these phoney groups may work to persuade others of the legitimacy of the polls. In the worst, independent election monitors may dispute a rosy assessment, but a good report may still create a rival narrative, reducing the impact of criticism emanating from more independent sources. In the world of political theatre, this is the equivalent of the magician who plants a member of their team in the audience to collude with their trick so that it seems more credible to everyone else.

By implementing all of these strategies at the same time, leaders can try and obscure the rigged foundations of their power. In turn, this reduces the cost of rigging and empowers the incumbent in two ways. Internationally, the regime can point to positive electoral assessments in order to secure access to the club of respectable election-holding nations, thereby tapping into financial assistance and foreign direct investment. Domestically, such endorsements can be used as part of the regime's public relations campaign. At the same time, the failure of international monitors to effectively defend democracy can have a demoralizing impact on the opposition, in part because it implies that the prospects for change are limited.

Not everyone cares as much about faking it, though. North Korea's Kim Jong-un, for example, or Vladimir Putin in Russia, don't much care whether the West validates their sham elections. They hold elections anyway, and bask in the glory of their comprehensive victories.

However, most leaders do try and play the electoral legitimacy game because, as we shall see in the conclusion, it boosts the prospects of regime survival. The challenge for counterfeit democrats is that not all leaders are able to do this equally effectively. While any government can try to obscure its activities by speaking the language of reform, securing international support depends in part on whether foreign powers can be given an incentive not to look too closely at the façade disguising the rot. Much like a magician performing an illusion, the effect of the Potemkin election works best if you are willing or susceptible to being deceived in the first place.

Over the past thirty years, a number of Western governments have invested considerable time and money into promoting democracy abroad. The amount spent on democracy-promotion activities by the lead US agency in this area, USAID, increased from $103 million in 1990 to $1 billion in 2005. While a lot of this money was spent in Afghanistan and Iraq, USAID's investment is indicative of a wider trend: in 2007, the 'member states of the European Union (EU) collectively spent around Euro 2,500 million on democracy assistance'.[9] As part of this remarkable effort, many smart and dedicated individuals have implemented a remarkable variety of projects designed to make democracy work, from strengthening civil society to making electoral commissions more independent and reducing the scale of vote buying.

Yet at the same time, there are cases in which democracy has clearly been sacrificed on the altar of another more pressing goal. The most obvious incentive for world powers to approve poor-quality polls is to maintain good relations with the government in order to access resources and pursue their geostrategic ambitions.[10] In this sense, a state's resource wealth and location play an important role in shaping whether the costs of rigging can be reduced. The significance of these factors becomes clear if we briefly return to the example of Azerbaijan. In 2013, Western monitors didn't simply endorse an election that seemed so clearly rigged because they were blind to its problems; they were blind to its problems because they deliberately did not open their eyes. The reason? Geopolitics.

Azerbaijan lies squarely in the energy-rich Caspian region and is therefore the linchpin of Europe's future oil and gas supplies. That makes it strategically important to the United States, too, because Azerbaijan acts as a counterweight to Europe's increasing dependence on Russian energy resources. From George W. Bush to Barack Obama, American foreign policy invested heavily in the Caspian basin as a means of undercutting Russian leverage across Europe.[11] Furthermore, Azerbaijan is in the process of developing the Southern Gas Corridor, a pipeline that connects the Shah Deniz gas field (which has between 1.5 and 3 billion barrels of natural gas reserves) to Italy.[12] In short, Azerbaijan got a free pass in part because Western countries prioritized their strategic relationship with the regime over their commitment to democratic principles.

This is clear from the fact that despite the pronouncements of the monitors, there was more than enough evidence of electoral malpractice to condemn the election as a sham vote – had the international community wanted to. Indeed, observers from the Organization for Security and Co-operation in Europe (OSCE) detected serious fraud or manipulation in an alarming 58 per cent of the polling locations that they visited.[13] In other words, on over half the occasions that an election observer showed up, they directly witnessed some form of election rigging. Despite this, other groups and major international players chose to emphasize the positives rather than the negatives.

Of course, strategic oil and gas reserves are not the only factors that can persuade the international community to pull its punches. Some elections receive a pass from Western governments because they take place in countries that occupy a strategic security position – as allies in the fight against terrorism, for example. Pakistan in the aftermath of 9/11 was a prime example of this type of thinking, but the logic even extends to countries like Uganda.[14] Other times, key trading partners receive undeserved praise for rigged elections. And of course, some countries, like Saudi Arabia, do not even bother holding elections, but still maintain a privileged position in the West because of a combination of economic and security ties.

Thus, leaders whose countries are insulated from international pressure – either because they have economic and political ties to Western states, or because of their resources and location[15] – find it easiest to get away with Potemkin elections. But here again it is important to recognize that international influence is not simply a static factor that autocrats have to take as they find it. Instead, it can be carefully cultivated. On the one hand, sound economic management to boost GDP, provide jobs and reduce dependency on Western aid can undercut the leverage of foreign powers that might otherwise seek to promote democracy. On the other hand, leaders may be able to make themselves seem indispensable by deliberately taking up a central role in supporting the ambitions of important partner states. They can do this by becoming foreign-policy chameleons, changing their colours based on the political stripes of prospective foreign sponsors.[16] In this way, wily autocrats in even poorer and less well-connected states can reduce the cost of rigging and strengthen their ability to withstand international pressure, facilitating electoral manipulation and the retention of power.

Defending the indefensible

When geopolitics comes into play, rigged elections may get a free pass in one of two ways. First, the observers themselves may turn a blind eye to corrupt and fraudulent practices, as was the case with some monitoring groups in Azerbaijan's 2013 vote. Second, even when observers get it right and take governments to task for rigging elections, Western governments may undercut that criticism by endorsing the election anyway for the sake of a broader diplomatic relationship.

Indeed, one of the problems facing international observers is that even when they do their jobs well and condemn a rigged election, more powerful figures within their governments back home may undermine their evaluation. To see this, let us return to Turkey's 2017 constitutional referendum. On several key fronts, there was compelling evidence that Turkey's referendum had been badly rigged. Western observers condemned it without mincing their words. The Council of Europe suggested that up to 2.5 million ballots were of dubious legitimacy, roughly double the margin by which the referendum passed.[17] Monitors from the OSCE also criticized the election, highlighting the illegality of allowing unstamped ballots and the unlevel playing field facing the opposition campaign.[18] In short, Western observers saw fraud, reported it, and condemned the election. The system of election observation worked precisely as it was intended to.

But in the end, this mattered little. Hours after the razor-thin referendum result was announced – with the changes narrowly passing – President Donald Trump called President

Erdoğan and congratulated him on his victory.[19] There was no mention of the flawed process or the undemocratic content of the referendum itself. Instead, it was unfettered praise from the most powerful man in the West, and it immediately undercut any criticism from the election monitors. After all, why would Erdoğan care about a report from the OSCE when the president of the United States offered an uncritical endorsement of the vote and validated its outcome with a congratulatory phone call?

Of course, unlike Turkey, which is rich in natural resources and sits at a crossroads between East and West, many countries in the world are strategically unimportant to the West. Yet even in some of these nations, counterfeit democrats have been able to position themselves as critical Western allies in order to reduce external pressure for democratization.

The Ugandan president Yoweri Museveni is a past master at this kind of strategy. In the 1990s, when faced with domestic and international pressure to introduce multiparty elections, Museveni forged strong alliances with Western and development programmes such as the UK's Department for International Development. By providing a 'proving ground' in which such programmes could be effectively implemented, his government generated much-needed success stories with which aid agencies could justify their budgets. In turn, this gave a number of powerful development organizations a stake in the continuity of the Museveni regime.

In the 2000s, when the effect of this strategy had started to wane, the president changed his colours yet again and repositioned himself as a crucial American ally in the war on terror. Notably, by providing the majority of the largest consignment of troops for the African Union Mission in Somalia (AMISOM), Museveni secured for himself the capacity to make or break international efforts to reduce the threat posed by the radical Islamist group al-Shabaab.[20] Partly as a result,

Western criticism of the poor-quality elections held under his leadership has been muted.

This is perfectly illustrated by the Ugandan elections of 2016. At present, Uganda is classified as 'not free' by Freedom House due to the many restrictions on the opposition imposed by the government of President Museveni (for more, see chapter 2, pp. 61–4).[21] For the latest polls, the European Union sent observers who were dispatched throughout the country to a small number of polling locations. They observed an election in which rigging was clearly present. Ballots arrived late, but seemingly only in opposition areas. The ruling regime arrested the opposition candidate, Kizza Besigye, multiple times.[22] And just in case anyone watching the polls might have thought that they were open and transparent, the chair of Uganda's supposedly non-partisan electoral commission publicly stated that the opposition candidate was not 'presidential material'.[23]

Things did not improve after the polls, when the ruling party's chairwoman, Justine Lumumba, warned that 'The state will kill your children' should they come out into the streets to protest the results of the election.[24] It is hard to imagine how anyone could classify such an election as free and fair.[25]

Further evidence of malpractice emerged during the course of voting. As we saw in the last chapter, in his political heartlands Museveni received a fantastic share of the vote based on an implausible turnout as a result of ballot-box stuffing. As usual, the European Union observer mission did a very good job of documenting these problems. However, the fact that observers are not supposed to directly intervene in the process, but rather document issues that can be addressed at a later stage, undermined their ability to prevent the abuses from occurring.[26]

At the same time, a desire not to ruin relations with the Ugandan government led the EU team to pull its punches in public; when asked by the press whether the election had been free and fair, the team deflected the question, directing the audience to read its report and 'and draw their own conclusions'.[27] While observers don't use the term 'free and fair' any more, preferring to talk about whether elections were 'credible' – a less controversial and more manageable threshold – the true answer was that the election was not good enough by any standard. Instead, the European Union opted not to step on any toes, and left its criticism to a lengthy and technical report that few will ever read.

President Museveni's ability to consistently 'wag the dog' serves as an important lesson that if counterfeit democrats play the chameleon well enough to blend in with the strategic aspirations of the West, they can get away with flawed elections. Indeed, in extreme cases – which are incredibly rare, but nonetheless problematic – disreputable election monitors have gone even further, directly interfering in the process for political ends. For example, in the 2010 presidential election in Haiti, monitors from the Organization of American States (OAS) – the regional body that represents thirty-five states in the Americas and is headquartered in Washington, DC – were tasked with observing the first-round elections, from which the top two candidates would go to a run-off. The election was highly contentious, as according to the initial tally the second- and third-place finishers were only separated by 0.7 per cent of the vote, which had been plagued by widespread irregularities. In an unprecedented step, the OAS established an 'Expert Verification Mission'.[28] That body did something unbelievable – it directly called for the results to be reversed, and suggested swapping the third-place finisher with the second, thereby changing which candidate would go to the second round.

Several analyses by the Center for Economic and Policy Research found that the decision was based on political considerations rather than statistical inference or any quantitative evidence. Worse, the Center's own analyses of the available statistical data suggested that the Expert Verification Mission came to precisely the wrong conclusion about the election. That finding helped ensure that the OAS recommendation was not followed, but the entire process shows the degree to which election monitors can become compromised by geopolitical motivations.[29]

The birth of election monitoring

This criticism of international observers should not be taken to imply that election monitoring should be scrapped. There is no question that the world would be less democratic were it not for the role played by monitors; there are a number of cases in which they have exposed election rigging, as when the European Union team cast doubt on the Kenyan election of 2007.[30] However, more needs to be done to free monitors from political concerns, and to enable them to better detect electoral manipulation. Indeed, although international observation has been around for many years, there have been very few improvements to the election-monitoring playbook in the last two decades. This is a particular problem, because election rigging over that same time period has grown significantly more sophisticated.

Election monitoring made its debut on the world stage in 1857, when European powers sent observers to witness the referendum that would unite Moldavia and Wallachia as Romania.[31] The practice did not recur in the modern era, however, until Costa Rica invited the Organization of American States to its 1962 election. But before the 1980s, fewer than one in ten elections had any form of observers.[32] On the rare occasions when monitors did operate during the Cold War, they were often just a way for the American government to legitimize the government of an allied state. That all changed at the end of the Cold War.

Between 1985 and 1995, the world saw a surge in election monitoring – from around 10 per cent of all elections being put under international scrutiny to more than half. By 2006, 80 per cent of all elections were being observed by international teams seeking to detect and expose fraud and rigging (see appendix 4).[33] Today, most major national-level elections are monitored by at least one international team, but in many cases multiple missions are deployed simultaneously. That is partly because of something political scientists call 'international norm diffusion' – or, plainly put, the expectation that governments would hold elections if they want to be seen as legitimate. When despots refuse to allow monitors to witness an election, it gives fresh ammunition to the opposition to suggest that the entire contest is rigged. As a result, the most alluring prospect for a strongman is to find ways to fix an election while receiving international endorsement. In many ways, this represents the Holy Grail for the leaders of counterfeit democracies: it diffuses criticism emanating from domestic groups and ensures that electoral controversy will not lead to the taps of international financial assistance being turned off.

The best election observation groups, such as the Carter Center, the European Union and OSCE, have, to their credit, tried to adopt new practices to detect rigged elections. Instead of monitors arriving in a country just days before ballots are cast, it is now commonplace to deploy 'long-term observer' teams throughout the country in the months before election day.[34] This is a key improvement, because it at least makes it more difficult for pre-election rigging to go undetected, and can prove critical in deterring media manipulation or a flawed voter registration period. Different missions are also increasingly likely to try and co-ordinate, both in terms of where they go and in terms of their evidence. This is important, because it makes no sense for election observers all to go to the same places; by pooling evidence, different teams can build up a better picture of how the whole process unfolded. Nonetheless, despite these efforts, many challenges remain.

Effective co-ordination is undermined by the fact that different missions judge elections using different standards, and some organizations are more likely to criticize than others. As the political scientist Judith Kelley has concluded, when a number of teams agree, 'their consensus can bolster their individual legitimacy as well as the legitimacy of the international norms they stress', but it is also true that 'the different biases, capabilities, and standards of organization sometimes can lead organizations to outright contradict each other or work at cross-purposes'.[35] In Africa, for example, African Union missions are known for giving more positive evaluations, in part because they do not want to establish a precedent that might be applied to their own countries further down the line.[36] This is a serious problem with regional monitoring organizations, which are usually comprised of at least some undemocratic member states. As a result, they tend to pull their punches.

Even when organizations are well intentioned and independent, they often do not have the resources to monitor effectively. Many are of such a small size (usually between 25 and 150 staff members) that they can only ever hope to cover a tiny fraction of polling stations. This problem is further exacerbated by the fact that international observation groups are typically subject to tight security regulations and cannot send their staff to more unstable or dangerous areas – which is often where electoral manipulation takes place.[37] As a result, evidence of rigging can fall through the cracks.

Escaping detection

Election observers also have to contend with wily ruling parties who are well-practised at hiding their activities. Unfortunately, the small size of observation teams – and the fact that they continue to follow the template of posting monitors to one polling station for the whole day – makes such missions predictable, and thus particularly easy to evade. It is usually clear the day before the poll which areas will be monitored, and this enables those seeking to rig elections simply to move their activities elsewhere. As a result, there is a growing body of research that suggests that monitors simply displace, rather than deter, election fraud. Like a game of whack-a-mole, stopping rigging in one precinct just makes it more likely to pop up in another, with the result that the 'right' result is still produced.[38]

Dictators are helped in this quest by the fact that even when geopolitical considerations are not at play the bar is often set pretty low, with election observers endorsing flawed elections that they would never endorse in their own countries. In off-the-record discussions with Brian, international monitors have admitted that in less stable states anything short of widespread state-sponsored violence will sometimes be tolerated if the alternative might destabilize a country. The risk of triggering political conflict, with all the negative political and economic consequences this would generate for ordinary citizens, is sometimes so high that even committed democrats think twice about blowing the whistle on electoral fraud. The technical report will, of course, cite all the violations observed, but few consequences will follow. Significantly, this danger is not simply something confected by overly anxious foreigners who overstate their own importance – recent research has found that election observation reports sometimes spark violence when they expose rigging.[39]

In addition to the political risks involved, observers' decisions are also shaped by their beliefs about the best way to make progress. In Uganda, for example, Museveni's military support was not the only reason why monitors pulled their punches: they were also motivated by a sense of what was achievable. Declaring the polls to have breached international standards would have had a number of important implications. On the one hand, it would have empowered Besigye and the opposition, potentially increasing the prospects for political conflict. In a region that has experienced both the Rwandan genocide and the 2007 electoral crisis in Kenya (chapter 3), monitors were understandably concerned about the prospect for instability. On the other hand, rejecting the results might well have led Museveni to expel Western donor missions and to reject international observation missions in the future, both of which could be liable to undermine the prospects for a more gradual process of democratization. By downplaying the abuses committed by Museveni's government, European Union observers ensured that they would continue to be able to engage with the NRM regime. But they did so at the cost of allowing a flawed poll to stand. The lack of political reform in Uganda over the past decade suggests that whatever influence the West is able to maintain by handling Museveni with kid gloves does not extend to the electoral arena.

In other cases, the thought process is somewhat lazier. As Thomas Carothers argued in the late 1990s, many observers witnessing voting in extremely impoverished regimes with a poor track record of democracy simply think, 'Well, what can you expect?'[40] This line of thinking, which is becoming less common but which continues to be a problem, tends to be particularly seductive in African countries, where some observers figure that it would be unfair to judge Gabon by the same criteria used for Germany. As a result, some of the standards applied are lower than they would be elsewhere: at times, polls need to be 'just good enough' for the international community to move on to the next country, rather than actually 'good'. In many cases, this means an improvement on the previous elections is acceptable – even if the latest polls were poor quality.

Taken together with their concern not to trigger political instability, this way of thinking has led international observation groups to condemn comparable types of rigging less frequently in Africa than elsewhere. Comparing all elections monitored by Western observers between 1989 and 2012, elections held in Africa were 4 per cent less likely to be branded as fraudulent – despite the fact that on average these polls are some of the lowest quality in the world. This is the 'Well, what can you expect?' principle in action. The fallout from this approach is what we call 'the curse of low expectations'. As counterfeit democrats rig elections and get away with it, they lose any incentive to reform the process. After all, if it worked last time, why do anything differently when the next vote comes around? In this way, the willingness of some monitors to allow flawed polls to 'pass', especially in poor and fragile countries, has actually incentivized leaders to do the bare minimum ahead of the following elections. This is an extremely dangerous situation from the point of view of democratic consolidation.

Those who rig elections understand the game and actively aim to convince monitors that flawed polls are clean. Take Belarus for example, often referred to as the 'last dictatorship in Europe'. When Brian was in Minsk in December 2015, high-level ex-government officials told him how the dictator, Alexander Lukashenko – who, as was documented in chapter 5, has publicly admitted to rigging – would manipulate elections with observers in mind. As we have seen (p. 160), he wanted to make sure that the final margin of victory was sufficiently large to demoralize the opposition, but sufficiently low as to seem plausible. As a result,

> Lukashenko instructs everyone as to what percentage he wants. Maybe it's 76 per cent. But then, his aides don't want to get in trouble in case someone fails to deliver. So they tell the regional staff to ensure that it's 79 per cent just to be safe. Then the regional staff tell the local staff to make sure Lukashenko wins 83 per cent. Then, everyone delivers, and Lukashenko gets 83 per cent.[41]

As in many of the other cases discussed here, Lukashenko was able to get away with this Potemkin election in part because he rigged cleverly, and in part because other considerations were at play. One high-level Western diplomat in Belarus explained it this way: 'The government let us "observe" the vote tallying from 50 metres away with a group of regime thugs blocking our view. All we could see was a bunch of butts from 50 metres – so obviously we couldn't see if the ballots were being counted correctly.' But, the official argued, 'Belarus is not Ukraine and we cannot allow it to become Ukraine.' In other words, observers may not have had the evidence that the election was manipulated, but they knew it had major problems and chose to avoid investigating further lest the country find itself in a destabilizing democratic transition.

The rise of 'zombie' election monitors

It is clear that the current system of international election observation leaves much to be desired. Unfortunately, in some ways the situation is becoming more difficult as counterfeit democracies devise new ways to cloud the picture. One of the most innovative of these strategies is the creation of 'zombie' election monitors whose sole role is to endorse rigged elections.[42] The idea is simple: if just a handful of Western election monitors (from the European Union, the Carter Center, and so on) are the sole observation groups, then rigged elections are more likely to be unanimously critiqued. But if there is a mix of Western groups and other monitors, and they split the verdict, it is easier to claim that there were conflicting interpretations of whether the election was problematic or not.

Thus, we have seen the rise of alternative monitors who are little more than the plants of autocratic regimes, their sole purpose to endorse undemocratic contests as democratic simply in order to complicate the Western narrative. As the political scientist Alexander Cooley has put it, 'Zombie monitors try to look like democratic observers, but serve autocratic purposes by pretending that clearly flawed elections deserve clean bills of health.'[43]

These groups have ornate names: the Inter-Commission Working Group on International Cooperation and Public Diplomacy of the Public Chamber of Russia Elections; and the Commonwealth of Independent States Observation Mission

(CIS-EMO). Both of those groups, by the way, gave full-throated endorsements of the rigged 2013 election in Azerbaijan. They are particularly effective because they are often supported by a number of different authoritarian governments, who back them because they know that if they help other autocrats enhance their own domestic and international legitimacy, they can reap the benefits of zombie monitor endorsement when their own elections roll around.

Moreover, some Western media outlets which do not know the difference between the OSCE and the CIS-EMO may simply treat them as equals, reporting that some outside groups endorsed a rigged election but others condemned it. When this happens, the narrative can quickly shift to imply that the process was a mixed bag, even if it was blatantly manipulated. Yet again, this recent development follows the logic of the Potemkin election – it does not matter whether the substance is democratic, so long as it can be made to *look* democratic to the outside world.[44]

Other times, the phenomenon of zombie monitors doesn't even require groups with official-sounding acronyms. In some cases, foreign governments have sought to curry favour with prospective trading or security partners by endorsing a clearly flawed election. In Cambodia's 2013 elections, for example, there was overwhelming evidence of rigging. The opposition leader was excluded and government rivals faced systematic media bias. There were also serious irregularities with the voter roll in opposition areas.

These problems were so obvious that the European Union (rightly) refused to legitimize the process and did not send observers. But Hungary and China did send monitors, at the invitation of Cambodia's government. China, a one-party state that doesn't even hold national elections, found that the Cambodian polls 'were conducted in a competitive, free, fair and transparent manner'. Hungary's delegation, which arrived one day before the election, found that 'The conduct of the National Assembly election was free, fair, acceptable and transparent . . . this was the victory of democracy.'[45] These were absurd statements given the wealth of evidence showing systematic rigging. But they were helpful in allowing the Cambodian government to dilute critical international statements condemning their rigged elections by playing up such flimsy endorsements in the domestic Cambodian media. With election observers, as with voters (see chapter 3), counterfeit democrats can divide and rule.

Strengthening democracy by watching the watchdogs

Unfortunately, the undermining of election monitoring has only worsened since the election of President Donald Trump in the United States. Beyond his congratulatory phone call to President Erdoğan in Turkey, Trump has made clear that he will not work to advance democratic principles abroad. This has been showcased in crystal-clear terms in Trump's first set of several foreign trips – which began, for the first time in modern American history, with a visit not to a democratic ally, but to the Kingdom of Saudi Arabia.

That visit was not exactly a powerful endorsement of the importance of democracy globally. Instead, it involved Trump banning American media from various events, and then taking part in a sword dance – this in a country that lacks a free press and whose ruling regime beheads dissidents with swords. Unlike previous American presidents (who, of course, also embraced the brutal Saudi regime), there was no pressure to hold elections or to improve the dismal Saudi human rights record.[46] A few months later, Trump travelled to Warsaw to deliver a major speech on the fate of 'the West'. He put Poland up on a pedestal as a model for others to follow, even though that country's illiberal populist ruling party had been sliding away from democracy and towards authoritarianism for years.[47] In his speech, Trump did not mention the word democracy even as he spoke about the West's survival. The signal could not have been clearer: Donald

Trump and his 'America First' administration do not really care very much about democracy, or the lack of it in other countries.

Trump's indifference to democracy abroad is an important shift, as the US government has been an important – albeit inconsistent – supporter of election observation. The American government has at various points responded to rigged elections by cutting off foreign aid, isolating regimes on the international stage, and slapping sanctions on ruling-party officials. Those consequences are a powerful deterrent for would-be election riggers, who fear that condemnation from Washington could have serious implications for trade deals and international power. Increasingly, though, it appears that the deterrent will need to come from Europe rather than the United States. That shift is problematic, however, because Europe lacks the economic influence of the US in many areas, and is itself dealing with a series of internal crises. As a result, the EU is poorly placed to step up and play a stronger role in places like Mozambique and Myanmar.

Furthermore, as Trump's America turns away from democracy promotion abroad, and Europe focuses on internal problems, China is beginning to shape global politics far more than in the past. Given that China actively seeks to oppress its own domestic pro-democracy reform movements, it should not be surprising that it does not support democracy abroad. As we discuss at greater length in the conclusion, this combination of factors means that there are far fewer international powers willing to invest time, political capital and money in genuine projects of democratic reform – and far more states that would prefer to undermine election monitoring and the pro-democracy reform agenda.[48]

However, the sky is not falling. Election monitors can, and sometimes do, condemn elections in important ways. In the Gambia's 2016 elections, for example, the presence of African Union monitors helped stop the incumbent Yahya Jammeh from backtracking on his initial pledge to accept the results.[49] In that instance, Jammeh was forced to leave office by international pressure – and the eventual threat of force from regional powers to back up the findings of the electoral commission and international monitoring teams deployed to watch the election.[50] However, even this success story demonstrates how much geopolitics matters: the Gambia is a tiny country, generally unimportant to international players. It's hard to imagine something similar happening in Nigeria or Iran or Thailand, where geostrategic thinking is far more likely to prevail.

In this sense, it is important to look at which kinds of organizations might be better suited to breaking free from geopolitics. Brian observed an election in Madagascar in 2013 with the Carter Center, which had a key advantage over other monitors on the ground in that it was not pressured by its funding government. That empowered the organization to assess the election on its merits. There may be significant upside to creating independently funded monitoring groups that are not beholden to specific governments, most notably limiting the influence of great-power politics on the legitimization of national elections. This is an area in which a new independent international monitoring body, funded by willing states or international organizations, could be instrumental in divorcing politics as much as possible from election observation reports.[51]

The problem with this suggestion is not so much logistics as political will: few governments would be prepared to support a process that they cannot politically control, and even fewer autocrats are likely to welcome such an independent group to their country. Given this, the task of protecting elections around the world may increasingly fall on domestic monitoring teams. While a number of governments have set up zombie observers, as documented above, there are many countries in which domestic teams do an incredible job under very trying conditions. And although these groups are often dependent on Western funding to survive, when they are run by independent civil society groups they often make clearer statements and less equivocal evaluations than their international counterparts.

Indeed, a recent study that compared the reports of international and domestic observation teams in six sub-Saharan African countries including Uganda found that on average it was the domestic groups that were more critical.[52] Given this, making sure that international monitors' reports reflect the concerns of local groups would be one way to strengthen their findings in a significant number of countries.

As the audience for election observation shifts from Western governments to the citizenry and civil society of the country holding an election, the focus of the work done by international observer groups will also need to evolve. One investment that is likely to pay dividends is to devote greater time and resources to strengthening and working with domestic election monitors in order to develop more effective anti-rigging strategies. With wider coverage and domestic buy-in to the process, monitors could try and build greater consensus around how elections should be run, establishing minimum standards that all parties can agree to. For example, the formation of cross-party committees to meet and agree on minimal reforms was critical to building opposition trust in the electoral process in Ghana, leading to incremental improvements over a number of years.[53]

These committees are most effective when they are domestically led, but they typically gain greater traction if international donors put their weight behind them too. Although the agreements that they give rise to are often modest, and always vulnerable to incumbent governments' last-minute backsliding, they can help to generate a set of standards against which political leaders agree to be judged, strengthening the hand of domestic and international monitors. And as information becomes even more difficult to block in the digital age, despotic regimes could then be held to account by election observation reports that expose manipulation – even if Western governments in the age of Trump pay less attention to what monitors say and do.

However, even if the audience shifts and domestic monitoring teams are strengthened, many of the challenges identified in this chapter will remain. Domestic groups can be co-opted by the ruling regime. They can also be fooled. At the same time, the problem of zombie monitors, and that of Western monitors endorsing obviously rigged elections in geopolitically important states, will not go away. As we discuss at greater length in the conclusion, when it comes to catching and appropriately condemning rigged elections, there are no quick fixes.

In recent years, only about one in five elections has been condemned by Western monitors – despite low scores for election quality in most regions and an across-the-board decline in the quality of democracy globally.[54] And in the Middle East, only about one in three elections has had monitors anyway, either because they were not welcomed by the host country or because no credible monitoring group would lend legitimacy to what have often been blatantly rigged, uncompetitive contests. In short, monitors aren't always welcomed; when they are, it's difficult for them to get it right; and when they do detect rigging, they're often ignored.[55]

It should therefore be clear that the phenomenon of Potemkin elections is an enormous challenge to the integrity of democracy. After all, if dictators, despots and counterfeit democrats are able to dupe observers into legitimizing rigged elections, then they can rig with impunity. Even if they buy votes, or exclude candidates, or even use violence that incorporates plausible deniability, they may still be able to win praise from monitors pursuing their own geostrategic goals. As a result, there's an enormous reckoning that must come, for both pro-democracy governments and election monitors themselves, on how to improve their methods in the face of innovative autocrats. With that in mind, we now refocus our analysis away from a discussion of how to rig an election towards an analysis of how to stop it.

CONCLUSION
How to stop election rigging

This book has explained how authoritarian leaders rig elections to stay in power by subverting democracy. Over half of all elections in counterfeit democracies fall well short of recognized international standards, and, since the end of the Cold War, incumbent leaders have only lost 11 per cent of all elections that have been held in those countries.[1] All too often, elections are used as ways to rubber-stamp an incumbent, designating them with a false sense of legitimacy after a stolen vote.

Unfortunately, low-quality elections are becoming the norm. The world's counterfeit democracies are not a minority – rather, they now constitute the majority of states. Moreover, the trend is bleak. As we noted in the introduction, in 2016 almost twice as many countries became more authoritarian than became more democratic.[2] This was not a blip. For eleven straight years, the authoritarian declines have outpaced the democratic gains. In other words, we are in the middle of a serious democratic recession. Today, nearly two in three citizens in the world live under a system of government that is not fully democratic.

The preceding chapters have demonstrated that the ability of power-hungry leaders to rig elections is rooted in the varying deployment of six distinct but complementary strategies enabling them to manipulate and win elections that they might otherwise lose. In most cases, no one tactic is enough on its own to ensure power is retained, and so leaders deploy different combinations to get the job done.

By gerrymandering electoral boundaries and excluding rival leaders who threaten to gain momentum, incumbents can give themselves a significant head start before the campaign has even begun (chapter 1). This advantage can then be consolidated by manipulating state access to resources to distribute patronage and gifts, outspending opposition parties (chapter 2). At the same time, incumbents may digitally manipulate the media and electoral process, taking advantage of the tendency of opposition parties and civil society groups to underestimate the vulnerability of new technology to subversion (chapter 4).

These strategies are likely to remain popular because they attract less criticism; gerrymandering happens well in advance of the campaign, and vote buying is often overlooked as an election ritual.

When these tactics prove to be insufficient, counterfeit democrats have two riskier options at their disposal. Political violence can be used to intimidate opponents, mobilise supporters and cow the media (chapter 3). Deploying repression can simultaneously divide the opposition and reinforce the unity of the ruling party. Finally, if that doesn't work, the last resort for the recalcitrant authoritarian is ballot-box stuffing (chapter 5). By getting regime loyalists to vote multiple times, or simply by announcing the wrong results, governments can quickly eradicate opposition gains. Of course, this is a particularly dangerous strategy because it is more likely to attract the attention of election observers, and hence generate international criticism. For this reason, smart authoritarians start early and have the contest sewn up well in advance of polling day.

And, while counterfeit democrats are busy rigging the election, they are also often running a parallel deception campaign internationally (chapter 6), hoping to earn a false veneer of democratic legitimacy from international partners or election monitors. If they can dupe observers or foreign governments into endorsing a rigged election, then they can reap every benefit of election rigging without facing any of the associated costs. In this sense, creating a Potemkin election is an overarching strategy: it allows incumbents to get away with all their other nefarious actions.

The effectiveness of these strategies means that counterfeit democrats are currently winning. In too many cases, they have figured out how to rig elections and get away with it. Despite the wide range of rigging strategies that have been documented in some of these countries, Western observation missions only raised the problem of fraud in 20 per cent of the elections, and foreign aid was only stopped in the aftermath of around 6 per cent, suggesting that in most cases where manipulation was detected the regime did not suffer financially.[3]

In response to this malaise, this conclusion draws together the different arguments that have been presented in the book regarding how the quality of elections can be improved and democracy strengthened. As we have set out in the conclusions to the preceding chapters, there are specific strategies that can be used to tackle each form of rigging. Here, we briefly summarize the most important of these before considering three broader strategies: developing more effective systems of election monitoring, harnessing digital technology, and empowering opposition parties and civil society groups. More specifically, we argue that international election observation can be revamped so that monitors have the tools they need to detect fraud, and more constructive ways to engage in counterfeit democracies. The international community can do far more to act on evidence of electoral malpractice and ensure that rigging is not a cost-free exercise. And digital technologies can be made to work for good rather than ill if they are put into the hands of independent civil society groups and opposition parties as well as electoral commissions.

But while there is much that could be done to turn the tables on the world's counterfeit democrats, it is also important to be realistic about the conditions necessary for these reforms to have a fighting chance. As we discuss in greater detail below, Western support for democracy is waning at the same time that the West's influence is declining relative to a number of rising global powers, many of which are undemocratic themselves and have no incentive to push for a more democratic world. There are therefore good reasons to be pessimistic about the global prospects for democracy in the twenty-first century. But there are also ways to ensure that such a dismal vision does not come to pass.

In this conclusion, we first make the case for protecting elections, and then explore how to do so.

Why protect elections?

At the end of the Cold War, it was blasphemy – at least in the West – to suggest that elections were not universally desirable. But today, given how effective authoritarian regimes have become at manipulating elections to maintain their grip on power, more people are openly asking whether we should even bother holding elections at all. This has been a perennial theme in the debate on electoral politics in places like Asia and Africa, where commentators have often questioned the 'feasibility of democracy'[4] and suggested that elections might do more harm than good.[5] In recent years, this argument has been gaining ground due to the number of authoritarian political systems delivering high levels of economic growth, notably in China but also in states such as Ethiopia and Rwanda.[6]

The success of these countries suggests to some that it might be better to abandon elections on the basis that they divert attention away from the task of governance and place pressure on governments to satisfy the short-term demands of voters rather than the long-term needs of the state. Perhaps, some argue, countries in Africa, Asia and Latin America would enjoy greater financial and infrastructural development under one-party states, which in turn would increase the prospects for democratic consolidation in the future. And, if authoritarian governments outperform their democratic counterparts, and elections are expensive and destabilizing events, why not make peace with benevolent dictators and give up on multiparty politics in the short term?

Many people have been seduced by this seemingly compelling argument. Some have even called for a post-democracy future or suggested that democracy has outlived its usefulness.[7] But whilst it is clearly true that some authoritarian governments outperform some democracies, this argument has a number of limitations. On average, democratic governments can be shown to have intrinsic and instrumental advantages over their authoritarian counterparts. Intrinsically, democracies are much more likely to respect the human rights of their citizens and in the vast majority of cases this is the type of political system that people want to live in.

For example, the Afrobarometer finds that a majority of people in *every single country that it surveys in Africa* believe that democracy is the best political system for their country.[8] Significantly, the majority of citizens both in countries that have yet to see the full benefit of democracy and in those where elections have generated conflict are strongly against reintroducing a form of military rule, one-party state or personal dictatorship.[9]

Similarly, the Americas Barometer, a survey carried out by the Latin American Public Opinion Project (LAPOP) of Vanderbilt University, finds that even though there is considerable support for strong leadership, citizens across Latin America aspire to live in democratic states.[10] The idea that democracy is a Western construct enforced on people who do not want it is therefore a myth – and it is a myth that serves to legitimize some of the most venal and abusive governments in the world. The evidence is clear: people across the world typically want a meaningful say in decisions that affect their lives, and it's not hard to imagine why. Moreover, just because some flawed democracies falter and occasionally fail doesn't mean that we should abandon democratic governance; rather it means that we should fix it.

Holding elections also has clear instrumental benefits. Indeed, when we move away from the small number of authoritarian states that deliver eye-catching economic growth to think about the full range of cases described in this book, it becomes clear that authoritarian success stories are the exception rather than the rule. On the whole, the repressive regimes that exist today do not justify their existence by promoting economic development or a cohesive national identity. For every China there is a Venezuela or a Zimbabwe, for every Rwanda a Turkmenistan or a Democratic Republic of Congo.

To see why this matters, try a simple thought experiment: you can choose which type of political system you'll be born into – democracy or authoritarianism – but you can't know in advance which country you will end up being born in. Few people would pick authoritarianism, hoping for a softer landing in Singapore, but knowing full well that they stand a good chance of finding themselves a citizen of Uzbekistan, North Korea or Syria.

The most recent quantitative studies available come to the same conclusion. In Africa, more-democratic states outperform their authoritarian counterparts when it comes to economic growth – and the longer countries remain democratic, the greater the boost to their economies, even when other factors such as aid and natural resources are taken into account.[11] The same pattern also holds globally. Researchers from the Varieties of Democracy (V-Dem) project have spent the last few years developing better measures of democracy. Based on a data set that features hundreds of different indicators for almost every country in the world for over 100 years, they have found that, in general, 'Democratic societies tend to be more prosperous than autocratic regimes',[12] and that this relationship is rooted in the holding of elections.[13]

It is therefore not a case of having to choose between democracy and development: the evidence suggests that the two can go hand in hand. One of the reasons for this is that countries that hold elections are more likely to provide key public services to their citizens. Even when competition is not fully free and fair, the pressure on governments to respond to public concerns leads to greater investment in areas such as health and education. Of course, this is not true of every country that holds elections, but on average the pattern persists.

For example, recent research on Africa has found that countries that hold elections invest more in education.[14] Indeed, the onset of multiparty politics was followed fairly soon after by the introduction of free primary education in a number of countries. This is particularly significant, given the fact that education is often found to be one of the factors that encourages pro-democratic attitudes.[15]

The post-Soviet states offer another instructive example. Those countries that went the way of the European Union, such as the Baltic nations of Estonia, Latvia and Lithuania, democratized rapidly and their economies swiftly developed. The story is quite different in those post-Soviet states that stayed authoritarian, such as Belarus. In 1995, for example, Lithuania's per capita GDP was about $2,000. Belarus wasn't far behind at about $1,400. But by 2016, the gulf between the countries had become enormous – with Lithuania's GDP soaring to nearly $15,000 while that of Belarus didn't even hit $5,000. Of course, joining the European Union trade zone accounts for some of this divergence, but these benefits were only possible because the Baltic states met EU accession criteria, including those on good governance and respect for human rights.

Given the strong public support for democracy and the instrumental benefits of elections, it does not make much sense to encourage the return of purely authoritarian political systems. Moreover, such a strategy would be unfeasible; the vast majority of countries around the world hold elections of one sort or another, and it makes more sense to ask how they can be improved than what other form of government could be put in their stead.[16] Doing so is likely to improve not only the quality of democracy but also the prospects for the economy. According to the V-Dem researchers mentioned above, the higher the quality of the elections that are held, the greater the positive impact of elections on development.[17] And of course, protecting elections also empowers people to have a say in the decisions that affect their lives, which is what almost all the available survey evidence tells us they want.

The abuse of democracy

As we have argued throughout this book, it also makes sense to be concerned about the quality of elections because at present rigged polls are helping to prolong the lifespan of authoritarian regimes. This point is well demonstrated by the example of Rwanda.

Around the 2017 Rwandan election, many journalists phoned us to discuss the polls, and most asked the same question: Why does President Paul Kagame bother holding elections at all? He had already won a fantastical 93 per cent of the vote in the 2013 election, and he had eliminated presidential term limits in 2010 meaning that he was legally allowed to stay in power until 2034. So why did he go through the motions of organizing a national poll that he was predestined to win? Why not just get rid of elections altogether?

When Kagame went on to take 99 per cent of the vote, these questions became even more pertinent.[18] Kagame had clearly not even bothered to try and manipulate the election in the clever ways described in previous chapters. Yet even in spite of this, he benefited from polls that had become little more than a political charade.

Most obviously, even the stage-managed 2017 contest was important to secure a base level of international legitimacy. While counterfeit democrats often behave arbitrarily, they like to be seen to be men – with a small number of exceptions they are almost always men – of order and responsibility. This means that leaders want to make it look as if they are following the rule of law even when they are not. Kagame is no exception.

In addition to respectability, holding rigged elections has six main instrumental benefits for autocrats. First, a number of regional organizations such as the European Union and the African Union (AU) have established minimum standards for countries to become members. These standards are often low, and are not always enforced, but governments nonetheless benefit from meeting them. The AU, for example, rarely speaks out about democratic backsliding, but does expel countries that experience an unconstitutional transfer of power, such as the removal of an elected government in a coup.[19] As a result, there is a price to be paid for being seen as an out-and-out dictator who cannot even pretend to be democratic.

Second, elections can also enable governments to access greater flows of aid and loans. This has become less of an issue following the rise of powers such as China that are willing to do business with authoritarian regimes, but it has been an important factor in the recent past. In the 1990s, when Western donors briefly focused on democracy promotion following the end of the Cold War and the collapse of the Soviet Union, countries such as the United States and United Kingdom withheld much-needed financial support in a bid to force authoritarian leaders in countries such as Kenya and Malawi to end their one-party states and introduce competitive polls.[20]

Third, a strong election win can be a powerful public relations tool. This may seem implausible in poor-quality elections, but it is often the case. Consider the Rwandan general election of August 2017. Ahead of the vote, President Paul Kagame's government endured some bad press over its poor human rights record.[21] In this context, the election campaign represented the perfect opportunity for Kagame's supporters to hit back at the president's critics by distributing images of large rallies on social media in a bid to persuade the world that Kagame is universally loved by his people.[22] And when Kagame won in an uncompetitive landslide, this also served a purpose. Within Rwanda, news of the president's domination of the poll communicated the strength of his grip on power.

Fourth, elections help leaders to establish tighter control of the ruling party itself: they give it a purpose. Rallies must be organized, T-shirts printed and networks revitalized. Through this process, the government can be reinvigorated. This is less of an issue for Kagame, whose RPF is known to be one of the more effective and professional parties on the continent. But in other countries in which political structures do little in between elections, campaigns help to rally party officials and supporters.[23] For example, in Thailand, where a military coup undermined democracy in 2014, campaigning has been banned for years. During that period, parties have been in disarray because they have no official reason to exist and no goal to pursue. But while many parties are effectively 'dormant . . . between elections', they come to life during campaigns.[24] Thus, holding an election can help to save the ruling party from a damaging process of institutional decay.

Fifth, and relatedly, elections facilitate processes of elite renewal. In many countries in which elections are rigged at the presidential level, legislative polls are more competitive. As we have seen, in some African nations roughly 50 per cent of legislators do not win re-election, even in countries where the president never loses (p. 76). Where members of parliament are elected on the basis of first-past-the-post constituencies, this level of competition encourages candidates to work harder to impress (or intimidate) the electorate. At the same time, the holding of party primaries – which are common, but not held everywhere – makes it possible to replace less popular legislators with more effective campaigners, and to inject young blood into the party in order to prevent its distancing from the broader population. In other words, elections actually help authoritarian ruling parties to remain fresh and, in some cases at least, more actively engaged with their support base. Elections can also be used as proving grounds – creating an electoral survival of the fittest to help ensure that the next generation of campaigners are effective.

The final advantage generated by holding elections is that it facilitates the deployment of divide-and-rule strategies. This is perhaps the most significant benefit of all. Purely authoritarian systems have a harder time demonstrating their legitimacy, and give opponents few options other than to campaign for regime change. As a result, ruling parties risk becoming a common enemy against which a diverse set of groups and individuals can come together. Without an election, the opposition is likely to unify for a common goal: political change. With an election, the prospects increase that opposition groups will turn on one another.

Indeed, the collapse of one-party states and military dictatorships is often preceded by the formation of broad movements in favour of change that bring together groups and leaders who would be unlikely to unite under other circumstances, including business leaders, trade unionists, religious leaders and opposition politicians.[25] The breadth of such reform movements gives them multiple sources of legitimacy and makes them particularly difficult to defeat, not least because they often attract international support.

However, things often change very rapidly once a leader has agreed to introduce minimal constitutional change and to hold multiparty elections. Faced with the possibility of winning power at the ballot box, pro-democracy movements have a tendency to fragment. Precisely because they are made up of strange bedfellows who have little in common bar their wish to remove the regime, such movements often split into their constituent parts. It may be that some elements can be co-opted into the government, while others can be encouraged to see each other as rivals. At the same time, clever autocrats actively foment disunity by sponsoring opposition parties. When Brian was in Belarus, members of several opposition parties told him that they believed that some of their counterparts were secretly stooges of the regime, and that their parties had been infiltrated by the security forces. Partly as a result, Belarusian elections normally feature a large number of presidential candidates – in 2010, the opposition vote was split sixteen ways.

This is important, because recent research has found that in countries that hold multiparty elections, transfers of power and transitions to greater levels of democracy often follow the formation of durable opposition coalitions.[26] Preventing opposition unity is therefore critical to the maintenance of authoritarian rule.

In other words, elections are, somewhat counterintuitively, useful to counterfeit democrats. The financial and reputational benefits of being seen to be more democratic, and the capacity of leaders to rig elections to blunt the process's transformative potential, helps to explain the puzzle with which we began this book: why authoritarian regimes that hold elections tend to last longer than those that do not. Given this, while it is clear that there is much more to democracy than elections, it is unlikely that the global democratic recession can be successfully addressed without improving their quality. To reinvigorate democracy, we have to make it harder to rig elections.

The shape of things to come

We have argued that the international community has an important role to play in creating the conditions under which democracy can be defended (chapter 6). Long-term democratic reform is almost always driven from within, but external actors can play an important role in helping to facilitate change. This can be done by refusing to financially and politically support governments that suppress the human rights of their citizens, and by speaking out more powerfully about obvious electoral abuses. International pressure will never be a silver bullet, but it can empower democrats on the ground if applied thoughtfully and carefully.

Consistency is crucial. If some flawed elections are endorsed while others are condemned, it creates the impression of unfair double standards. Moreover, if the West is willing to condemn gerrymandering in Zimbabwe, it also has to recognize and deal with the persistence of gerrymandering in America. Tackling the electoral abuses in Europe and the US needs to be a priority if Western partners want to be taken seriously in dealing with the more egregious abuses in new democracies.

Even then, the promotion of Western democracy risks being denounced as neo-colonial cultural imperialism, especially by savvy autocrats who understand the rhetorical power of this argument (chapter 3). As a result, international pressure is more likely to be effective if dozens of countries speak with one voice – and it is particularly important that the former colonial power not be the only voice heard.

For this reason, pro-democracy reformers should welcome the growing number of election observation groups from bodies such as the African Union, the Southern African Development Community (SADC) and the Association of Southeast Asian Nations (ASEAN) which are watching elections today. Whilst they are currently known for pulling their punches, these bodies offer one of the best hopes for the future, because if they can be persuaded to adopt higher standards they will be able to speak out with greater authority. This may sound like an overly optimistic goal, especially given some of the analysis in chapter 6, but there are already some positive signs in this regard. Most notably, the SADC recently revised its protocols to include long-term observation and the capacity to engage ICT experts, bringing it into line with international best practice.[27] ASEAN has also expressed a willingness to partner more closely with international democracy NGOs to improve its practices. Moreover, while criticism of vote buying and ballot-box stuffing has been limited, regional bodies have a better record of speaking out against the use of political violence. It could take another five or ten years before such groups are willing to expose and condemn evidence of electoral fraud, but it would be worth the wait.

Unfortunately, while some progress is being made in terms of building regional alliances to defend democracy, the broader international context has become significantly more problematic. This is both due to the rise of new economic powers that are unwilling to promote democracy abroad, and because Western support for high-quality elections has faltered.

For decades, the American government had a somewhat complicated approach to democracy support, backing democratic reform abroad when this did not conflict with American geostrategic goals, but simultaneously cosying up to brutal autocratic regimes like Saudi Arabia. This approach was not ideal, but it did serve to increase the pressure on a number of governments around the world to respect human rights and allow opposition parties to campaign.

More recently, this picture has been disrupted by the emergence of a number of world powers for which democracy and the quality of elections are not major concerns, including Brazil, Russia, China and India. This is most clearly the case with China, which began its latest phase of engagement in continents such as Africa and Latin America by stressing its solidarity with countries that had suffered colonial rule – in China's case, the 'semi-colonial' relations it was forced to endure with a number of countries including Britain and Japan – and its determination to avoid constructing relations of Western-style imperialism. A core component of this policy was the idea that China would help countries to achieve the goals that they had set for themselves, rather than the ones set for them by Western powers.

Over time, the notion of both partnership and non-interference has become increasingly difficult to sustain. On the one hand, China's thirst for importing raw materials, and the large trade surpluses that it enjoys with many trading partners as a result of the export of cheap manufactured goods, are reminiscent of unequal colonial economic relations. On the other, countries that have attempted to engage in foreign-policy activities that do not fit with China's own ambitions, for example by recognizing Taiwan as an independent state, have been threatened with economic and political sanctions.[28]

At the same time, the Chinese government has responded to international criticism, most notably of its economic support for President Omar al-Bashir's abusive and violent regime in Sudan, by moderating its policy, moving from a position of 'non-interference' to one of 'constructive engagement'.[29] As part of this shift, China began to participate in discussions regarding how Sudan's civil wars could be brought to an end, and, more recently, it provided troops to a United Nations-led peacekeeping mission in South Sudan in 2015, the first time that a Chinese infantry battalion had been sent on an external peacekeeping operation.

However, these caveats notwithstanding, the absence of democracy back home has ensured that China has been consistent in its refusal to pressure other states' governments to reform. Indeed, by providing uncritical support for police and military training, surveillance activity and the construction of prisons, China has helped to strengthen a number of authoritarian regimes' hold on power. Moreover, its 'constructive engagement' has typically been designed to protect China's own interests rather than those of the domestic population.[30] This is significant, because China is now a global player. China's international influence is best known in Africa, where the volume of trade has increased from just $10 million in 2010 to $220 billion in 2014, according to the China Africa Research Initiative at the Johns Hopkins School of Advanced International Studies in Washington.[31] What is less well known is that China's footprint is almost as significant in Latin America. Between 2000 and 2013, trade between China and Latin America and the Caribbean increased by twenty-two times, hitting $236.5 billion. This made China the region's second-largest trading partner after the United States, beating the European Union into third place.[32]

The growing economic significance of China around the world in terms of both trade and loans means that counterfeit democracies now have more financial options open to them than they did in the 1990s. This greater choice has reduced the dependency of economically weak authoritarian states on the financial support of those countries most likely to place political conditions on the provision of such assistance. In turn, this has weakened the capacity of countries such as the United Kingdom and the United States to engage in democracy promotion activities.

Moreover, China is just one of a number of countries that will play a greater role in counterfeit democracies in the future than they have in the past. Although the situation looks a little different when it comes to other members of the BRIC group – Brazil, Russia and India – all three have complicated democracy promotion efforts. Officially, Russia presents a policy not radically different from that of China, grounded in a rejection of Western imperialism. Unofficially, it has advanced 'a new type of authoritarianism at home and abroad with even more sophistication than the Soviet Union'.[33]

In the Russian case, such activity has not always been motivated by its economic investments and typically has more to do with a desire to challenge American hegemony and maintain its influence, particularly in post-communist Europe. Sadly, Russia is not alone and countries as diverse as Iran, Qatar and Saudi Arabia have all been accused of exporting a model of governance and set of political principles that is antithetical to democracy.

By contrast, Brazil and India are both fairly robust, if uneven, democracies and have no interest in promoting authoritarian rule abroad. Despite this, however, both have explicitly rejected the idea of applying political conditionality to aid and trade deals. Instead they have followed China's lead in stressing their solidarity with countries that have suffered Western colonialism or economic exploitation, speaking a language of partnership rather than paternalism. The net effect of the growing economic and political influence of these states has been to increase the number of options available to undemocratic governments, empowering them to play off potential benefactors against each other until they get the deal that they want.

The combined effects of these changes have been significant. In Venezuela, for example, the dictatorial regime of Nicolás Maduro (chapter 5, pp. 174–6) has been the subject of considerable international criticism over the way it has undermined democracy. But it has received considerable support from two of its most important economic partners, China and Russia.[34] This has included financial assistance and efforts to block international interventions such as sanctions against the Venezuelan government.[35] As Evan Ellis, a senior associate of the Center for Strategic and International Studies, put it when giving evidence to the Western Hemisphere subcommittee of the US Foreign Affairs Committee during a hearing on the political crisis in Venezuela, 'both Russia and China, in the pursuit of their commercial and strategic interests in Venezuela, have provided capital, goods, services, and political backing that has indirectly enabled the populist regime to ignore and ultimately destroy the mechanisms of democratic accountability'.[36]

However, it would be a mistake to think that international democracy promotion efforts have been undone because the rise of a group of less altruistic states has undermined the good work of the West; as we saw in chapter 6, some of the most significant threats to democracy promotion come from much closer to home. For one thing, Western support for democracy was never uniform or consistent. From French complicity in the Rwandan genocide to American support for authoritarian states as diverse as Uganda, Uzbekistan and Thailand that were willing to join the war on terror, Western governments have consistently traded democracy off against their core interests and security concerns.

Moreover, the catastrophic failures of Western interventions in Iraq, Afghanistan and Libya, combined with the violent instability produced by the Arab Spring, have undermined the appetite of some Western governments to sustain genuine pressure on undemocratic regimes. This paradigm shift has not been lost on the world's would-be strongmen. It is no coincidence that the quality of democracy around the world has fallen over the same period as these global shifts have taken place.

This already mixed picture looks set to become even more challenging over the next five years. As we explained in chapter 6, Donald Trump has vowed to put 'America First', a shift in American foreign policy that views the United States' international relationships through a purely transactional prism.

Consequently, Trump's administration has proposed a massive reduction in US foreign aid and the elimination of American democracy support programmes. As part of this shift, the State Department has pulled back from talking about 'shared democratic values' and is on course to remove democracy promotion from its mission statement.[37] The fate of these programmes will likely be decided by a Congress that is more supportive of investing in democracy, but the sea change in the White House will probably have a considerable negative impact on Western support for human rights and high-quality elections.

The implications of Trump's 'America First' turn are readily apparent to the counterfeit democrats of the world. In most of the countries where we have done field research, the elites in the governments' highest echelons pay close attention to what is happening in Western capitals – and Washington in particular – in determining what they can get away with. If the American president or the US State Department makes it clear that election rigging will prompt punitive action, there is more leverage to deter it. But over his first months as president in 2017, Donald Trump has sent a clear signal that he will be, at a minimum, permissive of authoritarian behaviour. In many cases, he praises it outright.

These signals matter, and they make it harder to combat election rigging. After all, if election observers condemn an election but the president of the United States calls to congratulate the leader anyway, then the value of election monitoring is severely undercut. In part, international election observation gets its power from the belief that foreign governments care about whether an election is rigged or not and are prepared to act in response to evidence of malpractice. Increasingly, that is not the case, which generates the risk that in future the detection and exposure of electoral manipulation could pose even less of a threat to authoritarian regimes than it has in the past.

Donald Trump is not alone in turning his back on the promotion of democratic values. While many European countries are steadfast in their commitments to democracy promotion, others are considering rolling back aid or programmes aimed at enhancing democracy, the rule of law and human rights abroad. In the European Union, internal crises and divides have prompted some leaders to suggest that they need to get their own house in order before worrying about what is happening beyond the continent's borders.[38] Such statements reflect the limited foreign-policy manpower and resources of European states, which are currently heavily invested in the negotiations surrounding the withdrawal of the United Kingdom.

European leaders are also dealing with the surge of populist parties at home who seem intent on rolling back democracy within Europe – notably in Hungary and Poland. Coming at the same time, Trump's belief that deals matter more than values will give political cover to European governments who wish to adopt the same approach.

Reining in rigging

Given the international climate, preventing governments with authoritarian instincts from illegitimately passing themselves off as democracies is not going to be an easy task. The longevity of many counterfeit democracies demonstrates that the problem of election rigging is not going away. This raises the question of how democrats can defend elections against subversion. As the analysis in the preceding chapters demonstrates, stopping election rigging is not easy. There are some places in which Western governments have colluded with authoritarian governments and knowingly condoned flawed elections (chapter 6, pp. 183–4), but there are also many places in which there have been concerted efforts by opposition parties, international donors and domestic civil society groups to reduce rigging.

These initiatives did not fail for lack of serious intent, or because those behind them were not brave. As we saw in chapter 3, some of those who have opposed authoritarian electoral manipulation have paid with their lives. Rather, the problem is more fundamental: election rigging is made possible by the prior existence of weak political institutions and democratic norms. It is the absence of effective checks and balances that enables ruling parties to undertake the corruption that funds vote rigging, politicized police forces that perpetrate political violence, and pliant judiciaries that fail to prosecute electoral offences. Delivering good-quality elections will require reforming the institutional context within which political competition takes place, and this is a huge undertaking.

Moreover, the challenge of how to strengthen democracy is compounded by the fact that authoritarians are adaptable. Having a number of tools at their disposal, counterfeit democrats will switch from one to another in order to evade the efforts of election observers. If, for example, ballot-box stuffing becomes easier to detect, then they switch to pre-election manipulation. Maybe the ruling party can ensure that electoral districts are distorted to such an extent that the parliamentary contest is from the outset not competitive. Or the government can interfere in the management of the polls so that only ruling-party strongholds receive valid voting identification cards in time for election day.

Failing that, governments can exclude rival candidates by banning them from competition under the guise of a legitimate rule change. If it is difficult to bully a court into disqualifying an opposition candidate, the regime can always lean on the police to jail the candidate on a trumped-up charge. And if monitors react to these tactics, then a savvy incumbent may move to digital rigging. In short, the strength of counterfeit democrats comes, at least in part, from the varied tools in the 'menu of manipulation' that they have at their disposal.[39]

By contrast, for the opposition to win, its leaders must overcome a number of major disadvantages, such as less funding and less access to state resources, while simultaneously trying to mobilize votes and deter rigging. Thus, while the ruling party can make a number of mistakes and still win, the opposition often loses even if it does everything right. This is why the deck is stacked against democracy in places where those who write the rules and run the elections are determined to cheat.

Incumbents will, however, lose if several strategies are simultaneously made unviable. To do so is a difficult task, because opposition parties, civil society groups and international actors typically have limited time and money. More often than not, this leads them to focus on trying to deal with the main strategy that the government used to rig the previous election. Such an approach is understandable: reformers identify the biggest threat to a good-quality election and concentrate their efforts on resisting that particular strategy in order to maximize their chances of generating positive results. But the tendency towards myopia often means that as one avenue of manipulation is closed off, ruling-party elites are able to open up others. As one experienced election observer said to Nic in Zimbabwe, 'We are always fighting the last election, but the regime is always looking ahead to the next.'[40]

These challenges are not a reason to be defeatist, but they are a reason to be realistic. Defending democracy will involve closing off one avenue of rigging after another until counterfeit democrats have nowhere left to turn. It is therefore likely to take the form of a prolonged and iterative process. The chapters that make up this book have highlighted a number of ways in which this can be done. As we explore in greater detail below, transferring some of the control over election scrutiny away from ruling parties and the electoral commissions that are often deferential to them, and into the hands of opposition parties, civil society organizations and independent domestic election monitors, is an important first step. This does not mean that it is not worth investing in electoral management bodies, which is the only way to build high-quality electoral systems in the long run. Instead, the point is that electoral commissions are more likely to improve their performance if they know that their every move is being watched.

These efforts can be buttressed by a number of others, including: establishing independent electoral boundaries commissions to prevent gerrymandering (chapter 1); encouraging the electorate that if they must take ruling-party bribes they should nonetheless vote with their conscience and so undermine the power of vote buying (chapter 2); using social media to inform citizens about the most common forms of rigging and how they can be avoided (chapter 1); strengthening fact-checking organizations and clamping down on the producers of fake news (chapter 4); encouraging regional organizations to act against human rights violations (chapter 3); and holding parallel vote tabulations to deter tallying fraud (chapter 5). Where digital manipulation of information and voting outcomes is a concern, enhancing the transparency of social media and strengthening the 'firewalls' around the information held by opposition parties and electoral commissions will also be essential (chapter 6).

Of course, these strategies are not easy to implement. They require well-funded opposition parties and a civil society that is at least semi-autonomous from the state. They also require that opposition parties and candidates have sufficient room within which to manoeuvre, and so will not be feasible in countries where the degree of authoritarian repression is so great that opposition parties cannot effectively mobilize.

Thus, as political scientists Philip Roessler and Marc Howard have argued, in countries in which ruling parties are so authoritarian that the opposition can only hope to secure a tiny proportion of the vote in elections – what we called 'dominant authoritarian regimes' in the introduction to this book – political change is very rare. Indeed, countries in this category have just a

5 per cent chance of experiencing a transfer of power or a transition to democracy in a given year.[41] It is therefore likely to be a very long time before states such as Rwanda evolve more-open political systems.

However, the prospects for democratization are far greater in more-competitive political environments that are not full democracies but nonetheless feature lower levels of authoritarian abuse. Countries in this category have a 16 per cent prospect of regime change in any given year – three times higher than the chances for dominant authoritarian regimes. This is important, because many of the countries discussed in this book fall into this group, including Kenya, Malaysia, Russia, Uganda, Zimbabwe and, at least until recently, Venezuela (appendix 15).

Moreover, there is hope even for some of the most problematic states. Roessler and Howard note that for all their authoritarian tendencies, dominant authoritarian systems rarely stop holding elections altogether.[42] Instead, if they experience political change they are more likely to become increasingly competitive over time. And once they become more competitive, the prospects for further political liberalization become significantly better.

Keep in mind that Tunisia, for instance, was a full-blown authoritarian state in 2010, but has rapidly become more democratic in the aftermath of the Arab Spring. And it's worth remembering that South Korea, Japan and Germany did not become fully fledged democracies overnight but rather over time – eventually becoming linchpins of the democratic world. We therefore have reasons to be hopeful, even in the case of countries that currently seem like lost causes.

Of course, this does not mean that all states are destined to be democracies, or that hybrid regimes which hold elections in an authoritarian context will necessarily become more open over time. If this book has demonstrated anything, it is the capacity of counterfeit democrats to hold onto power, and that the global trend is towards authoritarianism, not away from it.

But while it is important to be realistic about the scale of the challenge ahead, there is a good chance that if the tactics described in this conclusion can be put into action, they will increase the political cost of rigging, making it less attractive and thus increasing the prospects of democratic progress.

Reforming election monitoring

Inevitably, if election quality is to be improved, election monitors will need to play a leading role. After all, they are the election experts, and their role is to detect and, through exposure, to help prevent electoral fraud. If they were better able to expose poor-quality elections, it would increase the cost of rigging to authoritarian leaders. However, as the analysis in the preceding chapters has revealed, in recent years election monitors have often been the source of election controversy rather than the antidote to it. As more-assertive opposition parties have come up against resilient autocrats, observers have found themselves stuck in the middle.

As we discussed in chapter 6, this is in part because observers are inherently conservative. Operating at the pleasure of host governments, and careful to protect their reputation for neutrality, monitors are reluctant to challenge the validity of an election unless there is overwhelming evidence not just that there was malpractice, but that the malpractice changed the result. In addition to the political challenges that we have already identified, the system of international observation has three main problems that, if addressed, could considerably improve the prospects for protecting elections.

The first problem is that international monitoring has not really moved with the times. While the way that elections are rigged has changed significantly, the way they are monitored has evolved much more slowly. This generates a number of problems. Most obviously, few missions have the technical capacity they need for the battles to come. As we saw in chapters 4 and 5, the digital battleground for elections is a key new frontier in election rigging. But although the European Union does employ a data expert for its larger missions in countries that use digital technology on election day, most monitoring missions do not, and even EU teams tend to have just one person working in this area. In addition, it's incredibly difficult for a single individual on an election observation team to do the work of an intelligence agency and determine whether digital tampering or hacking was used.

Overwhelmingly, observers continue to follow a model in which the vast majority of the team are deployed to polling stations to watch voting take place and to monitor the count. In light of the examples of repression, vote buying and ballot-box stuffing provided in this book, this might sound like a good idea. But while there is some evidence that posting observers to a polling station reduces the level of election rigging *in that station*, there is also evidence that it simply displaces it elsewhere – especially in areas that are dominated by one party.[43]

This is possible because in most cases the size of international monitoring teams is small – below 150 – while there may be as many as 50,000 polling stations. As a result, it is fairly easy for election riggers simply to move their operations to areas where there are no observers. Moreover, because most election monitors have to stay in the polling station to which they are assigned, they cannot respond to the changing situation on the ground and go where they are most needed.

Thus, while it is good to have team members posted to different parts of the country in order to understand what is happening outside the capital, observers need to start hiring people with more technical skills so that they can police the deployment of biometric technology, computer logs and storage, and use their expertise to give an indication of whether there is a hidden digital pattern of electoral manipulation.

A second and more fundamental problem is that international monitors lack the means to ensure that the weaknesses and faults that they identify in the electoral system are rectified. Put simply, there is no enforcement mechanism available to observation groups. Instead, they are dependent on international donors and opposition parties taking up the cause, and a willingness on the part of ruling parties to reform. As a result, many of the well-thought-out criticisms and good suggestions made by monitors are effectively wasted. Indeed, the filing cupboards of the main observer groups are filled with reports urging the same reforms, election after election. It's like electoral Groundhog Day.

As we noted earlier, for election monitoring to be effective, it needs to be backed up by the international community, and more effectively integrated into the political process. One way of doing this would be for monitors to refuse to cover – and hence endorse – elections in countries that have made no changes and no formal response to previous election reports. This might result in a higher number of elections not featuring international observers, but it would end the current farce of monitors repeatedly observing elections featuring the same flaws.

The third problem is that there has been a proliferation of international observation groups, including the incumbent-created zombie observation teams (discussed in chapter 6, pp. 200–2). We have argued that this complex landscape is a strength, in that regional teams may be able to speak with more legitimacy than Western ones, but it also means that there can be multiple press conferences from different groups held on the same day, each giving a different message. Greater convergence around a common set of standards – for example, with joint statements – is required in order to generate a clear message that ruling parties will have to take notice of. This is currently a long way off, and represents a long-term goal that may only become possible once stronger electoral norms have evolved in the parts of the world in which election rigging remains common.

But if these changes can be made, it will significantly strengthen the effectiveness of international election observation, increasing the costs of rigging, and providing governments with stronger incentives to play by the rules of the game.

Digitizing elections

As we have seen, elections around the world are becoming increasingly digitized. This has negative implications when it comes to fake news and its circulation on social media (chapter 4), but also great potential to strengthen electoral systems against abuse (chapter 5). It is therefore important to think more broadly about how new technology can be harnessed to increase the costs of rigging.

One way to do this would be to introduce digital technology at every point of the electoral process. Many countries now employ biometric voter registration in order to clean up the electoral register; we have shown how this helped to remove millions of 'ghost voters' from the list in Nigeria (p. 166). A smaller number of countries are also using biometric software to verify voters using their fingerprints, ensuring that only those registered can actually vote, and that they can only vote once. Moreover, by connecting the kits that biometrically verify voters before they cast their ballot to a central server, it is possible to generate a measure of voter turnout in real time. This can then be used to work out whether an impossible number of people voted in a certain time period, indicating ballot-box stuffing.

Once we can be confident that the votes in ballot boxes are legitimate, the question is how to ensure that they are properly counted, and that there is no manipulation of the tallying process. One way to do this is to run a digital counting process alongside a manual one. For example, new mobile phone technology means that it is now possible to have returning officers at polling station level both record the results on a paper form, which can be sent to the relevant tallying centre, and at the same time enter them into a digital platform that automatically adds them to a live stream that can be viewed online, bypassing regional and national tallying centres. Election observers and political leaders can then compare the total number of votes produced through these two processes, with any large variation between the two numbers implying manipulation of the counting of the hard copies of the forms (which remain the official result).

Initially, election technology was fairly primitive. Each step of this process used to require a different piece of hardware or software. However, the latest technology on the market – integrated electoral management systems – does all three of these things simultaneously, allowing electoral commissions to register voters, verify them and transmit their votes with one piece of equipment.

But if this sounds too good to be true, that's because it is: as the contents of this book have laid bare, digital technology holds great promise but is no panacea. One of the weaknesses of all three of the strategies outlined above is that they typically fall under the control of the electoral commission. This is problematic, given that it is often the commission that is accused of being biased in favour of the ruling party, and thus of colluding in the rigging of elections. By sabotaging technology to ensure that it does not work, manipulating it to the advantage of the ruling party, or allowing the ruling party to hack into the system and change the figures, pliant electoral commissions can undermine the transformative potential of biometric processes. It all comes back to the same problem: if those who are being asked to introduce reforms are the same people who benefit from rigging, then the prospects for improvements are dim.

Indeed, looking beyond the potential that election technology offers, it is clear that it has often failed to protect the quality of elections. We have already documented how the use of an electronic transmission system in Venezuela presented no barrier to the ruling party simply making up the referendum result. In that case, the wider world was alerted to the abuse by the company that supplied the technology – but how many times has election technology been used to hide manipulation rather than to expose it? Evidence from countries in Africa suggests that this may be a real problem, because electoral commissions rarely take all of the steps required to make new technology function as intended. For example, if the electoral commission does not conduct an effective audit of the biometric registration process, multiple registrations may still make it onto the roll. This happened in Somaliland in 2008,[44] and also in the Democratic Republic of Congo in 2011, when 700,000 *doublons* (double registrations) were detected by the country's commission, which nonetheless ruled that it was too late to clean the register.[45] In these cases, elections received the credibility boost that comes from deploying new technology without any justification in terms of the quality of the electoral roll.

The vulnerability of digital processes to many of the same abuses that undermine manual processes is compounded by the limited knowledge of how new technology works in most new democracies. Rather than aiding transparency, the extremely high level of IT knowledge and expertise required to understand how integrated electoral management systems work, and what is implied about the process if they do not, means that opposition parties and international monitors are often poorly placed to evaluate the quality of the process – even in relatively technologically savvy states.

We must therefore not make the mistake of placing our faith in technical solutions to political problems. When opposition parties and donors invest in the transformative power of new scientific advances, they often overlook the fact that even the most advanced forms of election technology rely on human programming and management. And there is nothing about digital technology that means that those who use it are likely to be any more trustworthy or fair. As John Githongo, Kenya's former anti-corruption tsar, has put it: 'You cannot digitize integrity.'[46]

This does not mean that it is not worth investing in digital processes, but it does mean that it is important to evaluate whether the conditions on the ground mean that this technology is likely to be effectively utilized or subverted by those working in bad faith to undermine the election. It also suggests that while it makes sense for governments engaged in supporting democracy abroad to strengthen election management bodies, the best way to do this may be to empower domestic groups to better scrutinize the electoral process for themselves.

Empowering the opposition and civil society

Given the weaknesses inherent in digital processes when under the control of the electoral commission, and the uneven commitment of the international community to democratization, one way forward would be to put new technology in the hands of civil society groups and opposition parties. This is not to suggest that opposition parties are inevitably any more democratic or responsible than their authoritarian counterparts. As we have seen, opposition parties have engaged in vote buying, ballot-box stuffing and the use of political violence. We also know that in many cases changes of government in authoritarian states have led to little improvement in the quality of democracy, because the former opposition behaves just as badly as the old ruling party once it comes to power.

However, whilst we should resist the urge to lionize opposition parties, they are some of the few players that have a vested interest in promoting better-quality elections – if only while they are out of power. Harnessing this, and the capacity of pro-democracy civil society groups, is therefore one of the most effective ways to generate pressure for electoral reform.

Where civil society groups are concerned, international democracy supporters can assist domestic election monitors in harnessing new technology to conduct larger and more effective parallel vote tabulation, as they are already doing in many countries (pp. 177–9). Things are trickier when we move away from civil society groups, because there is limited direct support that international actors can provide to opposition parties. We have seen in Zimbabwe what happened to a movement that was accused of being the puppet of foreign interests (pp. 133–4). Given these dangers, international groups working to support democracy may be able to provide ideas and moral support, but not funding and equipment.

Opposition parties are therefore going to need to be increasingly well organized and innovative. This is possible. For example, by building a system of well-trained party agents and equipping them with new technology, opposition leaders can harness the potential of digital equipment and take it out of the hands of the ruling party. Ahead of the 2016 general elections in Ghana, the National Patriotic Party (NPP) used a specially designed smartphone app to collect a complete set of alternative results that demonstrated that it had won the election, and gave the electoral commission little option but to declare the defeat of the ruling party.[47] It was easier to do it there, where democracy has already started to consolidate and the opposition is relatively unconstrained, but parties in some of the more-open competitive authoritarian states may be able to deploy similar strategies.

For example, if electoral rules are changed to require results to be broken down to the lowest possible level – i.e. the individual polling station – opposition parties will have a fighting chance to hold ruling parties to account. By texting in the results and taking photos of them on their phones, opposition officials can construct their own tally. This makes it harder for the incumbent to rig during the tallying stage without getting caught. Of course, being able to demonstrate the real result of an election does not mean that the opposition necessarily wins. But at least it significantly levels the playing field.

The future of elections and election rigging

Now you know how to rig an election. Unfortunately, while some of the lessons in this book may be new to you, they are not new to the world's dictators, despots and counterfeit democrats. For decades, they have been fine-tuning their strategies in order to hold elections that only they can win. Over time, their trial-and-error efforts have produced rigging techniques that, unfortunately, work. The government prints the ballots, lets people show up to vote, and – almost without fail – wins and retains power. The hallmark of these elections is that we usually know who will win well before the counting ends. That's not how democracy is supposed to work.

In the twenty-first century, elections will be rigged with strategies both old and new, because autocrats have learnt a simple but sad truth: it is easier to stay in power by rigging elections than by not holding them at all. For that reason, we must learn an even more uncomfortable truth: right now, those who rig elections are outfoxing not only their own people but also the international community. Unless we learn how to identify these strategies and address them, then election quality will continue to decline. Over time, this is likely to call the basic legitimacy of democracy into question, as people grow frustrated with elections that fail to usher in change.

We know how to rig an election; we also know how to make it more difficult. If we care about democracy, we must act now. There is no time to waste.

APPENDICES

Appendix 1 Quantitative analysis methods and data sources

The quantitative data used in this volume are derived from a variety of qualitative and quantitative sources including media reports, the scholarly literature, election observation reports, and qualitative field interviews conducted by Professor Cheeseman in Kenya, Ghana, Malawi, Nigeria, Uganda, Zambia and Zimbabwe, and by Dr Klaas in Belarus, Thailand, Madagascar, Tunisia, Côte d'Ivoire, the United States and Zambia.

Our conclusions are also based on analysis and summary statistics of a specifically constructed database that incorporates the Center for Systemic Peace's Polity IV data (http://www.systemicpeace.org/polity/polity4.htm); the National Elections Across Democracy and Autocracy (NELDA) data set from Nikolay Marinov and Susan Hyde (http://www.nelda.co/); new data from the Varieties of Democracy Project (V-Dem), hosted at the University of Gothenburg and the University of Notre Dame (https://www.v-dem.net/en/); data from the Electoral Integrity Project (https://www.electoralintegrityproject.com/); International Election Observation data from Judith Kelley at Duke University; and Archigos data from Kristian Skrede Gleditsch and Giacomo Chiozza (http://www.rochester.edu/college/faculty/hgoemans/data.htm); as well as a series of specific variables drawn from World Bank, IMF, OECD and United Nations databases. For election-quality variables, we rely on a triangulation approach – examining variables within the V-Dem data and the Electoral Integrity Project but also looking at certain binary variables within NELDA for specific forms of electoral malpractice. In particular, the frequency of election-rigging strategies and the regional breakdown of them was conducted as our own analysis of V-Dem and NELDA data. We are indebted to the excellent researchers at all of these projects who made such analysis possible.

In each chapter, our conclusions reflect a combination of the quantitative and qualitative evidence available to us. We believe that this mixed-methods approach is crucial, particularly for a topic as opaque as election rigging. Even though we have interviewed autocrats and their allies, they rarely admit to specific tactics. Yet, by understanding the logic of incumbents, opposition parties, international monitors, diplomats, and the wide range of people involved in the battle for election integrity, we hope to provide a comprehensive and fair-minded assessment of election rigging.

For the countries that are included in each regional category, see appendix 2.

Appendix 2 Regional breakdown of countries used in statistical analysis

These are the regional breakdowns we used. The countries listed here do not include all the countries in the world. In rare instances, that is because of missing data. But for the most part, they are missing because they do not hold national-level elections (such as Saudi Arabia or Eritrea).

Sub-Saharan Africa

Angola, Benin, Botswana, Burkina Faso, Burundi, Central African Republic, Cameroon, Cape Verde, Chad, Comoros, Côte d'Ivoire, Democratic Republic of Congo, Djibouti, Equatorial Guinea, Ethiopia, Gabon, Gambia, Ghana, Guinea, Guinea-Bissau, Kenya, Liberia, Lesotho, Madagascar, Malawi, Mali, Mauritania, Mauritius, Mozambique, Namibia, Niger, Nigeria, Rwanda, Sao Tomé and Principe, Senegal, Seychelles, Sierra Leone, Somalia, South Africa, Swaziland, Tanzania, Togo, Uganda, Zambia, Zimbabwe

Middle East

Egypt, Iran, Iraq, Israel, Jordan, Kuwait, Lebanon, Oman, Syria, Turkey, Yemen

Latin America

Argentina, Bolivia, Brazil, Chile, Colombia, Costa Rica, Ecuador, El Salvador, Guatemala, Guyana, Honduras, Nicaragua, Panama, Paraguay, Peru, Uruguay, Venezuela

Europe (excluding post-Soviet states)

Albania, Austria, Belgium, Bosnia and Herzegovina, Bulgaria, Croatia, Cyprus, Czech Republic, Denmark, Finland, France, Germany, Greece, Hungary, Iceland, Ireland, Italy, Macedonia, Netherlands, Norway, Poland, Portugal, Romania, Serbia, Slovakia, Slovenia, Spain, Sweden, Switzerland, United Kingdom

Post-Soviet states

Armenia, Azerbaijan, Belarus, Estonia, Georgia, Kazakhstan, Kyrgyzstan, Latvia, Lithuania, Moldova, Russia, Tajikistan, Turkmenistan, Ukraine, Uzbekistan

Asia (excluding post-Soviet states)

Afghanistan, Bangladesh, Bhutan, Cambodia, India, Indonesia, Japan, Laos, Mongolia, Nepal, North Korea, Pakistan, Papua New Guinea, Philippines, Singapore, South Korea, Sri Lanka, Thailand, Timor-Leste, Vietnam

Appendix 3 Global total number of elections, by year

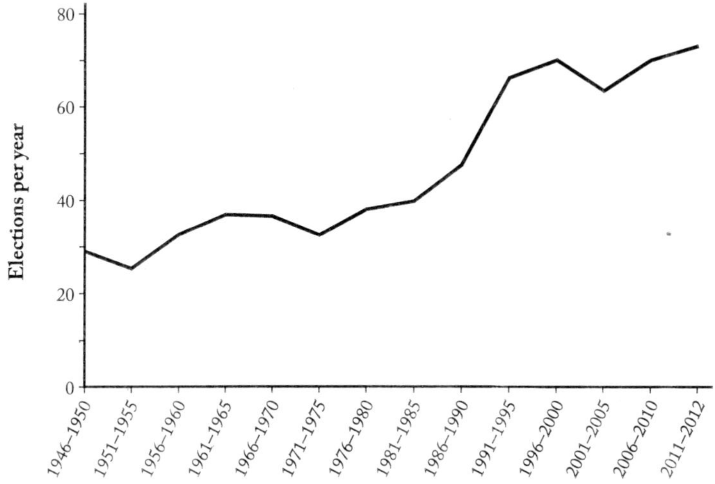

Source: National Elections Across Democracy and Autocracy (NELDA) dataset.

Appendix 4 Global number of elections monitored by international monitors, by year

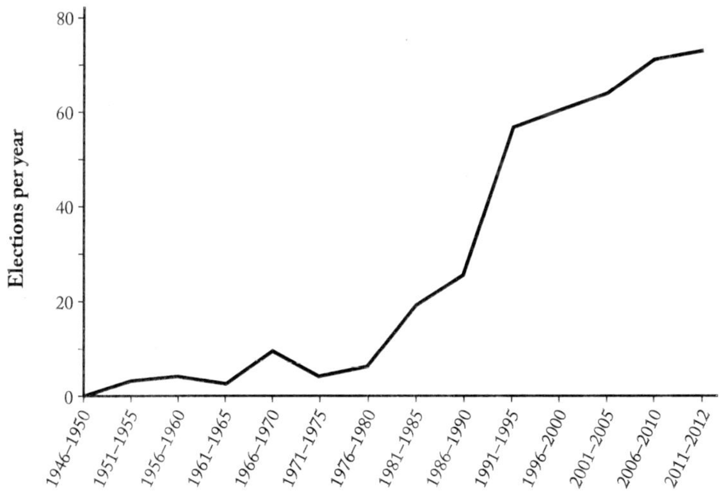

Source: National Elections Across Democracy and Autocracy (NELDA) dataset.

Appendix 5 Global percentage of elections lost by incumbents, by year

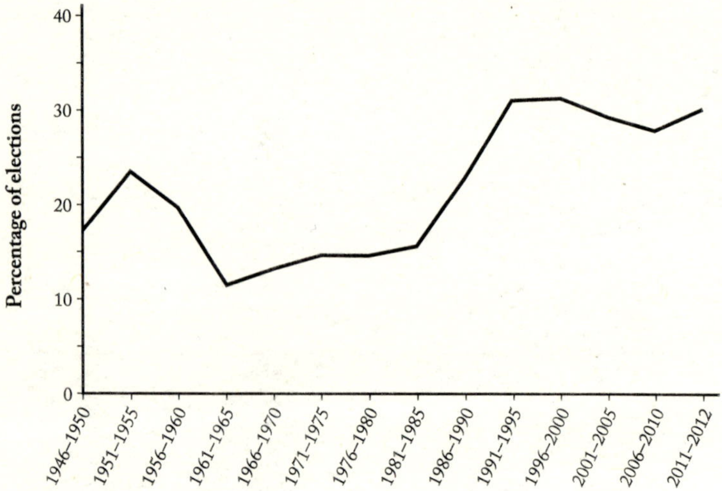

Source: National Elections Across Democracy and Autocracy (NELDA) dataset.

Appendix 6 Percentage of elections lost by incumbents in sub-Saharan Africa, by year

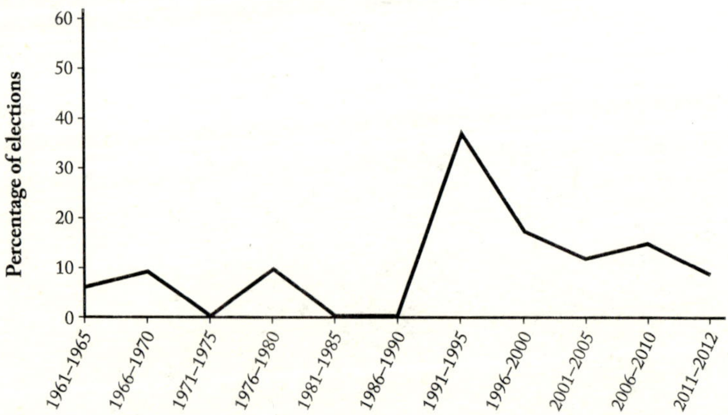

Source: National Elections Across Democracy and Autocracy (NELDA) dataset.

Appendix 7 Average election quality, by region, 2012–15

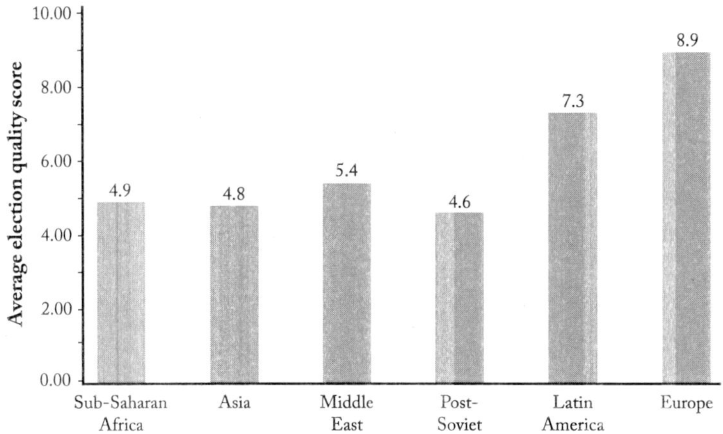

Source: Election Integrity Project. A score of 10 is a 'perfect' election.

Appendix 8 Global percentage chance of an election being rigged, by the number of years the incumbent has been in power, regression analysis 1989–2012

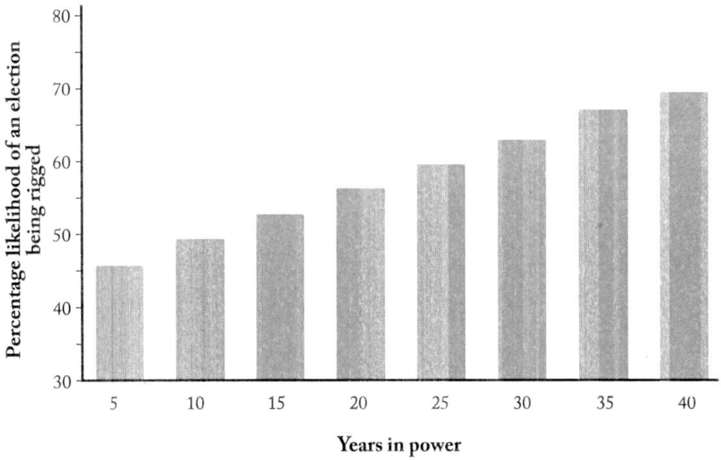

Source: Author regression analysis drawing on data from National Elections Across Democracy and Autocracy (NELDA), Varieties of Democracy (V-Dem) and Archigos.

Appendix 9 Percentage of elections with state control of the election management body, by region, 2012–16

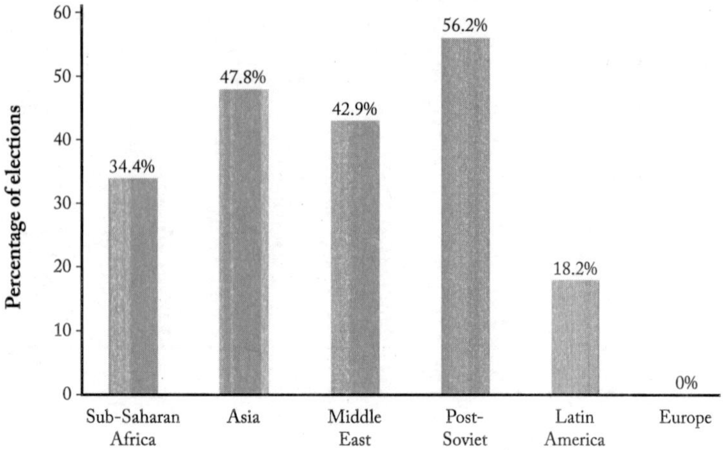

Source: Varieties of Democracy (V-Dem) dataset.

Appendix 10 Global percentage average of voter turnout over time

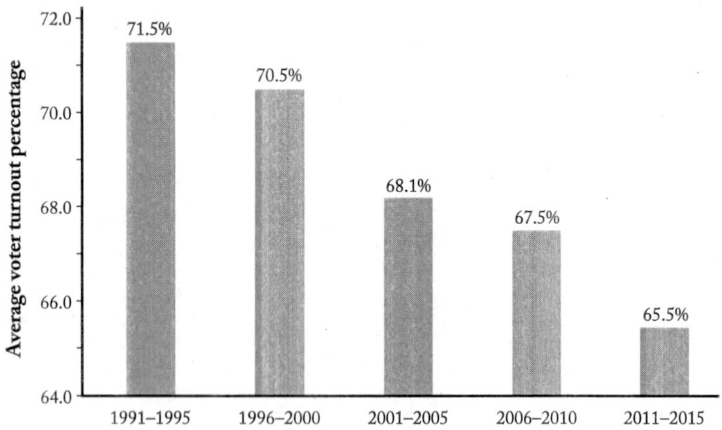

Source: Varieties of Democracy (V-Dem) dataset and Electoral Integrity Project.

Appendix 11 Percentage of elections with state targeting of the opposition with violence, intimidation or harassment

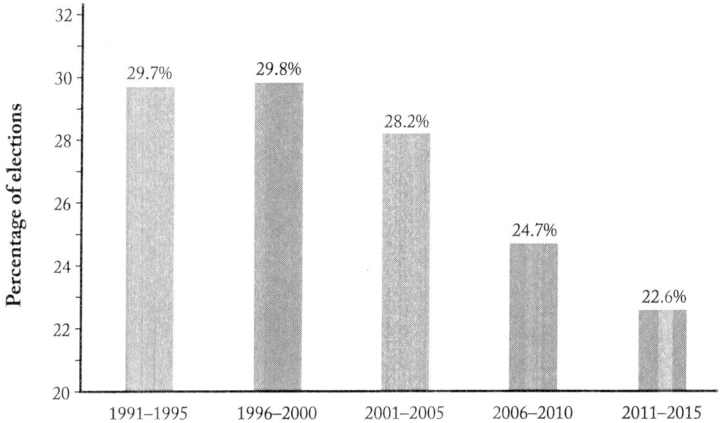

Source: National Elections Across Democracy and Autocracy (NELDA) dataset.

Appendix 12 Percentage of elections with state targeting of the opposition with violence, intimidation or harassment, by region, 2012–16

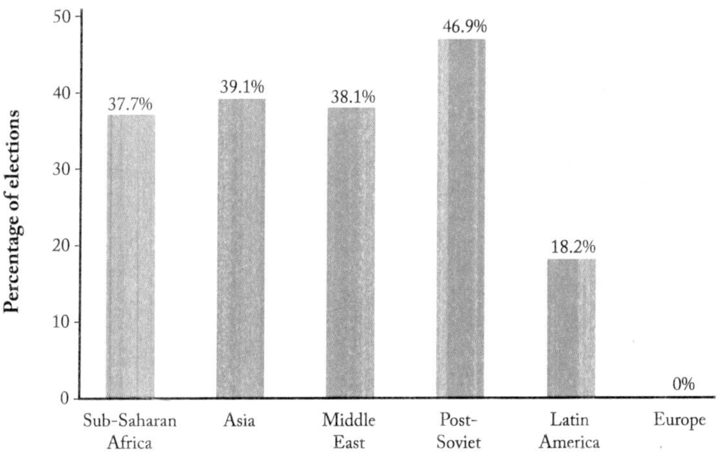

Source: National Elections Across Democracy and Autocracy (NELDA) dataset.

Appendix 13 Percentage of elections with election day irregularities, by region, 2012–16

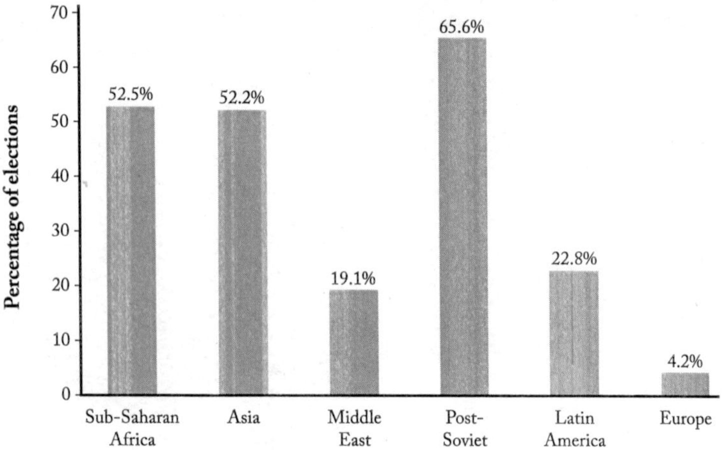

Source: Varieties of Democracy (V-Dem) dataset.

Appendix 14 Percentage of elections featuring vote buying, by region, 2012–16

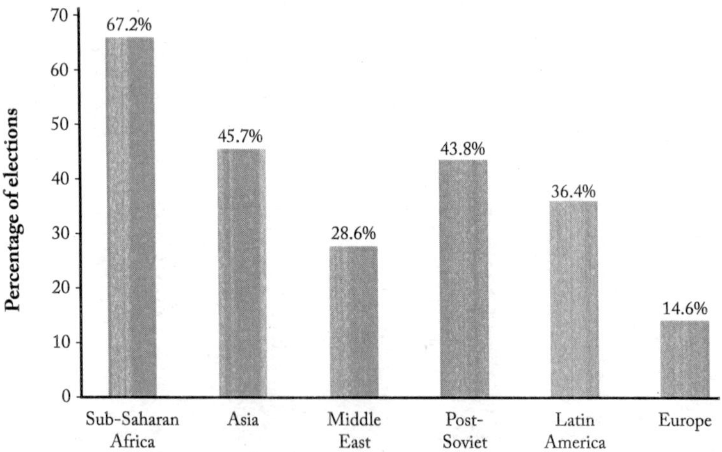

Source: Varieties of Democracy (V-Dem) dataset.

Appendix 15 Regime classification of cases discussed in depth in this book

Note: all classifications are based on the most recent data available, and may differ slightly from some of the historical examples given. Regime classification is based on Polity IV scores, which run from –10 (full dictatorship) to +10 (consolidated democracy). Our spectrum looks like this: closed authoritarian (–10 to –5), dominant authoritarian (–5 to 0), competitive authoritarian (0 to 5), electoral democracy (6 to 10).

Name	Classification	Freedom House rating
Australia	Electoral democracy	Free
Azerbaijan	Closed authoritarian	Not free
Belarus	Closed authoritarian	Not free
Brazil	Electoral democracy	Free
Cambodia	Competitive authoritarian	Not free
China	Closed authoritarian	Not free
Côte d'Ivoire	Competitive authoritarian	Partly free
Gambia	Closed authoritarian	Not free
Ghana	Electoral democracy	Free
Guatemala	Electoral democracy	Partly free
India	Electoral democracy	Free
Kazakhstan	Closed authoritarian	Not free
Kenya	Electoral democracy	Partly free
Madagascar	Electoral democracy	Partly free
Malaysia	Competitive authoritarian	Partly free
Mexico	Electoral democracy	Partly free
Namibia	Electoral democracy	Free
Nigeria	Electoral democracy	Partly free
North Korea	Closed authoritarian	Not free
Pakistan	Electoral democracy	Partly free
Papua New Guinea	Competitive authoritarian	Partly free

Russia	Competitive authoritarian	Not free
Rwanda	Dominant authoritarian	Not free
Sri Lanka	Electoral democracy	Partly free
Syria	Closed authoritarian	Not free
Tajikistan	Dominant authoritarian	Not free
Tanzania	Competitive authoritarian	Partly free
Thailand	Dominant authoritarian	Not free
Togo	Dominant authoritarian	Partly free
Turkey	Dominant authoritarian	Partly free
Turkmenistan	Closed authoritarian	Not free
Uganda	Dominant authoritarian	Not free
Ukraine	Competitive authoritarian	Partly free
United States	Electoral democracy	Free
Venezuela	Competitive authoritarian	Not free
Vietnam	Closed authoritarian	Not free
Zambia	Electoral democracy	Partly free
Zimbabwe	Competitive authoritarian	Partly free

Appendix 16 Electronic voting usage, global

Note: this table only includes cases where the act of voting is electronic; it does not include cases in which biometric technology is used to register or verify voters, or in which electronic technology is used in the collation of votes. 'DRE' stands for direct-recording electronic voting machine: this allows individuals to vote through a ballot made available through a mechanical or electro-optical mechanism, and then records this decision and processes it through a computer program.

Country	Date introduced	Classifications	Current status	Usage
Australia	2015	Remote internet voting	Used in parts of the country	NSW state elections
Brazil	1996	Voting machines	Used nationwide since 2000	Local, referendums, national
Canada	2003	Remote internet voting	Used in parts of the country	Local elections, referendums, First Nation elections
Estonia	2002	Remote internet voting	Used nationwide	Local, parliamentary, presidential and European elections (31.3 per cent usage in 2014 parliamentary)
Germany	1998	DRE voting machine	Discontinued	Used in local and European elections
India	2002	Electronic voting machines and remote internet voting	Used nationwide	All local, state and general parliamentary elections
Kazakhstan	2003	Indirect-recording voting system	Discontinued 2011	2011 presidential elections

Namibia	2014	Voting machines	Used nationwide	Presidential elections
Netherlands	1998	Voting machines	Discontinued 2017	For use by overseas voters only
Norway	2008	Remote internet voting	Currently being piloted	Local and parliamentary elections
Romania	2003	Remote internet voting	Used nationwide	For use by soldiers only
Switzerland	2000	Remote internet voting	Used in parts of the country	Municipal, cantonal and federal referendums
UAE	2011	Voting machines	Used nationwide	Federal National Council (FNC) elections
United States	2002	DRE voting machines	Used in parts of the country	General elections, in some states

ENDNOTES

Introduction: How do you solve a problem like elections?

1. Brian Klaas (2016), *The Despot's Accomplice: How the West is Aiding and Abetting the Decline of Democracy* (London: Hurst), p. 83; and Max Fisher (2013), 'Oops: Azerbaijan released election results before voting had even started', *Washington Post*, 9 October 2013; available online at http://www.washingtonpost.com/news/worldviews/wp/2013/10/09/oops-azerbaijan-released-election-results-before-voting-had-even-started (accessed 10 November 2017).
2. Authors' own calculation based on data from NELDA and Polity IV. See appendix 1 for more details.
3. See, for example, Steven Levitsky and Lucan Way (2002), 'The rise of competitive authoritarianism', *Journal of Democracy* 13, no. 2, pp. 51–65.
4. Michael Coppedge, John Gerring, Staffan I. Lindberg, Svend-Erik Skaaning, Jan Teorell, David Altman, Frida Andersson, Michael Bernhard, M. Steven Fish, Adam Glynn, Allen Hicken, Carl Henrik Knutsen, Kelly McMann, Valeriya Mechkova, Farhad Miri, Pamela Paxton, Daniel Pemstein, Rachel Sigman, Jeffrey Staton and Brigitte Zimmerman (2016), 'Varieties of Democracy (V-Dem) Codebook v6'; available online at https://www.v-dem.net/en/reference/version-6-mar-2016/ (accessed 17 December 2017).
5. Susan D. Hyde and Nikolay Marinov (2012), 'Which elections can be lost?', *Political Analysis* 20, no. 2, pp. 191–201.
6. For the origins of this phrase see Francis Fukuyama (1992), *The End of History and the Last Man* (New York: Free Press), pp. 1–20.
7. Freedom House (2017), 'Freedom in the world 2017'; available online at http://freedomhouse.org/report/freedom-world/freedom-world-2017 (accessed 29 January 2018).
8. Ibid.
9. See, for example, Dwight Y. King (2003), *Half-Hearted Reform: Electoral Institutions and the Struggle for Democracy in Indonesia* (Westport, CT: Praeger Publishers), p. 7.

10. Two of the most important recent contributions to this debate are Sarah Birch (2011), *Electoral Malpractice* (Oxford University Press) and Pippa Norris (2014), *Why Electoral Integrity Matters* (Cambridge University Press).
11. See Philip G. Roessler and Marc Morjé Howard (2009), 'Post-Cold War political regimes: when do elections matter?', in Staffan Lindberg (ed.) (2009), *Democratization by Elections: A New Mode of Transition* (Baltimore, MD: Johns Hopkins University Press), pp. 101–27, p. 120. The authors distinguish between three kinds of authoritarian system: closed authoritarian systems, which do not hold elections; hegemonic systems, which hold elections but do not allow them to be meaningfully contested; and competitive authoritarian systems, in which there is significant contestation but not under free and fair conditions. Based on the analysis of a global data set between 1987 and 2006, they found that hegemonic authoritarian systems that hold elections but tightly control them tend to be considerably more stable than closed authoritarian systems that do not hold elections at all. However, they also found that when elections under authoritarian rule become more open, as in competitive authoritarianism, the prospects of regime continuity fall considerably, a point to which we return in the conclusion.
12. See, for example, Birch (2011), *Electoral Malpractice*; Pippa Norris (2015), *Why Elections Fail* (Cambridge University Press); Susan Hyde (2011), *The Pseudo-Democrat's Dilemma: Why Election Observation Became an International Norm* (Ithaca, NY: Cornell University Press).
13. See Ferran Martínez i Coma and Ignacio Lago (2016), 'Gerrymandering in comparative perspective', *Party Politics*, DOI: https://doi.org/10.1177/1354068816642806 (accessed 17 December 2017).
14. See, for example, R. Michael Alvarez, Thad E. Hall and Susan D. Hyde (eds) (2008), *Election Fraud: Detecting and Deterring Electoral Manipulation* (Washington, DC: Brookings Institution Press).
15. The idea of a presidential toolbox of substitutable tools was first developed in collaboration with Paul Chaisty and Tim Power in relation to the way in which presidents manage legislative coalitions. See Paul Chaisty, Nic Cheeseman and Timothy Power (2014), 'Rethinking the "presidentialism debate": conceptualizing coalitional politics in cross-regional perspective', *Democratization* 21, no. 1, pp. 72–94; Paul Chaisty, Nic Cheeseman and Timothy Power (2018), *Coalitional Presidentialism in Comparative Perspective* (Oxford University Press).
16. See, for example, Ewan Harrison and Sara McLaughlin Mitchell (2013), *The Triumph of Democracy and the Eclipse of the West* (New York: Palgrave Macmillan), pp. 75–97.
17. For the classic text that named the 'third wave' see Samuel P. Huntington (1993), *The Third Wave: Democratization in the Late Twentieth Century* (Norman, OK: University of Oklahoma Press).
18. On post-materialist values see the influential work of Ronald Inglehart, in particular Ronald F. Inglehart (2008), 'Changing values among Western publics from 1970 to 2006', *West European Politics* 31, no. 1–2, pp. 130–46; Ronald Inglehart and Scott C. Flanagan (1987), 'Value change in industrial societies', *American Political Science Review* 81, no. 4, pp. 1289–319.
19. Defined as national-level legislative or executive elections that involve more than one candidate on the ballot from a different party to the

incumbent. Regional elections are not included, nor are national elections that only have the incumbent on the ballot.
20. Hyde and Marinov (2012), 'Which elections can be lost?'.
21. Carolyn Baylies and Morris Szeftel (1992), 'The fall and rise of multi-party politics in Zambia', *Review of African Political Economy* 19, no. 54, pp. 75–91.
22. See Larry Jay Diamond (2002), 'Thinking about hybrid regimes', *Journal of Democracy* 13, no. 2, pp. 21–35; Andreas Schedler (2013), *The Politics of Uncertainty: Sustaining and Subverting Electoral Authoritarianism* (Oxford University Press), introduction. For 'counterfeit democracy' see Klaas (2016), *The Despot's Accomplice*.
23. Gideon Maltz (2007), 'The case for presidential term limits', *Journal of Democracy* 18, no. 1, pp. 128–42.
24. See, for example, Nic Cheeseman (2010), 'African elections as vehicles for change', *Journal of Democracy* 21, no. 4, pp. 139–53.
25. Roessler and Howard (2009), 'Post-Cold War political regimes', pp. 118–22.
26. For the classic work on competitive authoritarian states see Steven Levitsky and Lucan A. Way (2010), *Competitive Authoritarianism: Hybrid Regimes after the Cold War* (Cambridge University Press).
27. Our scale is based on the presence or otherwise of multipartyism as well as the level of political rights and civil liberties at a given moment in time. It therefore does not map perfectly onto other democracy indices. However, for readers interested to know how this would translate into the Polity Index or Freedom House scores, using Polity IV Regime Type our spectrum looks like this: closed authoritarian (–10 to –5), dominant authoritarian (–5 to 0), competitive authoritarian (0 to 5), electoral democracy (6 to 10). For a discussion of Polity data and methodology see Monty G. Marshall (2014), 'Polity IV Project: political regime characteristics and transitions, 1800–2013', Polity IV; available online at http://www.systemicpeace.org/polity/polity4.htm (accessed 10 November 2017). For Freedom House (whose 1–14 scale combines scores for political rights and civil liberties, with lower scores being more free), the translation would be closed authoritarian (7 to 6), dominant authoritarian (5 to 4), competitive authoritarian (3), electoral democracy (2 to 1). For a discussion of Freedom House data and methodology see Freedom House (2012), 'Freedom in the world 2012: methodology'; available online at https://freedomhouse.org/report/freedom-world-2012/methodology (accessed 10 November 2017).
28. Roessler and Howard (2009), 'Post-Cold War political regimes', p. 119.
29. Ibid., p. 120.
30. Robert Dahl (1972), *Polyarchy: Participation and Opposition* (New Haven, CT: Yale University Press), p. 15.
31. This framework draws on Nic Cheeseman (2015), *Democracy in Africa: Successes, Failures, and the Struggle for Political Reform* (Cambridge University Press).
32. Paul Collier (2008), *Wars, Guns and Votes: Democracy in Dangerous Places* (New York: Random House), especially pp. 103–21.
33. George Packer (1985), 'Togo: the dictator's new clothes', *Dissent Magazine*, Fall, pp. 411–16.
34. Grant Podelco (2012), 'You crazy dictator: bread and circuses in Turkmenistan', *Atlantic*, 12 November; available online at https://www.

theatlantic.com/international/archive/2012/11/you-crazy-dictator-bread-and-circuses-in-turkmenistan/265125 (accessed 10 November 2017).

35. Michela Wrong (2009), *Our Turn to Eat: The Story of a Kenyan Whistleblower* (London: Fourth Estate).
36. Corruption figures are notoriously difficult to confirm precisely. Transparency International argues that Sani Abacha stole $3–$5 billion in just a short time in power, and tens of billions of dollars are missing from public coffers from oil and other energy payments over decades. One of the key sources they cite is Ignacio Jimu (2009), 'Managing proceeds of asset recovery: the case of Nigeria, Peru, the Philippines and Kazakhstan', Basel Institute of Governance/ICAR Working Paper Series no. 6, p. 7; available online at https://www.baselgovernance.org/sites/collective.localhost/files/publications/biog_working_paper_06.pdf (accessed 10 November 2017).
37. Alex Josey (2013), *Lee Kuan Yew: The Crucial Years* (New York: Marshall Cavendish International Asia Pte).
38. For an alternative perspective on why a number of authoritarian governments have failed to advance the standards of living of their people see James C. Scott (1998), *Seeing Like a State: How Certain Schemes to Improve the Human Condition Have Failed* (New Haven, CT: Yale University Press).
39. Brian Bennett (2012), *The Last Dictatorship in Europe: Belarus Under Lukashenko* (London: C. Hurst & Co.), pp. 219–30.
40. This is the situation in a number of states, where thirteen countries are governed by a leader who has been in power for a quarter-century or more, but it is not the case in most of the rest of the world.
41. Holger Bernt Hansen and Michael Twaddle (eds) (1995), *From Chaos to Order: The Politics of Constitution-making in Uganda* (Kampala: Fountain Publishers); Nic Cheeseman, Gabrielle Lynch and Justin Willis (2016), 'Museveni's NRM party still has support in rural Uganda', *The East African*, 16 January; available online at http://www.theeastafrican.co.ke/oped/comment/Museveni-NRM-party-still-has-huge-support-in-rural-Uganda-/434750-3036604-d65f7dz/index.html (accessed 15 December 2017).
42. In the African context, it is striking that when citizens in Ghana, Kenya and Uganda were asked what they thought was the most important factor for an election to be free and fair, the most popular answer in all three countries was 'a peaceful process'. The tendency to value peace and stability over competition is confirmed by a survey conducted by the Africa Centre for Open Governance (AfriCOG) shortly after Kenya's 2013 election, which found that 50.9 per cent of respondents felt that 'peace is more important than free and fair elections'. See Gabrielle Lynch, Nic Cheeseman and Justin Willis (forthcoming), 'The violence of electoral peace: the ballot, order and authority in Africa', *African Affairs*.
43. Robert Mattes and Michael Bratton (2016), 'Do Africans still want democracy? This new report gives a qualified yes', Afrobarometer Working Paper no. 36, p. 4; available online at http://afrobarometer.org/blogs/do-africans-still-want-democracy-new-report-gives-qualified-yes (accessed 18 November 2017). The Afrobarometer is a regular nationally representative survey that has been conducted in over thirty countries over multiple survey rounds. For information on its methods and the latest

data see the Afrobarometer (2017), online at http://www.afrobarometer.org (accessed 10 November 2017).

44. Rorisang Lekalake (2017), 'Still no alternative? Popular views of the opposition in Southern Africa's one-party dominant regimes', Afrobarometer Working Paper no. 38, p. 3.
45. Authors' own calculation based on the Archigos data set (see appendix 1 for more details).
46. For the case of Sudan see Lutz Oette (2010), 'Peace and justice, or neither? The repercussions of the al-Bashir case for international criminal justice in Africa and beyond', *Journal of International Criminal Justice* 8, no. 2, pp. 345–64; for a longer discussion of why ICC charges can make it harder to persuade a leader to step down see Mark Kersten (2012), 'The ICC and the Security Council: just say no?', *Justice in Conflict*, 29 February; available online at https://justiceinconflict.org/2012/02/29/the-icc-and-the-security-council-just-say-no/ (accessed 15 December 2017).
47. Data from Archigos, a data set of political leaders. See H.E. Goemans, Kristian Gleditsch and Giacomo Chiozza (2009), 'Introducing Archigos: a data set of political leaders', *Journal of Peace Research* 46, no. 2, pp. 169–83.
48. Harris Lentz (1999), *Encyclopedia of Heads of States and Governments: 1900 through 1945* (Jefferson, NC: McFarland), p. 219.
49. Calculated using the Polity Index and looking at those states in which oil contributes more than 3 per cent of a country's gross domestic product (GDP), and those in which oil contributes less than this. The score for oil-producing states falls to -3.1 if Norway, an oil outlier, is excluded from the data.
50. Data from Center for Systemic Peace, Polity IV project, see appendix 1. See also Michael Ross (2001), 'Does oil hinder democracy?', *World Politics* 53, no. 3, pp. 325–61; Sarah M. Brooks and Marcus J. Kurtz (2016), 'Oil and democracy: endogenous natural resources and the political "resource curse"', *International Organizations* 70, no. 2, pp. 279–311; and Anar K. Ahmadov (2014), 'Oil, democracy, and context: a meta-analysis', *Comparative Political Studies* 47, no. 9, pp. 1238–67.
51. Human Rights Watch (9 August 2002), 'Uzbekistan: two brutal deaths in custody'; available online at http://www.hrw.org/news/2002/08/09/uzbekistan-two-brutal-deaths-custody (accessed 10 November 2017); see also Thomas Carothers (2003), 'Promoting democracy and fighting terror', *Foreign Affairs*, January/February 2003; available online at https://www.foreignaffairs.com/articles/2003-01-01/promoting-democracy-and-fighting-terror (accessed 10 November 2017).
52. See, for example, Beth Whitaker (2010), 'Compliance among weak states: Africa and the counter-terrorism regime', *Review of International Studies* 36, no. 3, pp. 639–62.
53. For recent research on the role of economic shocks in toppling dictators see Sergei Guriev and Daniel Treisman (2015), 'How modern dictators survive: an informational theory of the new authoritarianism', National Bureau of Economic Research Working Paper no. 21136; available online at http://www.nber.org/papers/w21136 (accessed 10 November 2017).
54. Getting good information on the cost of bribes is difficult, because this varies across the country and is kept hidden by both those who give out bribes and those who receive them. However, anecdotal evidence suggests that there are

considerable cross-regional variations. For example, in the last Nigerian election, the modal bribe is estimated to have been around ₦500 ($3): see Michael Bratton (2008), 'Vote buying and violence in Nigerian election campaigns', *Electoral Studies* 27, no. 4, pp. 621–32. By contrast, in Colombia votes are said to cost between $8 and $65 per person: see Ivana Mellers (2016), 'The cost of corruption', *Americas Quarterly*; available online at http://americasquarterly.org/content/cost-corruption (accessed 10 November 2017). Similarly, in the 2013 general elections in Honduras the cost of vote buying ranged between $5 and $25: see Jason Wallach (2013), 'Anatomy of election fraud: stealing the 2013 Honduran election in five simple steps', *Foreign Policy in Focus*, 19 December; available online at http://fpif.org/anatomy-election-fraud-stealing-2013-honduran-election-five-simple-steps (accessed 10 November 2017). Of course, the cost of a bribe also depends on the income of candidates and the amount individuals have to spend on election campaigns. As we discuss elsewhere in this book, there is good reason to believe that the campaign budgets of African leaders are very high, and comparable to their Latin American counterparts.

55. See, for example, Fook Kwang Han (2017), 'The rise of Trump and its global implications: America at war with itself', *RSIS Commentary* no. 27, 10 February; available online at https://www.rsis.edu.sg/wp-content/uploads/2017/02/CO17027.pdf (accessed 10 November 2017).
56. Joanna M. Burkhardt (2017), 'History of fake news', *Library Technology Reports* 53, no. 8, pp. 5–9.
57. Nic Cheeseman (2008), 'The Kenyan elections of 2007: an introduction', *Journal of Eastern African Studies* 2, no. 2, pp. 166–84, p. 169; BBC News (2007), 'Kenya Muslims deny Sharia claims', 27 November; available online at http://news.bbc.co.uk/1/hi/world/africa/7115387.stm (accessed 5 December).
58. The EIU recognizes four categories of countries: full democracies, with only limited problems in democratic functioning; flawed democracies, in which democracy has significant faults; hybrid regimes, in which irregularities frequently prevent elections from being free and fair; and authoritarian regimes, in which pluralism has either vanished or is extremely limited. See 'Revenge of the deplorables: the 2016 Democracy Index report' (2016), Economist Intelligence Unit; available online at http://www.eiu.com/public/topical_report.aspx?campaignid=DemocracyIndex2016 (accessed 11 November 2017).
59. 'Declining trust in government is denting democracy', *Economist*, 25 January 2017; available online at http://www.economist.com/blogs/graphicdetail/2017/01/daily-chart-20 (accessed 11 November).
60. This phrase comes from Cheeseman (2010), 'African elections as vehicles for change'.
61. For the evidence on education see Robin Harding and David Stasavage (2013), 'What democracy does (and doesn't do) for basic services: school fees, school inputs, and African elections', *Journal of Politics* 76, no. 1, pp. 229–45. A longer discussion of these issues is provided in the conclusion.

1 Invisible rigging: How to steal an election without getting caught

1. Brian Whitmore (1998), 'St Pete poll plays double jeopardy', *Moscow Times*, 6 October; available online at http://old.themoscowtimes.com/

sitemap/free/1998/10/article/st-pete-poll-plays-double-jeopardy/284395.html (accessed 11 November 2017).

2. Brian Whitmore (1998), 'St Petersburg's reformers battle a Russian Tammany Hall', Jamestown Foundation, 13 November; available online at http://jamestown.org/program/st-petersburgs-reformers-battle-a-russian-tammany-hall (accessed 11 November 2017).
3. Whitmore (1998), 'St Pete poll plays double jeopardy'.
4. Ibid.
5. For a readable take on the life of Pitt see Jeremy Black (1992), *Pitt the Elder* (Cambridge University Press).
6. Richard A. Hogarty (2002), *Massachusetts Politics and Public Policy: Studies in Power and Leadership* (Amherst, MA: University of Massachusetts), p. 50.
7. 'Correspondence from John Adams to James Warren, 15 July 1776', National Archives Founders Online; available online at http://founders.archives.gov/documents/Adams/06-04-02-0162 (accessed 11 November 2017). [Original source: Robert J. Taylor (ed.) (1979), *The Adams Papers: Papers of John Adams*, vol. 4: *February–August 1776* (Cambridge, MA: Harvard University Press), pp. 382–3.]
8. Carl Huse (2016), 'Seeking to end gerrymandering's enduring legacy', *New York Times*, 25 January 2016; available online at http://www.nytimes.com/2016/01/26/us/politics/seeking-to-end-gerrymanderings-enduring-legacy.html (accessed 11 November 2017).
9. For more on gerrymandering see Erik J. Engstrom (2016), *Partisan Gerrymandering and the Construction of American Democracy* (Ann Arbor, MI: University of Michigan Press); for more on Gerry himself see George Athan Billias (1976), *Elbridge Gerry: Founding Father and Republican Statesman* (New York: McGraw-Hill).
10. David Lublin (1999), *The Paradox of Representation: Racial Gerrymandering and Minority Interests in Congress* (Princeton University Press).
11. Public Policy Polling (2013), 'Congress somewhere below cockroaches, traffic jams, and Nickelback in Americans' esteem'; available online at http://www.publicpolicypolling.com/pdf/2011/PPP_Release_Natl_010813_.pdf (accessed 11 November 2017).
12. Ballotpedia (2016), 'US House: post-election partisan control'; available online at http://ballotpedia.org/United_States_House_of_Representatives_elections,_2016 (accessed 11 November 2017).
13. Rick Pearson (2011), 'Federal court upholds Illinois congressional map', *Chicago Tribune*, 16 December; available online at http://articles.chicagotribune.com/2011-12-16/news/ct-met-congress-map-court-20111216_1_congressional-map-earmuff-shaped-new-map (accessed 11 November 2017).
14. Jowei Chen and David Cottrell (2016), 'Evaluating partisan gains from congressional gerrymandering: using computer simulations to estimate the effect of gerrymandering in the US House', *Electoral Studies* 44, pp. 329–30.
15. Jowei Chen and Jonathon Rodden (2013), 'Unintentional gerrymandering: political geography and electoral bias in legislatures', *Quarterly Journal of Political Science* 8, no. 3, pp. 239–69.
16. Laura Royden and Michael Li (2017), 'Extreme maps', Brennan Center for Justice, 9 May 2017; available online at http://www.brennancenter.org/publication/extreme-maps (accessed 11 November 2017).

17. Ballotpedia (2016), 'US House'.
18. Ibid.
19. Eliza Mackintosh (2017), 'Zimbabwe's military takeover was the world's strangest coup', CNN, 21 November; available online at http://edition.cnn.com/2017/11/20/africa/zimbabwe-military-takeover-strangest-coup/index.html (accessed 15 December 2017).
20. Most of the honorary degrees and the British knighthood have since been revoked. See Howard W. French (1988), 'Mugabe wins anti-hunger prize', *New York Times*, 16 September; available online at http://www.nytimes.com/1988/09/16/world/mugabe-wins-anti-hunger-prize.html (accessed 11 November 2017).
21. Nic Cheeseman and Blessing-Miles Tendi (2010), 'Power-sharing in comparative perspective: the dynamics of "unity government" in Kenya and Zimbabwe', *Journal of Modern African Studies* 48, no. 2, pp. 203–29.
22. Brian Raftopoulos (2007), 'Reflections on the opposition in Zimbabwe: the politics of the Movement for Democratic Change (MDC)', in Ranka Primorac and Stephen Chan (eds) (2007), *Zimbabwe in Crisis: The International Response and the Space of Silence* (London, New York: Routledge), pp. 125–48.
23. Dingilizwe Mathe (2008), 'Zimbabwe: the art of gerrymandering', *AfrikNews*, 22 March; available online at http://www.afrik-news.com/article12908.html (accessed 11 November 2017).
24. Ibid.
25. Richard Snyder and David J. Samuels (2004), 'Legislative malapportionment in Latin America', in Edward L. Gibson (ed.) (2004), *Federalism and Democracy in Latin America* (Baltimore, MD: Johns Hopkins University Press), pp. 131–72.
26. ACE Electoral Knowledge Network (2012), 'The ACE Encyclopaedia: boundary delimitation'; available online at http://aceproject.org/ace-en/topics/bd/onePage (accessed 11 November 2017).
27. The number of presidential systems globally is reviewed in Chaisty, Cheeseman and Power (2018), *Coalitional Presidentialism in Comparative Perspective*, introduction.
28. Michael J. Klarman (2004), *From Jim Crow to Civil Rights: The Supreme Court and the Struggle for Racial Equality* (Oxford University Press), p. 53.
29. Steve Annear (2017), 'Even Harvard students failed the 1964 Louisiana literacy test', *Boston Magazine*, 7 November; available online at http://www.bostonmagazine.com/news/blog/2014/11/07/harvard-students-failed-the-1964-louisiana-literacy-test (accessed 11 November 2017).
30. See Thom File (2013), 'The diversifying electorate: voting rates by race and Hispanic origin in 2012 (and other recent elections)', United States Census Bureau; available online at http://www.census.gov/prod/2013pubs/p20-568.pdf (accessed 11 November 2017); and William H. Frey (2013), 'Minority turnout determined the 2012 election', Brookings Institute; available online at http://www.brookings.edu/research/minority-turnout-determined-the-2012-election (accessed 11 November 2017).
31. Jens Manuel Krogstad and Mark Hugo Lopez (2016), 'Hillary Clinton won Latino vote but fell below 2012 support for Obama', Pew Research; available online at http://www.pewresearch.org/fact-tank/2016/11/29/hillary-clinton-wins-latino-vote-but-falls-below-2012-support-for-obama (accessed 11 November 2017).

32. Jordan Lebeau (2016), 'A state by state guide to voter restriction laws', Forbes, 7 November; see also Keith G. Bentele and Erin E. O'Brien (2013), 'Jim Crow 2.0? Why states consider and adopt restrictive voter access policies', *Perspectives on Politics* 11, no. 4, pp. 1088–116.
33. North Carolina State Board of Elections (2017), 'Post-election audit report'; available online at http://s3.amazonaws.com/dl.ncsbe.gov/sboe/Post-Election%20Audit%20Report_2016%20General%20Election/Post-Election_Audit_Report.pdf (accessed 11 November 2017).
34. Zoltan Hajnal, Nazita Lajevardi and Lindsay Nielson (2017), 'Voter identification laws and the suppression of minority votes', *The Journal of Politics* 79, no. 2, p. 369.
35. Christina A. Cassidy and Ivan Moreno (2017), 'Wisconsin voter ID law proved insurmountable for many', Associated Press, 14 May 2017; available online at http://www.jsonline.com/story/news/politics/2017/05/14/wisconsin-voter-id-law-proved-insurmountable-many/321680001 (accessed 11 November 2017). See also Ari Berman (2017), 'Rigged: how voter suppression threw Wisconsin to Trump', *Mother Jones*, November/December 2017; available online at http://www.motherjones.com/politics/2017/10/voter-suppression-wisconsin-election-2016 (accessed 11 November 2017).
36. Astrid Evrensel (ed.) (2010), *Voter Registration in Africa: A Comparative Analysis* (Johannesburg: EISA).
37. Wanjohi Githae (2016), 'Kenya: ODM cries foul over voter registration but minister denies bias claims', *Daily Nation*, 9 October; available online at http://allafrica.com/stories/201610090307.html (accessed 11 November 2017).
38. 'Zanu PF in "forced" voter registration', *Daily News*, 6 March 2017; available online at https://www.dailynews.co.zw/articles/2017/03/06/zanu-pf-in-forced-voter-registration (accessed 11 November 2017); for more recent problems see Maxwell Sibanda (2017), 'BVR not the panacea to Zim's electoral challenges', *Daily News*, 18 July; available online at https://www.dailynews.co.zw/articles/2017/07/18/bvr-not-the-panacea-to-zims-electoral-challenges (accessed 11 November 2017).
39. Bridget Mananavire (2015), 'Thousands of under-5s have no birth certificates', *Daily News*, 13 December; available online at https://www.dailynews.co.zw/articles/2015/12/12/thousands-of-under-5s-have-no-birth-certificates (accessed 11 November 2017).
40. 'No maternity fees, no birth record: is this legal?', *Zimbabwean*, 9 October 2015; available online at http://www.thezimbabwean.co/2015/10/no-maternity-fees-no-birth-record-is-this-legal (accessed 11 November 2017).
41. Sunday News Online (2017), 'Mudede dismisses politics in birth certificate registration', 23 July; available online at http://www.zimbabwesituation.com/news/zimsit-m-mudede-dismisses-politics-in-birth-certificate-registration/ (accessed 17 December 2017).
42. Nic Cheeseman, interview with former ZANU–PF official, Harare, Zimbabwe, July 2017.
43. Ibid.
44. Luke Anami (2017), 'Concern over high number of spoilt votes', *Standard*, 10 August; available online at http://www.standardmedia.co.ke/article/2001250839/concern-over-high-number-of-spoilt-votes (accessed 11 November 2017).

45. Wendy R. Weiser and Margaret Chen (2008), 'Voter suppression incidents, 2008', Brennan Center for Justice; available online at http://www.brennancenter.org/analysis/voter-suppression-incidents-2008 (accessed 11 November 2017).
46. John Wagner (2011), 'Ex-Ehrlich campaign manager Schurick convicted in Robocall case', *Washington Post*, 6 December; available online at http://www.washingtonpost.com/local/dc-politics/ex-ehrlich-campaign-manager-schurick-convicted-in-robocall-case/2011/12/06/gIQA6rNsaO_story.html (accessed 11 November 2017).
47. Richard R. Marcus (2004), 'Political change in Madagascar: populist democracy or neopatrimonialism by another name?', *Institute for Security Studies Papers* 89, p. 20.
48. Though this is not always impossible: in some countries voters can write in the name of their preferred leader onto the ballot, and if sufficient people do so then that person can win.
49. Jean-Loup Vivier (2010), *Madagascar, une île à la dérive: les années 2007–2010 – de Ravalomanana à Rajoelina* (Paris: L'Harmattan), p. 19.
50. Klaas (2016), *The Despot's Accomplice*, pp. 85–6.
51. 'Madagascar keeps politician out', BBC News, 7 October 2006; available online at http://news.bbc.co.uk/1/hi/world/africa/5416284.stm (accessed 11 November 2017).
52. See Bureau of Democracy, Human Rights, and Labor (2007), '2006 country reports on human rights practices: Madagascar', US Department of State; available online at http://www.state.gov/j/drl/rls/hrrpt/2006/78743.htm (accessed 11 November 2017).
53. Tim Marshal (2013), 'Iran's hand-picked presidential candidates', Sky News, 13 June; available online at https://news.sky.com/story/irans-hand-picked-presidential-candidates-10443107 (15 December 2017).
54. Abu B. Bah (2010), 'Democracy and civil war: citizenship and peacemaking in Côte d'Ivoire', *African Affairs* 109, no. 437, pp. 597–615.
55. Morris P. Fiorina and Samuel J. Abrams (2008), 'Political polarization in the American public', *Annual Review of Political Science* 11, pp. 563–88; Pew Research Centre (2014), 'Political polarization in the American public'; available online at http://assets.pewresearch.org/wp-content/uploads/sites/5/2014/06/6-12-2014-Political-Polarization-Release.pdf (accessed 11 November 2017).
56. Eric Lindgren and Priscilla Southwell (2014), 'The effect of electoral competitiveness on ideological voting patterns in the US House, 2002–10', *Politics & Policy* 42, no. 6, pp. 905–18; it is important to note that the study did not find a particularly strong effect.
57. Nolan McCarty, Keith T. Poole and Howard Rosenthal (2009), 'Does gerrymandering cause polarization?', *American Journal of Political Science* 53, no. 3, pp. 666–80.
58. Domenico Montanaro, Rachel Wellford and Simone Pathe (2014), '2014 midterm election turnout lowest in 70 years', PBS Newshour, 10 November; available online at http://www.pbs.org/newshour/updates/2014-midterm-election-turnout-lowest-in-70-years (accessed 11 November 2017).
59. Susanne D. Mueller (2008), 'The political economy of Kenya's crisis', *Journal of Eastern African Studies* 2, no. 2, pp. 185–210.
60. Donald L. Horowitz (2004), 'The alternative vote and interethnic moderation: a reply to Fraenkel and Grofman', *Public Choice* 121, no. 3,

pp. 507–17; Donald L. Horowitz (2003), 'Electoral systems: a primer for decision makers', *Journal of Democracy* 14, no. 4, pp. 115–27.

61. Jon Fraenkel and Bernard Grofman (2006), 'The failure of the alternative vote as a tool for ethnic moderation in Fiji: a rejoinder to Horowitz', *Comparative Political Studies* 39, no. 5, pp. 663–6; and Arend Lijphart (1991), 'The alternative vote: a realistic alternative for South Africa?', *Politikon: South African Journal of Political Studies* 18, no. 2, pp. 91–101.
62. David Welsh (1993), 'Domestic politics and ethnic conflict', *Survival* 35, no. 1, pp. 63–80; see also Samuel Mondays Atuobi (2008), 'Election-related violence in Africa', *Conflict Trends* 1, pp. 10–15.
63. Data from the NELDA dataset. See Susan Hyde and Nikolay Marinov (2012), 'Which elections can be lost?', *Political Analysis* 20, no. 2, pp. 191–210.
64. For a more in-depth discussion on broader problems with American elections see Pippa Norris (2017), *Why American Elections Are Flawed (and How to Fix Them)* (Ithaca, NY: Cornell University Press).
65. Barry Edwards, Michael Crespin, Ryan D. Williamson and Maxwell Palmer (2017), 'Institutional control of redistricting and the geography of representation', *Journal of Politics* 79, no. 2, pp. 722–6.
66. For further discussion of gerrymandering and independent commissions see James Ruley (2017), 'One person, one vote: gerrymandering and the independent commission, a global perspective', *Indiana Law Journal* 92, no. 2, pp. 783–816.
67. ACE Electoral Knowledge Network (2012), 'Boundary delimitation'.
68. Nicholas O. Stephanopoulos and Eric M. McGhee (2015), 'Partisan gerrymandering and the efficiency gap', *University of Chicago Law Review* 82, pp. 831–900.
69. See Metric Geometry and Gerrymandering Group (2017), 'Gerrymandering resources', Tufts University; available online at https://sites.tufts.edu/gerrymandr/resources (accessed 11 November 2017); and Shannon Najmabadi (2017), 'Meet the math professor who's fighting gerrymandering with geometry', *Chronicle of Higher Education*, 22 February 2017; available online at http://www.chronicle.com/article/Meet-the-Math-Professor/239260 (accessed 11 November 2017).
70. IFES (2014), 'Redefining boundaries'; available online at http://www.ifes.org/news/redefining-boundaries (accessed 11 November 2017).
71. Jamal Khurshid (2015), 'ECP facilitated gerrymandering of constituencies, SHC told', *News*, 20 September; available online at http://www.thenews.com.pk/print/63553-ecp-facilitated-gerrymandering-of-constituencies-shc-told (accessed 11 November 2017).
72. J. Gerald Hebert and Marina K. Jenkins (2010), 'The need for state redistricting reform to rein in partisan gerrymandering', *Yale Law & Policy Review* 29, p. 543; Samuel Issacharoff (2002), 'Gerrymandering and political cartels', *Harvard Law Review* 116, no. 2, pp. 593–648.
73. For an example see European Union Election Observation Mission in Kosovo (2017), 'Briefing of long-term election observers', 26 May; available online at http://eeas.europa.eu/election-observation-missions/eom-kosovo-2017/26981/briefing-long-term-election-observers_en (accessed 11 November 2017).
74. Stephen Chan (2017), 'If not free and fair? Selected African elections and their observation', Democracy in Africa, 28 January; available online at

http://democracyinafrica.org/wp-content/uploads/2017/01/If-not-free-and-fair-electoral-observation-FINAL.pdf (accessed 11 November 2017).

2 Buying hearts and minds: The art of electoral bribery

1. 'President Yoweri Museveni's sack of money sparks Uganda row', BBC News, 22 April 2013; available online at http://www.bbc.co.uk/news/world-africa-22245873 (accessed 11 November 2017).
2. Jake Maxwell Watts (2013), 'Ugandan president Yoweri Museveni hands out $100K in a sack full of cash', *Quartz*, 23 April; available online at https://qz.com/77205/ugandan-president-yoweri-museveni-hands-out-100k-in-a-sack-full-of-cash (accessed 11 November 2017).
3. The Stream (2013), 'Uganda's #sackofmoney hits a nerve', Al Jazeera, 23 April; available online at http://stream.aljazeera.com/story/201304231859-0022697 (accessed 11 November 2017).
4. BBC News (2013), 'President Yoweri Museveni's sack of money sparks Uganda row', 22 April; available online at http://www.bbc.co.uk/news/world-africa-22245873 (accessed 15 December 2017).
5. Kizito Michael George (2013), 'The cunning mediocrity of African presidents: Ugandan president Yoweri Museveni hands out $100K in a sack full of cash', *Watchman Africa* blog, 26 April 2013; available online at http://watchmanafrica.blogspot.co.ke/2013/04/the-cunning-mediocrity-of-african.html (accessed 11 November 2017).
6. Elliott Green (2010), 'Patronage, district creation, and reform in Uganda', *Studies in Comparative International Development* 45, no. 1, pp. 83–103.
7. Goran Hyden and Colin Leys (1972), 'Elections and politics in single-party systems: the case of Kenya and Tanzania', *British Journal of Political Science* 2, no. 4, pp. 389–420.
8. Joel D. Barkan and Frank Holmquist (1989), 'Peasant–state relations and the social base of self-help in Kenya', *World Politics* 41, no. 3, pp. 359–80.
9. Jeffrey Conroy-Krutz and Carolyn Logan (2012), 'Museveni and the 2011 Uganda election: did the money matter?', *Journal of Modern African Studies* 50, no. 4, p. 625.
10. The 2011 election was less repressive than its predecessor, but nonetheless occurred in a context of intimidation of the kind discussed in chapter 3. For more on how this form of competitive authoritarian government works in Uganda see Aili Mari Tripp (2010), *Museveni's Uganda: Paradoxes of Power in a Hybrid Regime* (Boulder, CO: Lynne Rienner Publishers).
11. Shaheen Mozaffar and Andreas Schedler (2002), 'The comparative study of electoral governance: introduction', *International Political Science Review* 23, no. 1, pp. 5–27.
12. Michael Bratton (2008), 'Vote buying and violence in Nigerian election campaigns', *Electoral Studies* 27, no. 4, pp. 621–32.
13. Frederic Charles Schaffer (ed.) (2007), *Elections for Sale: The Causes and Consequences of Vote Buying* (Boulder, CO: Lynne Rienner Publishers).
14. Frederic Charles Schaffer (2002), 'Might cleaning up elections keep people away from the polls? Historical and comparative perspectives', *International Political Science Review* 23, no. 1, pp. 69–84.
15. Of course, other factors are also important, such as how competitive elections are and the funding arrangements of political parties.

16. Nic Cheeseman, Gabrielle Lynch and Justin Willis (2016), 'Ghana shows a troubling willingness to accept political corruption our survey shows', *Washington Post*, 21 December; available online at https://www.washingtonpost.com/news/monkey-cage/wp/2016/12/21/yes-ghana-had-a-peaceful-transfer-of-power-but-its-citizens-accept-some-troubling-practices-as-part-of-democracy (accessed 11 November 2017).
17. Philip Golingai (2017), 'Who's driving Sabah's election campaign?', *Star Malaysia*, 25 February; available online at https://www.pressreader.com/malaysia/the-star-malaysia/20170225/281762744030037 (accessed 11 November 2017).
18. Duncan McCargo (2008), 'Thailand: state of anxiety', *Southeast Asian Affairs*, pp. 333–56.
19. Abdi Latif Dahir (2017), 'Kenya is set to hold one of the most expensive elections in Africa', *Quartz Africa*, 18 July; available online at https://qz.com/1030958/kenyas-elections-will-cost-1-billion-in-government-and-campaign-spend (accessed 11 November 2017).
20. Erick Oduor (2017), 'Millions of dollars at play as Kenyans go into their most expensive election yet', *East African*, 22 May; available online at http://www.theeastafrican.co.ke/news/Millions-of-dollars-at-play-as-Kenyans-go-to-the-polls/2558-3937572-as8pr8/index.html (accessed 11 November 2017).
21. 'India's election campaign spending could touch $5bn', *National*, 11 March 2014; available online at https://www.thenational.ae/world/india-s-election-campaign-spending-could-touch-5bn-1.451206 (accessed 11 November 2017).
22. Nic Cheeseman, interview with aspriring female member of parliament, Accra, Ghana, August 2013.
23. Thad Beyle and Jennifer M. Jensen (2015), 'Gubernatorial elections, campaign costs and winning governors of 2014', Council of State Governments; available online at http://knowledgecenter.csg.org/kc/system/files/Beyle%20Jensen%202015.pdf (accessed 11 November 2017).
24. Nicolas van de Walle (2007), 'Meet the new boss, same as the old boss? The evolution of political clientelism in Africa', in Herbert Kitschelt and Steven I. Wilkinson (eds) (2007), *Patrons, Clients and Policies: Patterns of Democratic Accountability and Political Competition* (Cambridge University Press), pp. 50–67.
25. Charles Hornsby (1989), 'The social structure of the National Assembly in Kenya, 1963–83', *Journal of Modern African Studies* 27, no. 2, pp. 275–96.
26. Jamin Raskin and John Bonifaz (1994), 'The constitutional imperative and practical superiority of democratically financed elections', *Columbia Law Review* 94, no. 4, pp. 1160–203; Susan E. Scarrow, 'Political finance in comparative perspective' (2007), *Annual Review of Political Science* 10, pp. 193–210.
27. Erik Eckholm (2012), 'Tea Party favorite wins Texas runoff', *New York Times*, 31 July; available online at http://www.nytimes.com/2012/08/01/us/politics/cruz-defeats-dewhurst-for-gop-nomination-in-texas-senate-race.html (accessed 11 November 2017).
28. Edward L. Glaeser and Raven E. Saks (2006), 'Corruption in America', *Journal of Public Economics* 90, no. 6, pp. 1053–72.
29. Chris C. Ojukwu and J.O. Shopeju (2010), 'Elite corruption and the culture of primitive accumulation in 21st century Nigeria', *International Journal of Peace and Development Studies* 1, no. 2, pp. 15–24.

30. OSCE Office for Democratic Institutions and Human Rights (2017), 'Republic of Armenia: parliamentary elections, 2 April 2017 – OSCE/ODIHR Election Observation Mission final report'; available online at http://www.osce.org/odihr/328226?download=true (accessed 11 November 2017).
31. 'Armenia votes to curb presidential powers in disputed referendum', *Guardian*, 7 December 2015; available online at https://www.theguardian.com/world/2015/dec/07/armenia-vote-disputed-referendum-president-powers (accessed 11 November 2017).
32. 'RFE/RL reporter roughed up while investigating vote buying in Armenia', Radio Free Europe/Radio Liberty, 14 May 2017; available online at https://www.rferl.org/a/armenia-rferl-reporter-roughed-up-vote-buying/28487648.html (accessed 11 November 2017).
33. This alliance included three parties, namely Prosperous Armenia, the Alliance Party, and the Mission Party.
34. OSCE Office for Democratic Institutions and Human Rights (2017), 'Republic of Armenia: parliamentary elections, 2 April 2017'.
35. 'Vote buying played main part in Armenian elections, says expert', Mediamax, 3 July 2017; available online at http://www.mediamax.am/en/news/society/24160 (accessed 11 November 2017).
36. Andrew Reynolds, Ben Reilly and Andrew Ellis (2008), *Electoral System Design: The New International IDEA Handbook* (Stockholm: International Institute for Democracy and Electoral Assistance), pp. 67, 176.
37. Paul Collier and Pedro C. Vicente (2012), 'Violence, bribery, and fraud: the political economy of elections in sub-Saharan Africa', *Public Choice* 153, no. 1, pp. 117–47.
38. OSCE Office for Democratic Institutions and Human Rights (2017), 'Republic of Armenia: parliamentary elections, 2 April 2017'.
39. Although no one was successfully prosecuted, it seems clear that considerable vote buying took place. See 'Vote buying played main part in Armenian elections, says expert', Mediamax.
40. Leonardo Arriola (2018), 'Financial institutions: economic liberalisation, credit and opposition party successes', in Nic Cheeseman (ed.) (2008), *Institutions and Democracy in Africa: How the Rules of the Game Shape Political Developments* (Cambridge University Press), pp. 92–115.
41. Ibid.
42. Eric C.C. Chang (2005), 'Electoral incentives for political corruption under open-list proportional representation', *Journal of Politics* 67, no. 3, pp. 716–30; Cheeseman (2015), *Democracy in Africa*, pp. 59–65.
43. 'Malaysia PM Najib Razak used $700M donation to win 2013 elections: WSJ', CNBC, 28 December 2015; available online at http://www.cnbc.com/2015/12/28/wsj-reports-malaysia-pm-najib-razak-used-700m-donation-to-win-2013-elections.html (accessed 11 November 2017); Tom Wright and Bradley Hope (2015), '1MDB and the money network of Malaysian politics', *Wall Street Journal*, 28 December; available online at https://www.wsj.com/articles/the-money-network-of-malaysian-politics-1451355113?mod=e2tw (accessed 11 November 2017).
44. Laurence Whitehead (2002), *Democratization: Theory and Experience* (Oxford University Press).
45. The ruling party was named the National Revolutionary Party until 1946.

46. Wayne A. Cornelius (2004), 'Mobilized voting in the 2000 elections: the changing efficacy of vote buying and coercion in Mexican electoral politics', in Jorge I. Domínguez and Chappell H. Lawson (eds) (2004), *Mexico's Pivotal Democratic Election: Candidates, Voters, and the Presidential Campaign of 2000* (Stanford University Press), pp. 47–67, p. 48.
47. Beatriz Magaloni (2008), *Voting for Autocracy: Hegemonic Party Survival and Its Demise in Mexico* (Cambridge University Press), p. 12.
48. John Ross (2003), 'No blood for oil', *Latin American Press*, 8 May; available online at http://www.latinamericapress.org/articles.asp?item=1&art=3427 (accessed 15 December 2017).
49. Jacqueline Peschard (2006), 'Control over party and campaign finance in Mexico', *Mexican Studies/Estudios Mexicanos* 22, no. 1, p. 97.
50. Ibid.
51. For a full discussion of the election see Domínguez and Lawson (2004), *Mexico's Pivotal Democratic Election*. For a short summary of the results see Joseph L. Klesner, 'The end of Mexico's one-party regime', Kenyon College Blog, no date; available online at http://www2.kenyon.edu/Depts/PSci/Fac/klesner/apsa97_Table1.htm (accessed 15 December 2017).
52. For an interesting debate on this topic see Simeon Nichter (2008), 'Vote buying or turnout buying? Machine politics and the secret ballot', *American Political Science Review* 102, no. 1, pp. 19–31; Susan C. Stokes (2005), 'Perverse accountability: a formal model of machine politics with evidence from Argentina', *American Political Science Review* 99, no. 3, pp. 315–25.
53. Bruce Baker (2001), *Escape from Domination in Africa: Political Disengagement and Its Consequences* (Trenton, NJ: Africa World Press), pp. 44–73. For comparative data on Africa see the Afrobarometer, http://afrobarometer.org (accessed 11 November 2017).
54. For a good summary of the challenges facing legislatures, and the disappointment of voters when they fail to meet them, see Joel D. Barkan, Robert Mattes, Shaheen Mozaffar and Kimberly Smiddy (2010), 'The African Legislatures Project, first findings', CSSR Working Paper no. 277; available online at https://open.uct.ac.za/handle/11427/19858 (accessed 11 November 2017).
55. Staffan I. Lindberg (2010), 'What accountability pressures do MPs in Africa face and how do they respond? Evidence from Ghana', *Journal of Modern African Studies* 48, no. 1, pp. 117–42.
56. Cheeseman (2015), *Democracy in Africa*, pp. 62–5.
57. See the website of the African Legislatures Project (ALP), at the Center for Democratic Governance and Leadership, online at http://microsites.bridgew.edu/cdgl/african-legislatures-project-alp (accessed 15 November 2017).
58. See Barkan et al. (2010), 'The African Legislatures Project'.
59. Cheeseman (2015), *Democracy in Africa*, pp. 57–86.
60. Nahomi Ichino and Noah L. Nathan (2013), 'Do primaries improve electoral performance? Clientelism and intra-party conflict in Ghana', *American Journal of Political Science* 57, no. 2, pp. 428–41.
61. Frederic C. Schaffer and Andreas Schedler (2007), 'What is vote buying? Empirical evidence', in Schaffer (ed.), *Elections for Sale*, pp. 17–30; Simeon

Nichter (2014), 'Conceptualizing vote buying', *Electoral Studies* 35, pp. 315–27.

62. Cheeseman, Lynch and Willis (2016), 'Ghana shows a troubling willingness to accept political corruption'.
63. Nic Cheeseman, Gabrielle Lynch and Justin Willis (2017), 'Ghana: the ebbing power of incumbency', *Journal of Democracy* 28, no. 2, pp. 92–104.
64. Ichino and Nathan (2013), 'Do primaries improve electoral performance?'.
65. John Malott (2013), 'Malaysia elections: what happened and what it means', *Islamic Monthly*, 7 May 2013; available online at http://theislamicmonthly.com/malaysia-elections-what-happened-and-what-it-means (accessed 11 November 2017).
66. Mong Palatino (2013), 'Malaysia's election "tsunami"', *Diplomat*, 10 May 2013; available online at http://thediplomat.com/2013/05/malaysias-election-tsunami (accessed 15 November 2017).
67. Ibid.
68. The coalition comprised three parties: the PKR, DAP and PAS.
69. Jeremy Grant (2013), 'Malaysia: the value of cash handouts – vote buying or an economic boost?', *Financial Times: World Blog*, 3 May; available online at https://www.ft.com/content/8254152d-c957-3d45-8ec8-ee696c5b6b13?mhq5j=e1 (accessed 10 July 2017).
70. Bridget Welsh (2013), 'Malaysia's elections: a step backward', *Journal of Democracy* 24, no. 4, pp. 136–50.
71. Bridget Welsh (2013), 'Buying support: Najib's "commercialisation" of GE13', *Malaysiakini*, 23 April 2013.
72. Welsh (2013), 'Malaysia's elections: a step backward', pp. 136–50.
73. Ibid.
74. Nichter (2008), 'Vote buying or turnout buying?'.
75. Valeria Brusco, Marcelo Nazareno and Susan Carol Stokes (2004), 'Vote buying in Argentina', *Latin American Research Review* 39, no. 2, pp. 66–88; Miguel R. Rueda (2015), 'Buying votes with imperfect local knowledge and a secret ballot', *Journal of Theoretical Politics* 27, no. 3, pp. 428–56.
76. Samuel Kwadwo Boaten Asante and W.W. Asombang (1989), 'An independent Namibia? The future facing SWAPO', *Third World Quarterly* 11, no. 3, pp. 1–19.
77. John Hatchard and Peter Slinn (1991), 'Namibia: the constitutional path to freedom', *Commonwealth Law Bulletin* 17, no. 2, pp. 644–65.
78. Henning Melber (2003), *Re-examining Liberation in Namibia: Political Culture Since Independence* (Uppsala: Nordic Africa Institute).
79. Gretchen Bauer (2001), 'Namibia in the first decade of independence: how democratic?', *Journal of Southern African Studies* 27, no. 1, pp. 33–55.
80. The authors are grateful to Ian Cooper for bringing this to their attention.
81. Joshua Bernard Forrest (1992), 'A promising start: the inauguration and consolidation of democracy in Namibia', *World Policy Journal* 9, no. 4, pp. 739–53.
82. Kate Baldwin (2013), 'Why vote with the chief? Political connections and public goods provision in Zambia', *American Journal of Political Science* 57, no. 4, pp. 794–809.
83. Edward Goldring and Michael Wahman (2016), 'Democracy in reverse: the 2016 general election in Zambia', *Africa Spectrum* 51, no. 3, pp. 107–21.

84. Dan Paget (2014), 'Zambia: dominance won and lost', in Renske Doorenspleet and Laurens Nijzink (eds) (2014), *Party Systems and Democracy in Africa* (Basingstoke: Palgrave), pp. 148–67.
85. Karen E. Ferree and James D. Long (2016), 'Gifts, threats, and perceptions of ballot secrecy in African elections', *African Affairs* 115, no. 461, pp. 621–45.
86. Michael Bratton and Eldred Masunungure (2006), 'Popular reactions to state repression: Operation Murambatsvina in Zimbabwe', *African Affairs* 106, no. 422, pp. 21–45.
87. Tavishi Bhasin and Jennifer Gandhi (2013), 'Timing and targeting of state repression in authoritarian elections', *Electoral Studies* 32, no. 4, pp. 620–31.
88. Norma Kriger (2005), 'ZANU (PF) strategies in general elections, 1980–2000: discourse and coercion', *African Affairs* 104, no. 414, pp. 1–34, p. 16.
89. Roger Southall (2013), 'How and why ZANU–PF won the 2013 Zimbabwe elections', *Strategic Review for Southern Africa* 35, no. 2, pp. 135–51, p. 135.
90. 'Parties warned against vote-buying ahead of poll', ABC News, 18 April 2013; available online at http://www.abc.net.au/news/2013-04-18/an-watchdog-warns-malaysian-parties-against-vote-buying/4638204 (accessed 19 December 2017).
91. Schaffer (2002), 'Might cleaning up elections keep people away from the polls?'.
92. Malott (2013), 'Malaysia elections'.
93. Charlotte Alter (2014), 'Voter turnout in midterm elections hits 72-year low', *Time*, 10 November; available online at http://time.com/3576090/midterm-elections-turnout-world-war-two/ (accessed 15 December 2017).
94. James Dray (2010), 'Voter turnout in sub-Saharan Africa', unpublished DPhil thesis (University of Oxford).
95. Robert M. Stein and Greg Vonnahme (2008), 'Engaging the unengaged voter: vote centers and voter turnout', *Journal of Politics* 70, no. 2, pp. 487–97.
96. Dray (2010), 'Voter turnout in sub-Saharan Africa'.
97. Cheeseman (2015), *Democracy in Africa*, pp. 182–9.
98. Allen Hicken, Stephen Leider, Nico Ravanilla and Dean Yang (2013), 'Combating vote-selling: a field experiment in the Philippines', CESifo Area Conference on Behavioural Economics, October; available online at https://www.povertyactionlab.org/evaluation/combating-vote-selling-philippines (accessed 17 December 2017).
99. For examples see Paul Collier, P.C. Vicente and J.C. Aker (2011), 'Is information power? A study of voter education using cell phones in Mozambique (IGC Policy Brief)', DFID Briefing; available online at https://www.gov.uk/dfid-research-outputs/is-information-power-a-study-of-voter-education-using-cell-phones-in-mozambique-igc-policy-brief (accessed 15 November 2017); 'Facilitating parliament, voter education and electoral observation', USAID News Update, 18 October 2016; available online at https://www.usaid.gov/kyrgyz-republic/fact-sheets/facilitating-parliament-voter-education-and-election-observation (accessed 15 November 2017).

100. Pedro C. Vicente and Leonard Wantchekon (2009), 'Clientelism and vote buying: lessons from field experiments in African elections', *Oxford Review of Economic Policy* 25, no. 2, pp. 292–305, p. 292.
101. In many cases, voter education is partial and does not reach a majority of citizens. It also tends to be conducted fairly late. There is also a risk that voter education generates more cynical, and in some cases less democratic, votes. Michael Bratton and Daniel Posner (1998), 'A first look at second elections in Africa, with illustrations from Zambia', in Richard Joseph (ed.) (1998), *State, Conflict, and Democracy in Africa* (Boulder, CO: Lynne Rienner), pp. 377–407. For a more positive view on the impact of voter education see Pedro C. Vicente and Leonard Wantchekon (2009), 'Clientelism and vote buying: lessons from field experiments in African elections', *Oxford Review of Economic Policy* 25, no. 2, pp. 292–305.
102. Homer Lawrence Morris (1921), *Parliamentary Franchise Reform in England from 1885 to 1918* (New York: Longmans, Green & Company), p. 200.
103. Charles Seymour and Donald Paige Frary (1918), *How the World Votes: The Story of Democratic Development in Elections*, vol. 1 (Springfield, MA: C.A. Nichols), p. 141.
104. For a critical review that finds that the expansion of the middle class (more specifically, the introduction of the secret ballot) was a relevant factor in electoral reform in the United States see Jan Teorell, Daniel Ziblatt and Fabrice Lehoucq (2017), 'An introduction to special issue: the causes and consequences of secret ballot reform', *Comparative Political Studies* 50, no. 5, pp. 531–54. Nic Cheeseman is grateful to Halfdan Lynge-Mangueira for very helpful discussions on this topic.
105. Chester Lloyd Jones (1913), 'The rotten boroughs of New England', *North American Review* 197, no. 689, pp. 486–98; Christopher Kam (2009), 'Partisanship, enfranchisement, and the political economy of electioneering in the United Kingdom, 1826–1906', unpublished typescript, University of British Columbia, p. 19; Christopher Kam (2017), 'The secret ballot and the market for votes at 19th-century British elections', *Comparative Political Studies* 50, no. 5, pp. 594–635.
106. On the importance of pro-poor growth, and a definition of the term, see Nanak Kakwani and Ernesto M. Pernia (2000), 'What is pro-poor growth?', *Asian Development Review* 18, no. 1, pp. 1–16; Roberto Perotti (1996), 'Growth, income distribution, and democracy: what the data say', *Journal of Economic Growth* 1, no. 2, pp. 149–87.
107. Cheeseman (2015), *Democracy in Africa*, pp. 1–5.
108. Pascal Fletcher (2013), 'Africa's emerging middle class drives growth and development', Reuters, 10 May 2013; available online at http://www.reuters.com/article/us-africa-investment/africas-emerging-middle-class-drives-growth-and-democracy-idUSBRE9490DV20130510 (accessed 15 November 2017); Lee Jong-Wha (undated), 'The bright future of Asia's middle class', *Huffington Post*; available online at https://www.huffingtonpost.com/lee-jongwha/future-asia-middle-class_b_6928250.html (accessed 15 November 2017).
109. The most famous of these is Barrington Moore (1993), *Social Origins of Dictatorship and Democracy: Lord and Peasant in the Making of the Modern World* (Boston, MA: Beacon Press).

110. African Development Bank (2011), 'The middle of the pyramid: dynamics of the middle class in Africa', p. 1; available online at https://www.afdb.org/fileadmin/uploads/afdb/Documents/Publications/The%20Middle%20of%20the%20Pyramid_The%20Middle%20of%20the%20Pyramid.pdf (accessed 15 November 2017).
111. Nic Cheeseman (2015), ' "No bourgeoisie, no democracy"? The political attitudes of the Kenyan middle class', *Journal of International Development* 27, no. 5, pp. 647–64.
112. Ibid., p. 648.
113. Alvarez, Hall and Hyde (2008), *Election Fraud*.
114. Norad (2010), 'Democracy support through the United Nations, literature review: what have we learnt about donors' support for democratic development?' (Oslo: Norwegian Agency for Development Cooperation), p. 49; available online at https://www.oecd.org/derec/norway/48085855.pdf (accessed 15 November 2017).

3 Divide and rule: violence as a political strategy

1. Aldar Kusainov (2005), 'Kazakhstan: mysterious murder mars presidential election campaign', EurasiaNet, 13 November 2005; available online at http://www.eurasianet.org/departments/insight/articles/eav111405.shtml (accessed 16 November 2017).
2. Rico Isaacs (2010), ' "Papa": Nursultan Nazarbayev and the discourse of charismatic leadership and nation-building in post-Soviet Kazakhstan', *Studies in Ethnicity and Nationalism* 10, no. 3, pp. 435–52.
3. Tor Bukkvoll (2004), 'Astana's privatised independence: private and national interests in the foreign policy of Nursultan Nazarbayev', *Nationalities Papers* 32, no. 3, pp. 631–50.
4. 'From Astana to "Syriana"', *New Yorker*, 12 April 2011; available online at http://archives.newyorker.com/?i=2001-07-09#folio=048 (accessed 16 November 2017).
5. See, for example, Sebastien Peyrouse (2012), 'The Kazakh neopatrimonial regime: balancing uncertainties among the "family", oligarchs and technocrats', *Demokratizatsiya* 20, no. 4, p. 345.
6. Peter Baker (2002), 'As Kazakh scandal unfolds, Soviet-style reprisals begin', *Washington Post*, 11 June; available online at http://articles.chicagotribune.com/2002-06-11/news/0206110214_1_nursultan-nazarbayev-oil-rich-former-soviet-republic-soviet-union (accessed 16 November 2017).
7. Edward Schatz (2009), 'The soft authoritarian tool kit: agenda-setting power in Kazakhstan and Kyrgyzstan', *Comparative Politics* 41, no. 2, pp. 203–22.
8. OSCE Office for Democratic Institutions and Human Rights (2005), 'Kazakhstan: presidential election, 4 December 2005 – Needs Assessment Mission report'; available online at http://www.osce.org/odihr/elections/kazakhstan/16553 (accessed 16 November 2017).
9. Collier (2008), *Wars, Guns and Votes*, p. 2.
10. Mahmood Mamdani (2014), *When Victims Become Killers: Colonialism, Nativism, and the Genocide in Rwanda* (Princeton University Press).
11. See Herman Schwartz (2000), *The Struggle for Constitutional Justice in Post-Communist Europe* (University of Chicago Press); Grzegorz Ekiert

(2013), 'The illiberal challenge in post-communist europe', *Taiwan Journal of Democracy* 8, no. 2, pp. 63–78.

12. Peace Medie (2008), 'The police: laws, prosecutions and women's rights in Liberia', in Nic Cheeseman (ed.) (2008), *Institutions and Democracy in Africa* (Cambridge University Press), pp. 137–48.
13. For an early analysis see Joel G. Verner (1984), 'The independence of supreme courts in Latin America: a review of the literature', *Journal of Latin American Studies* 16, no. 2, pp. 463–506. For the Mexican case see Julio Ríos-Figueroa (2007), 'Fragmentation of power and the emergence of an effective judiciary in Mexico, 1994–2002', *Latin American Politics and Society* 49, no. 1, pp. 31–57. It is important to note that serious challenges remain. For a summary of these see William C. Prillaman (2000), *The Judiciary and Democratic Decay in Latin America: Declining Confidence in the Rule of Law* (Westport, CT: Greenwood Publishing Group).
14. For more information see the website of the International Crisis Group, online at https://www.crisisgroup.org (accessed 16 November 2017).
15. Emilie Hafner-Burton, Susan D. Hyde and Ryan S. Jablonski (2014), 'When do governments resort to election violence?', *British Journal of Political Science* 44, no. 1, pp. 149–79.
16. Steven Levitsky and Lucan A. Way (2006), 'Linkage versus leverage: rethinking the international dimension of regime change', *Comparative Politics* 38, no. 4, pp. 379–400; Steven Levitsky and Lucan Way (2005), 'International linkage and democratization', *Journal of Democracy* 16, no. 3, pp. 20–34.
17. William Reno (1995), *Corruption and State Politics in Sierra Leone* (Cambridge University Press).
18. For more information on the ICC see William A. Schabas (2011), *An Introduction to the International Criminal Court* (Cambridge University Press).
19. Nomazulu Thata (2016), 'Tribalism or ethnic disharmony retards Zimbabwe's development – Part 4.3', *Bulawayo 24 News*, 13 June; available online at http://bulawayo24.com/Opinion/Columnist/90143 (accessed 15 December 2017).
20. Klaas (2016), *The Despot's Accomplice.*
21. Neil DeVotta (2009), 'The Liberation Tigers of Tamil Eelam and the lost quest for separatism in Sri Lanka', *Asian Survey* 49, no. 6, pp. 1021–51.
22. Centre for Monitoring Election Violence (CMEV) (undated), 'Election violence in Sri Lanka'; available online at https://cmev.org (accessed 16 November 2017).
23. Ibid.
24. 'Sri Lanka pre-election attack leaves one person dead', BBC News, 12 January 2010; available online at http://news.bbc.co.uk/1/hi/8454285.stm (accessed 16 November 2017).
25. 'Violence flares before Sri Lankan election', ABC News, 23 January 2010; available online at http://www.abc.net.au/am/content/2010/s2799549.htm (accessed 16 November 2017); 'Tiran Alles residence comes under grenade attack', TamilNet, 22 January 2010; available online at https://www.tamilnet.com/art.html?catid=13&artid=31033 (accessed 16 November 2017).
26. Commonwealth Secretariat (2010), 'Report of the Commonwealth Expert Team: Sri Lanka presidential election'; available online at http://reliefweb.int/sites/reliefweb.int/files/resources/96C7C3124913DE58852576CB0064E67B-Full_Report.pdf (accessed 17 November 2017).

27. Ibid.
28. Ibid.
29. Lanka Election (2013), 'Sri Lankan presidential election'; available online at http://www.lankaelection.com/presidential_election/2010/ (accessed 15 December 2017).
30. Centre for Monitoring Election Violence (CMEV) (undated), 'Election violence in Sri Lanka'; available online at https://cmev.org (accessed 16 November 2017).
31. John Hickman (2009), 'Is electoral violence effective? Evidence from Sri Lanka's 2005 presidential election', *Contemporary South Asia* 17, no. 4, pp. 429–35.
32. CTV News (2012), '22 murders in 2 months connected to Brazilian municipal elections: report', 3 September; available online at https://www.ctvnews.ca/world/22-murders-in-2-months-connected-to-brazilian-municipal-elections-report-1.940948 (accessed 15 December 2017).
33. Teresa P.R. Caldeira and James Holston (1999), 'Democracy and violence in Brazil', *Comparative Studies in Society and History* 41, no. 4, pp. 691–729.
34. Hannah Stone (2011), 'Drug gangs cast shadow over Guatemala campaign funding', InSight Crime, 6 September; available online at http://www.insightcrime.org/news-analysis/drug-gangs-cast-shadow-over-guatemala-campaign-funding (accessed 16 November 2017).
35. ACE Electoral Knowledge Network, 'Case study of electoral violence in Guatemala'; available online at http://aceproject.org/ace-en/focus/elections-and-security/case-study-electoral-violence-in-guatemala (accessed 16 November 2017).
36. International Crisis Group (2011), 'Guatemala: drug trafficking and violence', 2011 Briefing; available online at https://www.crisisgroup.org/latin-america caribbean/central-america/guatemala/guatemala-drug-trafficking-and-violence (accessed 11 November 2017).
37. Anna-Claire Bevan (2011), 'Politics is a death sentence in Guatemala', *New Internationalist*, 7 July; available online at https://newint.org/blog/2011/07/07/guatemala-election-violence (accessed 16 November 2017).
38. International Crisis Group (2011), 'Guatemala: drug trafficking and violence'.
39. 'Mayor in Russia sent to prison for corruption', Associated Press, 3 August 2016; available online at http://www.dailymail.co.uk/wires/ap/article-3721275/Mayor-Russia-sent-prison-corruption.html (accessed 16 November 2017).
40. 'Russian mayor who left ruling party arrested on corruption charges', Radio Free Europe/Radio Liberty, 3 July 2013; available online at https://www.rferl.org/a/yaroslavl-urlashov-arrest-putin/25035230.html (accessed 16 November 2017).
41. 'Once Russian opposition's hope, ex-Yaroslavl mayor gets lengthy jail sentence', Radio Free Europe/Radio Liberty, 3 August 2016; available online at at https://www.rferl.org/a/russia-yaroslavl-mayor-jailed-bribery/27897703.html (accessed 16 November 2017).
42. David M. Herszenhorn (2013), 'Russian mayor, an opposition figure, is arrested', *New York Times*, 3 July; available online at http://www.nytimes.com/2013/07/04/world/europe/russian-mayor-an-opposition-figure-is-arrested.html (accessed 16 November 2017).

43. Lawrence P. Markowitz (2012), 'Tajikistan: authoritarian reaction in a postwar state', *Democratization* 19, no. 1, pp. 98–119.
44. Cholpon Orozobekova (2016), 'Tajikistan? The iron first closes', *The Diplomat*, 8 June; available online at https://thediplomat.com/2016/06/tajikistan-the-iron-fist-closes/ (accessed 16 December 2017).
45. Human Rights Watch (2013), 'Tajikistan: end crackdown ahead of election'; available online at https://www.hrw.org/news/2013/10/21/tajikistan-end-crackdown-ahead-election (accessed 16 November 2017).
46. Ibid.
47. Ibid.
48. Freedom House (2014), 'Nations in transit 2014: Tajikistan'; available online at https://freedomhouse.org/report/nations-transit/2014/Tajikistan (accessed 16 November 2017).
49. Human Rights Watch (2012), 'Tajikistan: rights group forced to close', 25 October; available online at https://www.hrw.org/news/2012/10/25/tajikistan-rights-group-forced-close (15 December 2017).
50. Freedom House (2013), 'Freedom in the world 2013: Tajikistan'; available online at https://freedomhouse.org/report/freedom-world/2013/Tajikistan (accessed 16 November 2017).
51. Shahram Akbarzadeh (2006), 'Geopolitics versus democracy in Tajikistan', *Demokratizatsiya* 14, no. 4, pp. 563–78, p. 563.
52. Daniel Branch and Nic Cheeseman (2008), 'Democratization, sequencing, and state failure in Africa: lessons from Kenya', *African Affairs* 108, no. 430, pp. 1–26.
53. Jacqueline M. Klopp and Elke Zuern (2007), 'The politics of violence in democratization: lessons from Kenya and South Africa', *Comparative Politics* 39, no. 2, pp. 127–46.
54. Stephen Brown (2001), 'Authoritarian leaders and multiparty elections in Africa: how foreign donors help to keep Kenya's Daniel arap Moi in power', *Third World Quarterly* 22, no. 5, pp. 725–39.
55. Branch and Cheeseman (2008), 'Democratization, sequencing, and state failure in Africa'.
56. Mueller (2008), 'The political economy of Kenya's crisis'.
57. For a theoretically rich discussion of how this mobilization occurred see Catherine Boone (2011), 'Politically allocated land rights and the geography of electoral violence: the case of Kenya in the 1990s', *Comparative Political Studies* 44, no. 10, pp. 1311–42.
58. Ibid.
59. Joel D. Barkan (1993), 'Kenya: lessons from a flawed election', *Journal of Democracy* 4, no. 3, pp. 85–99.
60. Kenya Human Rights Commission (2009), 'Surviving after torture: a case digest on the struggle for justice by torture survivors in Kenya'; available online at http://resource.khrc.or.ke:8181/khrc/bitstream/handle/123456789/83/HUMAN%20RIGHTS%20REPORT-VOLUME%201%20NUMBER%203.pdf?sequence=1 (accessed 16 November 2017).
61. Susanne D. Mueller (2011), 'Dying to win: elections, political violence, and institutional decay in Kenya', *Journal of Contemporary African Studies* 29, no. 1, pp. 99–117; Kenyan Commission of Inquiry into Post Election Violence (2008), 'Report of the Commission of Inquiry into Post-Election Violence (CIPEV)'; available online at https://searchworks.stanford.edu/

view/7911942 (accessed 16 November 2017); Human Rights Watch (1993), 'State-sponsored ethnic violence in Kenya'; available online at https://www.hrw.org/report/1993/11/01/divide-and-rule-state-sponsored-ethnic-violence-kenya (accessed 16 November 2017).

62. David W. Throup and Charles Hornsby (1998), *Multi-Party Politics in Kenya: The Kenyatta and Moi States and the Triumph of the System in the 1992 Election* (London: James Currey), p. 93.
63. Cheeseman (2015), *Democracy in Africa*, pp. 185–6.
64. Walter O. Oyugi (1997), 'Ethnicity in the electoral process: the 1992 general elections in Kenya', *African Journal of Political Science/Revue Africaine de Science Politique* 2, no. 1, pp. 41–69, pp. 49–53.
65. Maurice N. Amutabi (2009), 'Beyond imperial presidency in Kenya: interrogating the Kenyatta, Moi and Kibaki regimes and implications for democracy and development', *Kenya Studies Review* 1, no. 1, p. 64.
66. Throup and Hornsby (1998), *Multi-Party Politics in Kenya*, pp. 142–60.
67. UNHCR, 'Kenya: aftermath of the elections', 15 March 2007; available online at http://archive.li/yTK7O (accessed 15 December 2017).
68. One of the classic discussions of anti-colonial political organization is provided by Thomas L. Hodgkin (1956), *Nationalism in Colonial Africa* (London: Muller).
69. Cherry J. Gertzel and Morris Szeftel (1984), *The Dynamics of the One-Party State in Zambia* (Manchester University Press); Jan Pettman (1974), 'Zambia's second republic: the establishment of a one-party state', *Journal of Modern African Studies* 12, no. 2, pp. 231–44.
70. Gwendolen Margaret Carter and Charles F. Gallagher (eds) (1962), *African One-Party States*, vol. 2, no. 2 (Ithaca, NY: Cornell University Press).
71. This section draws heavily on Cheeseman (2015), *Democracy in Africa*, chapter 5.
72. Peter Uvin (1999), 'Ethnicity and power in Burundi and Rwanda: different paths to mass violence', *Comparative Politics* 31, no. 3, pp. 253–71.
73. Scott Straus (2013), *The Order of Genocide: Race, Power, and War in Rwanda* (Ithaca, NY: Cornell University Press), pp. 197–9.
74. Alison Des Forges (1999), 'Leave none to tell their story: genocide in Rwanda' (New York: Human Rights Watch), p. 54.
75. Christine L. Kellow and H. Leslie Steeves (1998), 'The role of radio in the Rwandan genocide', *Journal of Communication* 48, no. 3, pp. 107–28.
76. A number of other international governments have been criticized for being slow to respond, including the United States, but the French appear to have been the most complicit in the genocide itself. See Daniela Kroslak (2007), *The Role of France in the Rwandan Genocide* (London: Hurst & Co.); Stephen D. Goose and Frank Smyth (1994), 'Arming genocide in Rwanda', *Foreign Affairs* 75, no. 5, pp. 86–96.
77. Cheeseman (2015), *Democracy in Africa*, pp. 157–62.
78. Des Forges (1999), 'Leave none to tell their story', p. 54.
79. Ibid.
80. Peter Robinson and Golriz Ghahraman (2008), 'Can Rwandan President Kagame be held responsible at the ICTR for the killing of President Habyarimana?', *Journal of International Criminal Justice* 6, no. 5, pp. 981–94; René Lemarchand (1995), 'Rwanda: the rationality of genocide', *African Issues* 23, no. 2, pp. 8–11.

81. Linda Melvern (2006), *Conspiracy to Murder: The Rwandan Genocide* (London: Verso), pp. 44–6.
82. Kriger (2005), 'ZANU (PF) strategies in general elections, 1980–2000'.
83. Cheeseman and Tendi (2010), 'Power-sharing in comparative perspective'.
84. Ian Scoones (2015), 'Zimbabwe's land reform: new political dynamics in the countryside', *Review of African Political Economy* 42, no. 144, pp. 190–205; for a longer treatment see Charles Laurie and Stephen Chan (2016), *The Land Reform Deception: Political Opportunism in Zimbabwe's Land Seizure Era* (Oxford University Press).
85. Jocelyn Alexander, Joanne McGregor and Terence Osborn Ranger (2000), *Violence and Memory: One Hundred Years in the 'Dark Forests' of Matabeleland, Zimbabwe* (Melton: Heinemann and James Currey).
86. Terence Ranger (2004), 'Nationalist historiography, patriotic history and the history of the nation: the struggle over the past in Zimbabwe', *Journal of Southern African Studies* 30, no. 2, pp. 215–34.
87. Blessing-Miles Tendi (2010), *Making History in Mugabe's Zimbabwe: Politics, Intellectuals, and the Media* (New York: Peter Lang), p. 2.
88. Ibid.
89. Cheeseman (2015), *Democracy in Africa,* pp. 161–2.
90. Michael Bratton and Eldred Masunungure (2008), 'Zimbabwe's long agony', *Journal of Democracy* 19, no. 4, pp. 41–55.
91. Nic Cheeseman (2008), 'The Kenyan elections of 2007: an introduction', *Journal of Eastern African Studies* 2, no. 2, pp. 166–84.
92. Susanne D. Mueller (2014), 'Kenya and the International Criminal Court (ICC): politics, the election and the law', *Journal of Eastern African Studies* 8, no. 1, pp. 25–42.
93. Nic Cheeseman, Gabrielle Lynch and Justin Willis (2014), 'Democracy and its discontents: understanding Kenya's 2013 elections', *Journal of Eastern African Studies* 8, no. 1, pp. 2–24.
94. It is important to note that violence related to political competition resulted in around 500 deaths in the Tana River area, but these occurred in advance of the election and were not co-ordinated by national political leaders in the manner of the 2007/8 clashes. Lynch, Cheeseman and Willis (forthcoming), 'The violence of electoral peace'.
95. Branch and Cheeseman (2008), 'Democratization, sequencing, and state failure in Africa'.
96. Evelyn Kwamboka (2011), 'Lawyers battle claims of Kalenjin "networks"', *Standard*, 8 September; available online at https://www.standardmedia.co.ke/business/article/2000042419/lawyers-battle-claims-of-kalenjin-network (accessed 16 November 2017); Gabrielle Lynch (2014), 'Electing the "alliance of the accused": the success of the Jubilee Alliance in Kenya's Rift Valley', *Journal of Eastern African Studies* 8, no. 1, pp. 93–114.
97. Cheeseman, personal correspondence with Kenyan scholars, June and July 2012.
98. Veritas (2013), 'ZESN 2013 advance harmonised election report'; available online at http://www.veritaszim.net/node/926 (accessed 16 November 2017).
99. Freedom House (2013), 'Freedom in the world 2013: Zimbabwe'; available online at https://freedomhouse.org/report/freedom-world/2013/zimbabwe (accessed 16 November 2017).

100. André Mbata Mangu (2014), 'The African Union and the promotion of democracy and good political governance under the African Peer-Review Mechanism: 10 years on', *Africa Review* 6, no. 1, pp. 59–72, p. 69.
101. 'Full AU election observer mission report', *New Zimbabwe*, 1 November 2013; available online at http://www.newzimbabwe.com/opinion-12875-Full+AU+election+observer+mission+report/opinion.aspx (accessed 16 November 2017).
102. Michael Bratton (2008), 'Vote buying and violence in Nigerian election campaigns', *Electoral Studies* 27, no. 4, pp. 621–32; Alejandro Trelles and Miguel Carreras (2012), 'Bullets and votes: violence and electoral participation in Mexico', *Journal of Politics in Latin America* 4, no. 2, pp. 89–123.
103. Emilie M. Hafner-Burton, Susan D. Hyde and Ryan S. Jablonski (2016), 'Surviving elections: election violence, incumbent victory and post-election repercussions', *British Journal of Political Science*, DOI: 10.1017/S000712341600020X, pp. 1–30.
104. Dawn Brancati and Jack L. Snyder (2013), 'Time to kill: the impact of election timing on postconflict stability', *Journal of Conflict Resolution* 57, no. 5, pp. 822–53.
105. Jane Duncan (2014), *The Rise of the Securocrats: The Case of South Africa* (Auckland Park: Jacana Media (Pty) Ltd).
106. Cheeseman (2015), *Democracy in Africa*, p. 117.
107. Human Rights Watch (2012), ' "Tell them that I want to kill them": two decades of impunity in Hun Sen's Cambodia'; available online at https://www.hrw.org/report/2012/11/13/tell-them-i-want-kill-them/two-decades-impunity-hun-sens-cambodia (accessed 16 November 2017).
108. Human Rights Watch (2015), '30 years of Hun Sen: violence, repression, and corruption in Cambodia'; available online at https://www.hrw.org/report/2015/01/12/30-years-hun-sen/violence-repression-and-corruption-cambodia (accessed 16 November 2017).
109. International Republican Institute (1999), 'Kingdom of Cambodia parliamentary elections: July 26, 1998 – observation report'; available online at http://www.iri.org/sites/default/files/fields/field_files_attached/resource/cambodias_1998_national_assembly_elections.pdf (accessed 16 November 2017).
110. Ibid., p. 6.
111. Eli Lake (2017), 'Thank Trump for enforcing Obama's "red line" in Syria', *Bloomberg View*, 7 April; available online at https://www.bloomberg.com/view/articles/2017-04-07/thank-trump-for-enforcing-obama-s-red-line-in-syria (accessed 16 November 2017).
112. John Irish (2017), 'French Intelligence says Assad carried out sarin attack', Reuters, 26 April; available online at https://www.reuters.com/article/us-mideast-crisis-syria-intelligence/french-intelligence-says-assad-forces-carried-out-sarin-attack-idUSKBN17S0RY (15 December 2017).
113. Luke Harding (2017), '"It had a big impact on me" – story behind Trump's whirlwind missile response', *Guardian*, 7 April; available online at https://www.theguardian.com/world/2017/apr/07/how-pictures-of-syrias-dead-babies-made-trump-do-unthinkable (accessed 16 November 2017).
114. Zoya Sheftalovich (2017), 'Boris Johnson: "no doubt" Assad behind Syria sarin gas attack', *Politico*, 30 June; available online at http://www.

politico.eu/article/boris-johnson-no-doubt-assad-behind-syria-sarin-gas-attack (accessed 16 November 2017).

115. David Smith (2017), 'As warplanes return to scene of attack, Trump defends missile launch', *Guardian*, 9 April; available online at https://www.theguardian.com/world/2017/apr/08/syria-khan-sheikun-sarin-attack-strike-trump-views-unclear (accessed 16 November 2017).
116. Bruce Broomhall (2003), *International Justice and the International Criminal Court: Between Sovereignty and the Rule of Law* (Oxford University Press), pp. 5–10.
117. Chris Mahony (2010), *The Justice Sector Afterthought: Witness Protection in Africa* (Tshwane: Institute for Security Studies); available online at https://oldsite.issafrica.org/siteimages/WitnessProt.pdf (accessed 16 November 2017).
118. BBC News (2013), 'Claims of witnesses in Kenya ICC trial "disappearing"', 8 February; available online at http://www.bbc.co.uk/news/world-africa-21382339 (accessed 17 December 2017).
119. Cenap Çakmak (2017), *A Brief History of International Criminal Law and International Criminal Court* (London: Palgrave), pp. 213–38; Adam Branch (2004), 'International justice, local injustice', *Dissent* 51, no. 3, pp. 22–6.
120. Abel Escribà-Folch and Joseph Wright (2010), 'Dealing with tyranny: international sanctions and the survival of authoritarian rulers', *International Studies Quarterly* 54, no. 2, pp. 335–59.
121. Adam Branch (2011), 'Neither liberal nor peaceful? Practices of "global justice" by the ICC', in Susanna Campbell, David Chandler and Meera Sabaratnam (eds), *A Liberal Peace? The Problems and Practices of Peacebuilding* (New York: Zed Books), pp. 121–38.
122. Tor Krever (2016), 'Africa in the dock: on ICC bias', *Critical Legal Thinking*, 30 October; available online at http://criticallegalthinking.com/2016/10/30/africa-in-the-dock-icc-bias (accessed 16 November 2017).
123. Ed Cropley (2016), 'ICC's toughest trial: Africa vs. "Infamous Caucasian Court"', Reuters, 28 October; available online at http://www.reuters.com/article/us-africa-icc-idUSKCN12S1U3 (accessed 16 November 2017).

4 Hack the election: Fake news and the digital frontier

1. Jordan Robertson, Michael Riley and Andrew Willis (2016), 'How to hack an election', *Bloomberg Businessweek*, 31 March; available online at https://www.bloomberg.com/features/2016-how-to-hack-an-election (accessed 16 November 2017).
2. Ibid.
3. Jonathan Watts and David Agren (2016), 'Hacker claims he helped Enrique Peña Nieto win Mexican presidential election', *Guardian*, 1 April; available online at https://www.theguardian.com/world/2016/mar/31/mexico-presidential-election-enrique-pena-nieto-hacking (accessed 17 November 2017).
4. Betsy Woodruff, Ben Collins, Kevin Poulsen and Spencer Ackerman (2017), 'Trump campaign staffers pushed Russian propaganda days before the election', *Daily Beast*, 18 October; available online at https://www.

thedailybeast.com/trump-campaign-staffers-pushed-russian-propaganda-days-before-the-election (accessed 16 November 2017).

5. Ben Collins, Gideon Resnick, Kevin Poulson and Spencer Ackerman (2017), 'Exclusive: Russians appear to use Facebook to push Trump rallies in 17 U.S. cities', *Daily Beast*, 20 September; available online at https://www.thedailybeast.com/russians-appear-to-use-facebook-to-push-pro-trump-flash-mobs-in-florida (accessed 17 December 2017).
6. Some authors have suggested that media outlets operating in a free environment should refuse to publish hacked material, to minimize its impact. See, for example: Nathaniel A.G. Zelinsky (2017), 'Foreign cyber attacks and the American press: why the media must stop reprinting hacked material', *Yale Law Journal* 127, pp. 286–314.
7. Statistics for international penetration can be found at Internet World Stats: Usage and Population Statistics (2017), online at http://www.internetworldstats.com/stats.htm (accessed 16 November 2017).
8. For more information on CyberBerkut see Elina Lange-Ionatamishvili and Sanda Svetoka (2015), 'Strategic communication and social media in the Russia Ukraine conflict', in Kenneth Geers (ed.) (2015), *Cyber War in Perspective: Russian Aggression against Ukraine* (Tallinn: NATO CCD COE Publications), pp. 103–11.
9. Andy Greenberg (2017), 'Everything we know about Russia's election-hacking playbook', *Wired*, 6 September; available online at https://www.wired.com/story/russia-election-hacking-playbook (accessed 17 November 2017).
10. Sam Bright (2017), 'After Trump, "big data" firm Cambridge Analytica is now working in Kenya', BBC News, 3 August; available online at http://www.bbc.co.uk/news/blogs-trending-40792078 (accessed 15 December 2017).
11. For a critique on the over-embracing of the notion of 'Twitter revolutions' see Jared Keller (2010), 'Evaluating Iran's Twitter "revolution"', *Atlantic*, 18 June; available online at https://www.theatlantic.com/technology/archive/2010/06/evaluating-irans-twitter-revolution/58337 (accessed 16 November 2017).
12. For further discussion of this see William J. Dobson (2012), *The Dictator's Learning Curve: Inside the Global Battle for Democracy* (New York: Random House); and Klaas (2016), *The Despot's Accomplice*.
13. 'Fake news is damaging public confidence and social media companies need to do more', Creativepool, 1 June 2017; available online at https://creativepool.com/magazine/socialmedia/fake-news-is-damaging-public-confidence-and-social-media-companies-need-to-do-more.14440 (accessed 16 November 2017).
14. Bryan Naylor (2017), 'Intelligence chiefs, "stand more resolutely" behind finding of Russia election hacking', NPR, 5 January; available online at http://www.npr.org/2017/01/05/508355408/intelligence-chiefs-stand-more-resolutely-behind-finding-of-russia-election-hack (accessed 16 November 2017).
15. Samanth Subramanian (2017), 'Inside the Macedonian fake-news complex', *Wired*, 15 February; available online at https://www.wired.com/2017/02/veles-macedonia-fake-news (accessed 16 November 2017).
16. For a debunking story about this fake news see Shawn Rice (2017), 'Pope Francis forbidding Catholics from voting for Hillary Clinton is a hoax',

Business 2 Community, 21 October; available online at https://www.business2community.com/us-news/pope-francis-forbidding-catholics-voting-hillary-clinton-hoax-01686561 (15 December 2017).

17. Ibid. See also Alexander Smith and Vladimir Banic (2016), 'Fake news: how a partying Macedonian teen earns thousands publishing lies', NBC News, 9 December; available online at http://www.nbcnews.com/news/world/fake-news-how-partying-macedonian-teen-earns-thousands-publishing-lies-n692451.
18. Jeremy B. White (2017), 'Facebook says 126 million Americans may have been exposed to Russia-linked US election posts', *Independent*, 31 October; available online at http://www.independent.co.uk/news/world/americas/us-politics/facebook-russia-adverts-americans-exposed-trump-us-election-2016-millions-a8028526.html (accessed 15 December 2017).
19. Andrew Higgins, Mike McIntire and Gabriel J.X. Dance (2016), 'Inside a fake news sausage factory: "this is all about income"', *New York Times*, 25 November; available online at https://www.nytimes.com/2016/11/25/world/europe/fake-news-donald-trump-hillary-clinton-georgia.html (accessed 16 November 2017).
20. Laura Sydell (2016), 'We tracked down a fake-news creator in the suburbs. Here's what we learned', NPR, 23 November; available online at http://www.npr.org/sections/alltechconsidered/2016/11/23/503146770/npr-finds-the-head-of-a-covert-fake-news-operation-in-the-suburbs (accessed 16 November 2017).
21. Estimating the precise impact of fake news is extremely difficult, in part because the secret ballot means that we have to take people's word for how they voted – and we know that some people disguise their preferences. The following articles do not make the claim that fake news changes the way that people vote on a sufficient scale to change an election outcome, but they do demonstrate the spread of fake news and its impact on the beliefs of recipients. Meital Balmas (2014), 'When fake news becomes real: combined exposure to multiple news sources and political attitudes of inefficacy, alienation, and cynicism', *Communication Research* 41, no. 3, pp. 430–54; Hunt Allcott and Matthew Gentzkow, 'Social media and fake news in the 2016 election', *Journal of Economic Perspectives* 31, no. 2, pp. 211–36.
22. Allcott and Gentzkow (2017), 'Social media and fake news'.
23. Craig Silverman (2016), 'This analysis shows how viral fake election news stories outperformed real news on Facebook', BuzzFeed News, 16 November; available online at https://www.buzzfeed.com/craigsilverman/viral-fake-election-news-outperformed-real-news-on-facebook (accessed 16 November 2017).
24. Allcott and Gentzkow (2017), 'Social media and fake news'.
25. 'Donald Trump tax records show he could have avoided taxes for nearly two decades, The Times found', *New York Times*, 1 October 2017; available online at https://www.nytimes.com/2016/10/02/us/politics/donald-trump-taxes.html (15 December 2017).
26. Hannah Ritchie (2016), 'Read the biggest fake news stories of 2016', CNBC News, 30 December; available online at https://www.cnbc.com/2016/12/30/read-all-about-it-the-biggest-fake-news-stories-of-2016.html (accessed 16 November 2017).
27. Sarah Wheaton (2016), 'Trump not convinced of Russian hacking', *Politico*, 26 September; available online at http://www.politico.com/story/

2016/09/trump-debate-russia-hacking-228737 (accessed 16 November 2017).

28. See Peter Pomerantsev (2015), 'The Kremlin's information war', *Journal of Democracy* 26, no. 4, pp. 40–50.
29. Massimo Calabresi (2017), 'Inside Russia's social media war on America', *Time*, 18 May; available online at http://time.com/4783932/inside-russia-social-media-war-america (accessed 16 November 2017).
30. Alessandro Bessi and Emilio Ferrara (2016), 'Social bots distort the 2016 US presidential election online discussion', *First Monday* 21, no. 11; available online at at http://firstmonday.org/ojs/index.php/fm/article/view/7090/5653 (accessed 16 November 2017).
31. Steve Tesich (1992), 'A government of lies', *Nation* 254, no. 1, pp. 12–14.
32. 'Oxford Dictionaries Word of the Year 2016 is . . .', Oxford Dictionaries, 16 November 2016; available online at https://www.oxforddictionaries.com/press/news/2016/12/11/WOTY-16 (accessed 16 November 2017).
33. Richard Kreitner (2016), 'Post-truth and its consequences: what a 25-year-old essay tells us about the current moment', *Nation*, 30 November; available online at https://www.thenation.com/article/post-truth-and-its-consequences-what-a-25-year-old-essay-tells-us-about-the-current-moment (accessed 16 November 2017).
34. For further discussion on the North Korean personality cult see Daniel Byman and Jennifer Lind (2010), 'Pyongyang's survival strategy: tools of authoritarian control in North Korea', *International Security* 35, no. 1, pp. 44–74.
35. See, for example, Steven Heydemann and Reinoud Leenders (eds) (2013), *Middle East Authoritarianisms: Governance, Contestation, and Regime Resilience in Syria and Iran* (Stanford University Press); and Lisa Wedeen (1998), 'Acting "as if": symbolic politics and social control in Syria', *Comparative Studies in Society and History* 40, no. 3, pp. 503–23.
36. 'China invents the digital totalitarian state', *The Economist*, 17 December 2016; available online at https://www.economist.com/news/briefing/21711902-worrying-implications-its-social-credit-project-china-invents-digital-totalitarian (accessed 16 November 2017).
37. Lucy Hornby (2017), 'China changes tack on "social credit" scheme plan', *Financial Times*, 4 July; available online at https://www.ft.com/content/f772a9ce-60c4-11e7-91a7-502f7ee26895 (accessed 16 November 2017).
38. Nathan VanderKlippe (2015), 'China seeks to export its vision of the internet', *Globe and Mail*, 1 January; available online at https://beta.theglobeandmail.com/report-on-business/international-business/china-seeks-to-export-its-vision-of-the-internet/article22269080 (accessed 16 November 2017); David Rohde (2011), 'China's newest export: internet censorship', Reuters, 17 November; available online at http://blogs.reuters.com/david-rohde/2011/11/17/chinas-newest-export-internet-censorship (accessed 16 November 2017).
39. Jaclyn Kerr (2014), 'The digital dictator's dilemma: internet regulation and political control in non-democratic states', Center for International Security and Cooperation (CISAC), Stanford University Social Science Seminar Series, 16 October; available online at http://cisac.fsi.stanford.edu/sites/default/files/kerr_-_cisac_seminar_-_oct_2014_-_digital_dictators_dilemma.pdf (accessed 18 January 2018).

40. Kaveh Waddell (2016), 'Why some people think a typo cost Clinton the election', *Atlantic*, 13 December; available online at https://www.theatlantic.com/technology/archive/2016/12/why-some-people-think-a-typo-cost-clinton-the-election/510572 (accessed 16 November 2017).
41. Russell Brandom (2016), 'The phishing email that hacked the account of John Podesta', CBS News, 28 October; available online at http://www.cbsnews.com/news/the-phishing-email-that-hacked-the-account-of-john-podesta (accessed 16 November 2017).
42. Eric Lipton, David Sanger and Scott Shane (2016), 'The perfect weapon: how Russian cyberpower invaded the US', *New York Times*, 13 December; available online at https://www.nytimes.com/2016/12/13/us/politics/russia-hack-election-dnc.html (accessed 16 November 2017).
43. William M. Arkin, Ken Dilanian and Cynthia McFadden (2016), 'US officials: Putin personally involved in US election hack', NBC News, 15 December; available online at https://www.nbcnews.com/news/us-news/u-s-officials-putin-personally-involved-u-s-election-hack-n696146 (accessed 17 November 2017).
44. Sam Thielman (2016), 'FBI and Homeland Security detail Russian hacking campaign in new report', *Guardian*, 29 December; available online at https://www.theguardian.com/technology/2016/dec/29/fbi-dhs-russian-hacking-report (accessed 16 November 2017).
45. 'US intel report identifies Russians who gave emails to WikiLeaks – officials', Reuters, 6 January 2017; available online at http://www.reuters.com/article/us-usa-russia-cyber-celebrate-idUSKBN14P2NI (accessed 16 November 2017).
46. Aaron Sharockman (2016), 'It's true: WikiLeaks dumped Podesta emails hour after Trump video surfaced', PolitiFact, 18 December; available online at http://www.politifact.com/truth-o-meter/statements/2016/dec/18/john-podesta/its-true-wikileaks-dumped-podesta-emails-hour-afte (accessed 16 November 2017).
47. See, for example: Carol Lee and Julia Ainsley (2017), 'Focus on Flynn, Trump timeline suggests obstruction is on Mueller's mind', NBC News, 11 December; available online at https://www.nbcnews.com/news/us-news/18-crucial-days-what-did-president-know-when-did-he-n828261 (accessed 18 December 2017).
48. Eli Watkins and Marshall Cohen (2017), 'As Russia probe looms, Roger Stone touts relationship to WikiLeaks', CNN, 15 March; available online at http://edition.cnn.com/2017/03/10/politics/roger-stone-wikileaks-russia/index.html (accessed 16 November 2017).
49. Alan Yuhas (2017), 'Roger Stone claims he has "perfectly legal back channel" to Julian Assange', *Guardian*, 5 March; available online at https://www.theguardian.com/us-news/2017/mar/05/roger-stone-trump-adviser-julian-assange (accessed 16 November 2017).
50. Tom Lobianco and Mary Clare Jalonick (2017), 'Roger Stone asserts that Trump campaign did not collude with Russia', *Time*, 26 September; available online at https://www.yahoo.com/news/roger-stone-asserts-trump-campaign-194719709.html (accessed 16 November 2017).
51. Ashley Parker, Carol D. Leonnig, Philip Rucker and Tom Hamburger (2017), 'Trump dictated son's misleading statement on meeting with Russian lawyer', *Washington Post,* 31 July; available online at https://www.washingtonpost.com/politics/trump-dictated-sons-misleading-

statement-on-meeting-with-russian-lawyer/2017/07/31/04c94f96-73ae-11e7-8f39-eeb7d3a2d304_story.html (accessed 16 November 2017).

52. 'Read the emails on Donald Trump Jr's Russia meeting', *New York Times*, 11 July 2017; available online at https://www.nytimes.com/interactive/2017/07/11/us/politics/donald-trump-jr-email-text.html (accessed 16 November 2017).
53. Shehab Khan (2017), 'Donald Trump held press conference promising more dirt on Clinton hours after Donald Trump Jr's Russia emails', *Independent*, 12 July; available online at http://www.independent.co.uk/news/world/americas/us-politics/donald-trump-jr-hillary-clinton-russia-email-press-conference-dirt-democratic-us-president-election-a7836826.html (accessed 16 November 2017).
54. Ivan Nechepurenko (2017), 'Russian lawyer who met Donald Trump Jr once represented spy agency', *New York Times*, 21 July; available online at https://www.nytimes.com/2017/07/21/world/europe/trump-russian-lawyer-fsb-kgb.html (accessed 16 November 2017).
55. Judd Legum (2017), 'Trump mentioned WikiLeaks 164 times in last month of election, now claims it didn't impact one voter', ThinkProgress, 8 January; available online at https://thinkprogress.org/trump-mentioned-wikileaks-164-times-in-last-month-of-election-now-claims-it-didnt-impact-one-40aa62ea5002 (accessed 16 November 2017).
56. David Folkenflik (2017), 'Behind Fox News' baseless Seth Rich story: the untold tale', NPR, 1 August; available online at http://www.npr.org/2017/08/01/540783715/lawsuit-alleges-fox-news-and-trump-supporter-created-fake-news-story (accessed 16 November 2017).
57. 'Washington gunman motivated by fake news "Pizzagate" conspiracy', *Guardian*, 5 December 2016; available online at https://www.theguardian.com/us-news/2016/dec/05/gunman-detained-at-comet-pizza-restaurant-was-self-investigating-fake-news-reports (accessed 16 November 2017).
58. Nicholas Confessore and Danny Hakim (2017), 'Data firm says "secret sauce" aided Trump; many scoff', *New York Times*, 6 March; available online at https://www.nytimes.com/2017/03/06/us/politics/cambridge-analytica.html (accessed 17 November 2017).
59. Carole Cadwalladr (2017), 'The great British Brexit robbery: how our democracy was hijacked', *Observer*, 7 May; available online at https://www.theguardian.com/technology/2017/may/07/the-great-british-brexit-robbery-hijacked-democracy (accessed 16 November 2017).
60. Jamie Doward and Alice Gibbs (2017), 'Did Cambridge Analytica influence the Brexit vote and the US election?', *Guardian*, 4 March; available online at https://www.theguardian.com/politics/2017/mar/04/nigel-oakes-cambridge-analytica-what-role-brexit-trump (accessed 15 December 2017).
61. Sam Bright (2017), 'After Trump, "big data" firm Cambridge Analytica is now working in Kenya', *BBC News*, 3 August; available online at http://www.bbc.co.uk/news/blogs-trending-40792078 (accessed 17 November 2017).
62. Privacy International (2017), 'Texas media company hired by Trump created Kenyan president's viral "anonymous" attack campaign against rival, new investigation reveals', 13 December; available online at https://www.privacyinternational.org/node/1563 (accessed 15 December 2017).
63. 'Technology against tricksters' (2016), *Africa Confidential* 57, no. 18; available online at https://www.africa-confidential.com/article/id/11772/Technology_against_tricksters (accessed 17 November 2017).

64. Oliver Wright (2011), 'Cameron's favourite pollsters hand dictator 96 per cent approval rating', *Independent*, 24 November; available online at http://www.independent.co.uk/news/world/europe/camerons-favourite-pollsters-hand-dictator-96-per-cent-approval-rating-6267065.html (accessed 17 November 2017).
65. Ibid.
66. Scott Shackelford, Bruce Schneier, Michael Sulmeyer, Anne E. Boustead, Ben Buchanan, Amanda Craig, Trey Herr and Jessica Zhanna Malekos Smith (2016), 'Making democracy harder to hack', *University of Michigan Journal of Legal Reform* 50, pp. 629–60.
67. Ibid.
68. Dustin Volz and Julia Edwards Ainsley (2017), 'Russians targeted 21 election systems, US official says', Reuters, 21 June; available online at http://www.reuters.com/article/us-usa-cyber-congress-idUSKBN19C1Y3 (accessed 17 November 2017).
69. Jason Murdock (2016), 'Mexico election hack: political party behind leak of 93.4 million voter records?', *International Business Times*, 25 April; available online at http://www.ibtimes.co.uk/mexico-election-hack-political-party-behind-leak-93-4-million-voter-records-1556608 (accessed 17 November 2017).
70. Scott Shackelford et al (2016), 'Making democracy harder to hack: should elections be classified as 'critical infrastructure?', Kelley School of Business Research Paper no. 16-75; available online at https://papers.ssrn.com/sol3/papers.cfm?abstract_id=2852461 (accessed 18 January 2018).
71. 'Statement by Secretary Jeh Johnson on the designation of election infrastructure as a critical infrastructure subsector', US Department of Homeland Security, 6 January 2017; available online at https://www.dhs.gov/news/2017/01/06/statement-secretary-johnson-designation-election-infrastructure-critical (accessed 17 November 2017).
72. Benjamin Wittes and Susan Hennessey (2017), 'Jeff Sessions just confessed his negligence on Russia', *Foreign Policy*, 20 October; available online at http://foreignpolicy.com/2017/10/20/jeff-sessions-just-confessed-his-negligence-on-russia (accessed 17 November 2017).
73. Shackelford et al. (2016), 'Making democracy harder to hack', p. 629.
74. For more on Africa Check see https://africacheck.org (accessed 17 November 2017).
75. For more on the International Fact-Checking Network (IFCN) see Poynter, 'International Fact-Checking Network fact-checkers' code of principles'; available online at https://www.poynter.org/international-fact-checking-network-fact-checkers-code-principles (accessed 17 November 2017).
76. Josh Constine (2017), 'Facebook tries fighting fake news with publisher info button on links', TechCrunch, 5 October; available online at https://techcrunch.com/2017/10/05/facebook-article-information-button (accessed 17 November 2017).
77. Alex Hern (2017), 'Google acts against fake news on search engine', *Guardian*, 25 April; available online at https://www.theguardian.com/technology/2017/apr/25/google-launches-major-offensive-against-fake-news (accessed 17 November 2017).
78. Daisuke Wakabayashi and Linda Qiu (2017), 'Google serves fake news ads in an unlikely place: fact-checking sites', *New York Times*, 17 October;

available online at https://www.nytimes.com/2017/10/17/technology/google-fake-ads-fact-check.html (accessed 17 November 2017).

5 Ballot-box stuffing: the last resort

1. Thomas P. Wolf (2009), '"Poll poison"?: politicians and polling in the 2007 Kenya election', *Journal of Contemporary African Studies* 27, no. 3, pp. 279–304.
2. Cheeseman (2008), 'The Kenyan elections of 2007'.
3. Oscar Obonyo (2008), 'If Kivuitu were to speak, what would be the punch?', 14 December; available online at https://www.standardmedia.co.ke/article/1144001701/if-kivuitu-were-to-speak-what-would-be-the-punch (accessed 15 December 2017); 'Curtain falls on unrepentant Kivuitu', *The Star*, 27 February 2013.
4. Daniel Branch and Nic Cheeseman (2008), 'Democratization, sequencing, and state failure in Africa: lessons from Kenya', *African Affairs* 108, no. 430, pp. 1–26, p. 17.
5. David W. Throup (2008), 'The count', *Journal of Eastern African Studies* 2, no. 2, pp. 290–304.
6. Cheeseman was serving as an election monitor, and was in the room when those watching the official announcement of the election results were ordered to leave.
7. Abiya Ochola and Elizabeth Mwai (2008), 'Kenya: poll lacks credibility, says EU observers', *East African Standard*, 2 January 2008; available online at http://allafrica.com/stories/200801020008.html (accessed 17 November 2017).
8. Branch and Cheeseman (2008), 'Democratization, sequencing, and state failure in Africa'.
9. 'No recount in Kenya vote, says Annan', CNN, 12 February 2008; available online at http://edition.cnn.com/2008/WORLD/africa/02/12/kenya (accessed 17 November 2017).
10. The power-sharing deal split cabinet positions equally, but Kibaki's party demanded to be given the most influential ministries including Finance, Foreign Affairs, and Internal Security.
11. By this point, Kibaki had stepped down, having served two terms in office.
12. Alberto Simpser (2013), *Why Governments and Parties Manipulate Elections: Theory, Practice, and Implication* (New York: Cambridge University Press), pp. 170–2.
13. As quoted in Ashlea Rundlett and Milan W. Svolik (2016), 'Micromotives and macrobehaviour in electoral fraud', *American Political Science Review* 110, no. 1, pp. 180–97.
14. Ibid.
15. S.Y. Quraishi (2016), 'Controversy over Karnataka RS polls is an opportunity to bring in crucial electoral reforms', *Indian Express*, 8 June; available online at http://indianexpress.com/article/opinion/columns/rajya-sabha-polls-karnataka-sting-election-commission-2840031 (accessed 17 November 2017).
16. Brian Klaas, interview with Béatrice Atallah, Antananarivo, Madagascar, 7 February 2013.
17. Her promotion was recorded but little analysed in the Zambian press: see Jimmy Chibuye (2015), 'Irene Mambilima is chief justice', *Zambia Daily*

Mail, 2 February; available online at https://www.daily-mail.co.zm/ rene-mambilima-chief-justice (accessed 17 November 2017). On the Zambian elections see John Bwalya and Brij Maharaj (2018), 'Not to the highest bidder: the failure of incumbency in the Zambian 2011 elections', *Journal of Contemporary African Studies* 36, no. 1, pp. 1–16; Nic Cheeseman, Robert Ford and Neo Simutanyi (2014), 'Is there a "populist threat" in Zambia?', in Christopher Adam, Paul Collier and Michael Gondwe (eds), *Zambia: Building Prosperity from Resource Wealth* (Oxford University Press), pp. 493–512.

18. Sishuwa Sishuwa (2018), 'Zambia's 2016 elections: is a disputed outcome now inevitable?', *African Arguments*, 1 June; available online at http://africanarguments.org/2016/06/01/zambias-2016-elections-is-a-disputed-outcome-now-inevitable (accessed 17 November 2017).
19. 'Appointment of Esau Chulu as Electoral Commission of Zambia chairperson receives overwhelming support', *Lusaka Times*, 16 April 2015; available online at https://www.lusakatimes.com/2015/04/16/appointment-of-esau-chulu-as-electoral-commission-of-zambia-chairperson-receives-overwhelming-support (accessed 17 November 2017).
20. 'A former president and ECZ Essau Chulu helped Lungu rig elections – HH', *Lusaka Times*, 9 September 2016; available online at http://www.lusakatimes.com/2016/09/09/former-president-ecz-essau-chulu-helped-lungu-rig-elections-hh (accessed 17 November 2017).
21. 'Donors risk funding a fix' (2017), *Africa Confidential* 58, no. 16; available online at http://www.africa-confidential.com/article-preview/id/12071/Donors_risk_funding_a_fix (accessed 17 November 2017).
22. Ibid.
23. The letter was published in *The Times*: Richard Henry Dana Jr (1859), 'The ballot in the United States', *The Times*, 27 August. The earliest reported use appears to be by William Porter Miles, a member of the Confederate States House of Representatives, in 1858. For a fuller account of these issues see Tracy Campbell (2005), *Deliver the Vote: A History of Election Fraud, an American Political Tradition, 1742–2004* (New York: Basic Books).
24. In fact, as we saw in chapter 1, voting requirements in the US are particularly high. For more on the president's allegations and their flaws see Nicholas Fandos (2017), 'Trump won't back down from his voting fraud lie. Here are the facts', *New York Times*, 24 January; available online at http://www.nytimes.com/2017/01/24/us/politics/unauthorized-immigrant-voting-trump-lie.html (accessed 17 November 2017).
25. Nic Cheeseman, interview with senior US official, Oxford, August 2009.
26. Ibid.
27. National Democratic Institute (2007), 'Final NDI report on Nigeria's 2007 elections', p. 17; available online at https://www.ndi.org/sites/default/files/2313_ng_report_election07_043008.pdf (accessed 17 November 2017).
28. Ibid., p. 18.
29. As discussed later in the chapter, when the electoral commission came under new leadership and conducted a thorough operation to clean the register and remove duplicates, it found well over 4 million 'ghosts'. The introduction of a different system subsequently led to the removal of 10 million names. See 'New voter ID cleaned 10m names from Nigeria's

register!', Peace FM, 16 December 2015; available online at http://www.peacefmonline.com/pages/politics/politics/201512/264083.php (accessed 17 November 2017).

30. 'Ghost voter fears in Nigeria', BBC News, 17 September 2002; available online at http://news.bbc.co.uk/2/hi/africa/2263157.stm (accessed 17 November 2017).
31. 'Huge win for Nigeria's Yar'Adua', BBC News, 23 April 2007; available online at http://news.bbc.co.uk/1/hi/world/africa/6584393.stm (accessed 15 December 2017).
32. Stephen Mulvey (2004), 'Analysis: divided Ukraine', BBC News, 25 November; available online at http://news.bbc.co.uk/1/hi/world/europe/4043315.stm (accessed 17 November 2017).
33. 'Ukrainian opposition leader claims victory', *Guardian*, 23 November 2004; available online at https://www.theguardian.com/world/2004/nov/23/ukraine (accessed 17 November 2017).
34. Office for Democratic Institutions and Human Rights (OSCE) (2005), 'Ukraine: presidential election 31 October, 21 November and 26 December 2004 – OSCE/ODIHR election observation mission final report'; available online at http://www.osce.org/odihr/elections/ukraine/14674?download=true (accessed 17 November 2017).
35. 'Invisible ink: how they rigged the vote', *Sydney Morning Herald*, 2 December 2004; available online at http://www.smh.com.au/news/World/Invisible-ink-how-they-rigged-the-vote/2004/12/02/1101923247133.html (accessed 17 November 2017).
36. Ibid.
37. Ibid.
38. Steven Lee Myers (2004), 'Ukrainian court orders new vote for presidency, citing fraud', *New York Times*, 4 December; available online at http://www.nytimes.com/2004/12/04/world/europe/ukrainian-court-orders-new-vote-for-presidency-citing-fraud.html (accessed 17 November 2017).
39. Metin Heper and Şule Toktaş (2003), 'Islam, modernity, and democracy in contemporary Turkey: the case of Recep Tayyip Erdoğan', *Muslim World* 93, no. 2, pp. 157–85. For a longer discussion see Soner Cagaptay (2017), *The New Sultan: Erdogan and the Crisis of Modern Turkey* (New York: I.B. Tauris).
40. Tezcan Gumus (2017), 'Turkey is about to use democracy to end its democracy', *Quartz*, 5 April; available online at http://qz.com/950313/turkey-is-preparing-to-vote-on-a-constitutional-referendum-that-gives-president-recep-tayyip-erdogan-unprecedented-power (accessed 17 November 2017).
41. Patrick Kingsley (2017), 'Videos fuel charges of fraud in Erdogan's win in Turkey', *New York Times*, 18 April; available online at http://www.nytimes.com/2017/04/18/world/europe/turkey-referendum-is-haunted-by-allegations-of-voter-fraud.html (accessed 17 November 2017).
42. Ibid.
43. Kadir Yildrim (2017), 'How Erdogan won more power but lost legitimacy in Turkey's constitutional referendum', *Washington Post*, 17 April; available online at http://www.washingtonpost.com/news/monkey-cage/wp/2017/04/20/how-erdogan-won-more-power-but-lost-legitimacy-in-turkeys-constitutional-referendum (accessed 17 November 2017).

44. Cheeseman, interview with former election observer, Nairobi, Kenya, October 2017.
45. Alex Scacco and Bernd Beber (2012), 'What the numbers say: a digit-based test for election fraud', *Political Analysis* 20, no. 2, pp. 235–47.
46. Nicole Beardsworth and Nic Cheeseman (2016), 'How to win an election in Uganda', *Newsweek*, 16 March; available online at http://www.newsweek.com/uganda-elections-2016-yoweri-museveni-437049 (accessed 17 November 2017).
47. Edris Kiggundu and Sulaiman Kakaire (2016), 'Museveni voted for by poorest Ugandans', *Observer* (Uganda), 29 February; available online at http://observer.ug/news-headlines/42872-museveni-voted-for-by-poorest-ugandans (accessed 15 December 2015).
48. See Charles Hornsby (2011), *Kenya: A History Since Independence* (London: I.B. Tauris), p. 534.
49. 'Venezuela vote: authorities reject inflation claim', BBC News, 3 August 2017; available online at http://www.bbc.com/news/world-latin-america-40808752 (accessed 17 November 2017).
50. 'Venezuela vote: turnout figure tampered with', BBC News, 2 August 2017; available online at http://www.bbc.co.uk/news/world-latin-america-40804812 (accessed 15 December 2017).
51. Girish Gupta (2017), 'Exclusive: Venezuelan vote data casts doubt on turnout at Sunday poll', Reuters, 2 August 2017; available online at http://www.reuters.com/article/us-venezuela-politics-vote-exclusive-idUSKBN1AI0AL (accessed 17 November 2017).
52. Amanda Erickson (2017), '8 important keys to understanding Venezuela's controversial election', *Washington Post*, 29 July; available online at https://www.washingtonpost.com/news/worldviews/wp/2017/07/29/8-important-keys-to-understanding-venezuelas-controversial-election/?utm_term=.b5f0e6e7e134 (accessed 15 December 2017).
53. For a discussion of coalition formation and MPs' attitudes to legislative majorities see Paul Chaisty, Nic Cheeseman and Tim Power, *Coalitional Presidentialism in Comparative Perspective: Minority Presidents in Multiparty Systems* (Oxford University Press), pp. 46–75 and 120–42.
54. Nic Cheeseman, Gabrielle Lynch and Justin Willis (forthcoming), 'Digital dilemmas: the unintended consequences of election technology', *Democratization*.
55. Cheeseman, Lynch and Willis (2017), 'Ghana: the ebbing power of incumbency'.
56. The NDI is loosely affiliated to the Democratic Party and received considerable state funding to support democracy and elections abroad. For more on how and where it conducts PVTs see NDI (2017), 'Parallel vote tabulations'; available online at https://www.ndi.org/pvt (accessed 17 November 2017).
57. Commonwealth Observer Group (2015), 'Nigeria elections 2015: arrival statement'; available online at http://thecommonwealth.org/media/news/nigeria-elections-2015-arrival-statement-commonwealth-observer-group (accessed 17 November 2017).
58. This optimism is well summarized in Alan Gelb and Julia Clark (2013), 'Identification for development: the biometrics revolution', Center for Global Development Working Paper no. 315; available online at https://www.cgdev.org/sites/default/files/1426862_file_Biometric_ID_for_

Development.pdf (accessed 17 November 2017); and Alan Gelb and Anna Diofasi (2016), 'Biometric elections in poor countries: wasteful or a worthwhile investment?', Center for Global Development Working Paper no. 435; available online at https://www.cgdev.org/sites/default/files/biometric-elections-poor-countries-wasteful-or-worthwhile-investment.pdf (accessed 12 January 2018).

6 Potemkin elections: How to fool the West

1. Michael David-Fox (undated), 'The myth of the Soviet Potemkin village', Université Paris 1 Panthéon Sorbonne and ENS 'La Russie aux XIXe et XXe siècles: politique intérieure et influences internationales' seminar series; available online at http://www.histoire.ens.fr/IMG/file/Coeure/David-Fox%20Potemkin%20villages.pdf (accessed 17 November 2017).
2. Freedom House (2013), 'Freedom in the world 2013'; available online at https://freedomhouse.org/report/freedom-world/freedom-world-2013 (accessed 17 November 2017).
3. Andrew Hough (2010), 'Azerbaijan president's son, 12, "buys £30m worth of luxury Dubai property"', *Daily Telegraph*, 5 March; available online at http://www.telegraph.co.uk/news/worldnews/middleeast/azerbaijan/7379847/Azerbaijan-presidents-son-12-buys-30m-worth-of-luxury-Dubai-property.html (accessed 17 November 2017).
4. Joshua Keating (2013), 'Azerbaijan accidentally releases election results before vote . . . the president does even better', *Slate*, 10 October; available online at http://www.slate.com/blogs/the_world_/2013/10/10/azerbaijan_election_rigging_president_does_even_better_than_the_early_results.html (accessed 17 November 2017).
5. Fisher (2013), 'Oops'.
6. Ibid.
7. Council of Europe (2013), 'Presidential election in Azerbaijan: joint statement by PACE and EP delegations'; available online at https://www.coe.int/en/web/portal/-/presidential-election-in-azerbaijan-joint-statement-by-pace-and-ep-delegations (accessed 17 November 2017).
8. Alexander Cooley (2015), 'Countering democratic norms', *Journal of Democracy* 26, no. 3, pp. 49–63. See also Christopher Walker (2016), 'The hijacking of "soft power"', *Journal of Democracy* 27, no. 1, pp. 49–63.
9. Cheeseman (2015), *Democracy in Africa*, pp. 114–15.
10. See, for example, Thomas Carothers (2011), *Aiding Democracy Abroad: The Learning Curve* (Washington, DC: Carnegie Endowment for International Peace).
11. Samuel Ramani (2016), 'Three reasons the US won't break with Azerbaijan over its violations of human rights and democratic freedoms', *Washington Post*, 20 January; available online at https://www.washingtonpost.com/news/monkey-cage/wp/2016/01/20/3-reasons-the-u-s-wont-break-with-azerbaijan-over-its-violations-of-human-rights-and-democratic-freedoms (accessed 17 November 2017).
12. 'FACTBOX – Azerbaijan's main gas fields', Reuters, 24 February 2017; available online at http://uk.reuters.com/article/azerbaijan-gas-idUKL8N1G53VT (accessed 17 November 2017).
13. David M. Herszenhorn (2013), 'Observers differ on fairness of election in Azerbaijan', *New York Times*, 10 October; available online at http://www.

nytimes.com/2013/10/11/world/asia/observers-say-azerbaijan-election-marred-by-fraud.html (accessed 17 November 2017).

14. Carothers (2003), 'Promoting democracy and fighting terror'.
15. Levitsky and Way (2006), 'Linkage versus leverage'.
16. Carothers (2003), 'Promoting democracy and fighting terror'.
17. 'Observer says 2.5 million Turkish referendum votes could have been manipulated', Reuters, 18 April 2017; available online at http://www.reuters.com/article/us-turkey-politics-referendum-observers-idUSKBN17K0JW?il=0 (accessed 18 November).
18. OSCE Office for Democratic Institutions and Human Rights (2017), 'Lack of equal opportunities, one-sided media coverage and limitations on fundamental freedoms created unlevel playing field in Turkey's constitutional referendum, international observers say'; available online at http://www.osce.org/odihr/elections/turkey/311726 (accessed 18 November 2017).
19. Carol Morello (2017), 'Trump calls Erdogan to congratulate him on contested referendum, Turkey says', *Washington Post*, 17 April; available online at https://www.washingtonpost.com/world/national-security/trump-calls-turkeys-erdogan-to-congratulate-him-on-contested-referendum/2017/04/17/f997d306-2397-11e7-a1b3-faff0034e2de_story.html (accessed 18 November 2017).
20. For the use of peacekeeping as a strategy to gain international leverage see Kasaija Philip Apuuli (2017), 'Uganda in regional and international peacekeeping operations', *The Round Table* 106, no. 5, pp. 505–15. For the 2016 election specifically see Ty McCormick (2016), 'Is the U.S. military propping up Uganda's "elected" autocrat?', *Foreign Policy*, 18 February; available online at http://foreignpolicy.com/2016/02/18/is-the-us-military-propping-up-ugandas-elected-autocrat-museveni-elections/ (accessed 17 December 2017).
21. Freedom House (2017), 'Freedom in the world 2017: Uganda'; available online at https://freedomhouse.org/report/freedom-world/2017/uganda (accessed 18 November 2017).
22. 'Ugandan opposition leader under house arrest to stop him holding rallies', *Guardian*, 15 October 2015; available online at https://www.theguardian.com/world/2015/oct/15/uganda-opposition-leader-besigye-house-arrest-stop-rallies (accessed 18 November 2017).
23. Stephen Wandera (2016), 'Uganda: Besigye not presidential material – Kiggundu', *Monitor*, 17 February; available online at http://allafrica.com/stories/201602171025.html (accessed 18 November 2017).
24. Nelson Wesonga (2016), 'Lumumba shoot-to-kill threat sparks outrage', *Daily Monitor*, 1 February; available online at http://www.monitor.co.ug/SpecialReports/Elections/Lumumba-shoot-to-kill-threat-sparks-outrage/859108-3056812-blgevl/index.html (accessed 18 November 2017).
25. Nic Cheeseman (2016), 'Besigye's campaign and the lessons for Africa's opposition parties', *Daily Nation*, 21 February; available online at http://www.nation.co.ke/oped/Opinion/Besigye-campaign-and-lessons-for-Africa-opposition-parties/440808-3086048-ou88iuz/index.htm (accessed 18 November 2017).
26. See the 'Rules of conduct for international observers' in the 'Electoral integrity' section of the encyclopedia of the Administration and Cost of

Elections (ACE) Electoral Knowledge Network, available at http://aceproject.org/ace-en/topics/ei/eid/eid06/eid06a (accessed 17 December 2017).

27. Nic Cheeseman, Gabrielle Lynch and Justin Willis (2015), 'How election monitors are failing', *Foreign Policy*; available online at http://foreignpolicy.com/2016/04/29/how-election-monitors-are-failing-uganda (accessed 18 November 2017).
28. Alan Barber (2011), 'CEPR examines OAS report on Haiti's election, finds it "inconclusive, statistically flawed, and indefensible"', Center for Economic Policy Research (CEPR); available online at http://cepr.net/blogs/haiti-relief-and-reconstruction-watch/cepr-examines-oas-report-on-haitis-election-finds-it-qinconclusive-statistically-flawed-and-indefensibleq-summary (accessed 18 November 2017).
29. David Rosnik (2010), 'The Organization of American States in Haiti: election monitoring on political interventions', Center for Economic and Policy Research (CEPR); available online at http://cepr.net/documents/publications/haiti-oas-2011-10.pdf (accessed 18 November 2017).
30. European Union External Action (2017), 'EU election observation mission to Kenya in 2007'; available online at https://eeas.europa.eu/headquarters/headquarters-homepage/26127/eu-election-observation-mission-kenya-2007_en (accessed 18 November 2017).
31. Arturo Santa-Cruz (2013), *International Election Monitoring, Sovereignty, and the Western Hemisphere: The Emergence of an International Norm* (New York: Routledge), p. 3.
32. Susan D. Hyde (2011), 'Catch us if you can: election monitoring and international norm diffusion', *American Journal of Political Science* 55, no. 2, pp. 356–69.
33. Hyde (2017), *The Pseudo-Democrat's Dilemma*.
34. See, for example, Ursula E. Daxecker (2014), 'All quiet on election day? International election observation and incentives for pre-election violence in African elections', *Electoral Studies* 34, pp. 232–43.
35. Judith Green Kelley (2009), 'The more the merrier? The effects of having multiple international election monitoring organizations', *Perspectives on Politics* 7, no. 1, pp. 59–64.
36. Judith Green Kelley (2012), *Monitoring Democracy: When International Election Observation Works, and Why It Often Fails* (Princeton University Press), p. 48.
37. In both Kenya (2017) and Nigeria (2015) Cheeseman talked to election observation teams that were not able to go to parts of the country that were seen to be particularly unsafe as a result of chronic crime and terrorism issues.
38. Joseph Asunka, Sarah Brierley, Miriam Golden, Eric Kramon and George Ofosu (2017), 'Electoral fraud or violence: the effect of observers on party manipulation strategies', *British Journal of Political Science*, DOI: 10.1017/S0007123416000491, pp. 1–23. See also Joseph Asunka, Sarah Brierley, Miriam Golden, Eric Kramon and George Ofosu (2014), 'Protecting the polls: the effect of observers on election fraud' (unpublished manuscript, University of California), pp. 8–9.
39. Ursula E. Daxecker (2012), 'The cost of exposing cheating: international election monitoring, fraud, and post-election violence in Africa', *Journal of Peace Research* 49, no. 4, pp. 503–16.

40. Thomas Carothers (1997), 'The observers observed', *Journal of Democracy* 8, no. 3, pp. 17–31.
41. Klaas, interview with anonymous government official, Minsk, Belarus, 11 December 2015.
42. Patrick Merloe (2015), 'Election monitoring vs. disinformation', *Journal of Democracy* 26, no. 3, pp. 79–93.
43. Cooley (2015), 'Countering democratic norms'.
44. Sarah S. Bush and Lauren Prather (2017), 'The promise and limits of election observers in building election credibility', *Journal of Politics* 79, no. 3, pp. 921–35.
45. Lauren Crothers (2013), 'China and Hungary call national election "free and fair"', *Cambodia Daily*, 31 July; available online at https://www.cambodiadaily.com/elections/china-and-hungary-call-national-election-free-and-fair-37664 (accessed 18 November 2017).
46. Abby Phillip and David Nakamara (2017), 'Autocrats hear a clear message during Trump trip: US will not "lecture" on human rights', *Washington Post*, 22 May; available online at https://www.washingtonpost.com/politics/autocrats-hear-a-clear-message-during-trump-trip-us-will-not-lecture-on-human-rights/2017/05/22/1c7328b4-3f0c-11e7-8c25-44d09ff5a4a8_story.html (accessed 18 November 2017).
47. Ellen Hinsey and Rafal Pankowski (2016), 'Poland's illiberal challenge', *New England Review* 37, no. 4, pp. 73–88. See also Ishaan Tharoor (2017), 'Poland's war on democracy was aided by Trump', *Washington Post*, 24 July; available online at https://www.washingtonpost.com/news/worldviews/wp/2017/07/24/polands-war-on-democracy-was-aided-by-trump (accessed 18 November 2017).
48. See, for example, Aijan Sharshenova and Gordon Crawford (2017), 'Undermining Western democracy promotion in Central Asia: China's countervailing influences, powers and impact', *Central Asian Survey*, pp. 1–20; Michael J. Boyle (2016), 'The coming illiberal order', *Survival* 58, no. 2, pp. 35–66. For a broader discussion on the dim prospects for liberal democracy currently see Marc F. Plattner (2017), 'Liberal democracy's fading allure', *Journal of Democracy* 28, no. 4, pp. 5–14.
49. The African Union was one of the only delegations to observe the election, as the European Union and the Economic Community of West African States did not attend. The presence of these monitors was significant, because it helped to harden the stance of the African Union regarding the need for Jammeh to stand down. See Alex Vines (2016), 'Gambia's election result is a sign of democracy advancing in Africa', Chatham House Expert Comment, 9 December; available online at https://www.chathamhouse.org/expert/comment/gambias-election-result-sign-democracy-advancing-africa (accessed 11 January 2018).
50. See Niklas Hultin, Baba Jallow, Benjamin N. Lawrance and Assan Sarr (2017), 'Autocracy, migration, and the Gambia's "unprecedented" 2016 election', *African Affairs* 116, no. 463, pp. 321–40; and Sheriff Kora and Momodou Darboe (2017), 'The Gambia's electoral earthquake', *Journal of Democracy* 28, no. 2, pp. 147–56.
51. This proposal did not, however, gain traction when it was discussed at the end of the Cold War. See Judith Kelley (2009), 'The more the merrier? The effects of having multiple international election monitoring organizations', *Perspectives on Politics* 7, no. 1, pp. 59–64.

52. Laura Brunts (2011), 'Watchdogs of democracy: a comparative study of election monitoring groups in Africa' (unpublished Masters thesis, University of Oxford).
53. Cheeseman, Lynch and Willis (2017), 'Ghana: the ebbing power of incumbency'.
54. Hyde and Marinov (2012), 'Which elections can be lost?'.
55. For an in-depth analysis of the challenges and failures of international election monitoring see Kelley (2012), *Monitoring Democracy*.

Conclusion: How to stop election rigging

1. Author's own calculation based on data from NELDA and Polity IV. See appendix 1 for more details.
2. Arch Puddington and Tyler Roylance (2016), 'Anxious dictators, wavering democracies: global freedom under pressure', in 'Freedom in the world 2016', Freedom House, pp. 1–9; available online at https://freedomhouse.org/sites/default/files/FH_FITW_Report_2016.pdf (accessed 18 November 2017).
3. Author's own calculation based on data from NELDA. See appendix 1 for more details.
4. For a thoughtful discussion about whether democracy can be made to work in Africa see Claude Ake (2000), *The Feasibility of Democracy in Africa* (Dakar: Council for the Development of Social Science Research in Africa). For a debate between leading scholars including Francis Fukuyama, Thomas Carothers, Edward D. Mansfield and Jack Snyder and Sheri Berman (2007) see 'The debate on "sequencing"', *Journal of Democracy* 18, no. 3; available online at http://carnegieendowment.org/files/Sequencing_Exchange.pdf (accessed 18 November 2017).
5. Amy Chua (2004), *World on Fire: How Exporting Free Market Democracy Breeds Ethnic Hatred and Global Instability* (New York: Doubleday).
6. For more see ODI (2007–2012), 'African power and politics programme', online at https://www.odi.org/projects/africa-power-and-politics-programme (accessed 18 November 2017).
7. Frank Karsten and Karel Beckman (2012), *Beyond Democracy: Why Democracy Does Not Lead to Solidarity, Prosperity and Liberty But to Social Conflict, Runaway Spending and a Tyrannical Government* (London: CreateSpace); Jarno Lang (2014), 'Democracy and Southeast Asia are not incompatible', *Fair Observer*, 8 December; available online at https://www.fairobserver.com/region/asia_pacific/southeast-asia-and-democracy-53098 (accessed 18 November 2017); Andrew Green (2014), 'Why Western democracy can never work in the Middle East', *Daily Telegraph*, 16 August; available online at http://www.telegraph.co.uk/news/worldnews/middleeast/11037173/Why-Western-democracy-can-never-work-in-the-Middle-East.html (accessed 18 November 2017).
8. Mattes and Bratton (2016), 'Do Africans still want democracy?'.
9. Ibid.
10. LAPOP data and analysis are available online at https://www.vanderbilt.edu/lapop/ (accessed 17 December 2017). It is worth noting, though, that support for democracy is significantly lower in Brazil, Chile, Guatemala and Paraguay: Margarita Corral (2011), 'The state of democracy in Latin America: a comparative analysis of attitudes of elites and citizens', *Boletin PNUD & Instituto De Iberoamérica* 1; available online at http://www.

vanderbilt.edu/lapop/insights/030711.PNUD_PELA_Report.pdf (accessed 18 November 2017).

11. Takaaki Masaki and Nicolas van de Walle (2014), 'The impact of democracy on economic growth in sub-Saharan Africa, 1982–2012', UNU-WIDER working paper 2014/057 (Helsinki: UNU-WIDER); available online at https://www.wider.unu.edu/publication/impact-democracy-economic-growth-sub-saharan-africa-1982-2012 (accessed 18 November 2017).
12. It is important to note that this work was published very recently (2017) and has not yet appeared in a peer-reviewed journal; see Eric Bader and Anna Lührmann (2017), 'Democratic institutions at local and national levels: drivers for economic development?', V-Dem Institute Policy Brief no. 9; available online at https://www.v-dem.net/media/filer_public/45/0b/450b2941-3345-4e2b-ade6-423b91a1684e/v-dem_policy-brief_9_2017.pdf (accessed 18 November 2017).
13. Carl Henrik Knutsen, John Gerring, Svend-Erik Skaaning, Jan Teorell, Matthew Maguire, Michael Coppedge and Staffan I. Lindberg (2015), 'Economic development and democracy: an electoral connection', V-Dem Institute Working Paper Series 2015:16; available online at http://people.bu.edu/mwm/docs/2015_V-Dem_Modernization.pdf (accessed 18 November 2017).
14. Harding and Stasavage (2013), 'What democracy does (and doesn't do) for basic services'.
15. Geoffrey Evans and Pauline Rose (2012), 'Understanding education's influence on support for democracy in sub-Saharan Africa', *Journal of Development Studies* 48, no. 4, pp. 498–515; Cheeseman (2015), '"No bourgeoisie, no democracy"?'.
16. Cheeseman (2015), *Democracy in Africa*, pp. 167–70.
17. Knutsen et al. (2015), 'Economic development and democracy', p. 13.
18. 'Rwanda Elections 2017: President Kagame to win one-horse race?', BBC News, 3 August 2017; available online at http://www.bbc.com/news/av/world-africa-40801529/rwanda-elections-2017-president-kagame-to-win-one-horse-race (accessed 18 November 2017).
19. Thomas Legler and Thomas Kwasi Tieku (2010), 'What difference can a path make? Regional democracy promotion regimes in the Americas and Africa', *Democratization* 17, no. 3, pp. 465–91.
20. Barbara Grosh and Stephen Orvis (1996), 'Democracy, confusion, or chaos: political conditionality in Kenya', *Studies in Comparative International Development* 31, no. 4, pp. 46–65.
21. Ismail Akwei (2017), 'Kagame's female challenger faces exclusion from Rwanda's presidential race', *Africa News*, 28 June 2017; available online at http://www.africanews.com/2017/06/28/kagame-s-female-challenger-faces-exclusion-from-presidential-race (accessed 18 November 2017).
22. 'August 2017 presidential elections: pride of the Rwandan choice', *RPF Inkotanyi*, 23 July 2017; available online at http://rpfinkotanyi.rw/index.php?id=187&tx_ttnews%5Btt_news%5D=481&cHash=9c677e18ce14c271293d61adfc8b9fea (accessed 17 December 2017).
23. Levitsky and Way (2010), *Competitive Authoritarianism*.
24. Lise Rakner, Lars Svåsand and Nixon S. Khembo (2007), 'Fissions and fusions, foes and friends: party system restructuring in Malawi in the 2004 general elections', *Comparative Political Studies* 40, no. 9, pp. 1112–37, p. 1114.

25. Richard Joseph (1997), 'Democratization in Africa after 1989: comparative and theoretical perspectives', *Comparative Politics* 29, no. 3, pp. 363–82.
26. Marc Morjé Howard and Philip G. Roessler (2006), 'Liberalizing electoral outcomes in competitive authoritarian regimes', *American Journal of Political Science* 50, no. 2, pp. 365–81.
27. SADC (2017), 'SADC Electoral Observation Mission (SEOM) launches in the Kingdom of Lesotho for the 2017 national assembly elections'; available online at https://www.sadc.int/news-events/news/sadc-electoral-observation-mission-seom-launches-kingdom-lesotho-2017-national-assembly-elections (accessed 18 November 2017).
28. John Reed (2016), 'China intervenes in Zambian election', *Financial Times*, 5 September; available online at https://www.ft.com/content/d6d5d176-3d0a-11db-8239-0000779e2340?mhq5j=e6 (accessed 17 December 2017).
29. Daniel Large (2009), 'China's Sudan engagement: changing northern and southern political trajectories in peace and war', *China Quarterly* 199, pp. 610–26.
30. Colum Lynch (2014), 'UN peacekeepers to protect China's oil interests in South Sudan', *Foreign Policy*, 16 June; available online at http://foreignpolicy.com/2014/06/16/u-n-peacekeepers-to-protect-chinas-oil-interests-in-south-sudan (accessed 18 November 2017).
31. David Pilling (2017), 'Chinese investment in Africa: Beijing's testing ground', *Financial Times*, 13 July; available online at https://www.ft.com/content/0f534aa4-4549-11e7-8519-9f94ee97d996?mhq5j=e6 (17 December 2017).
32. Cary Huang (2016), 'Why China is cosying up to Latin America', *South China Morning Post*, 11 December; available online at http://www.scmp.com/week-asia/opinion/article/2053391/why-china-cosying-latin-america (accessed 18 November 2017).
33. Rachel Vanderhill (2013), *Promoting Authoritarianism Abroad* (Boulder, CO: Lynne Rienner Publishing), p. 4.
34. For the growing Russian financial engagement in Venezuela see Marianna Parraga and Alexandra Ulmer (2017), 'Special report: Vladimir's Venezuela – leveraging loans to Caracas, Moscow snaps up oil assets', Reuters, 11 August; available online at http://www.reuters.com/article/us-venezuela-russia-oil-specialreport/special-report-vladimirs-venezuela-leveraging-loans-to-caracas-moscow-snaps-up-oil-assets-idUSKBN1AR14U (accessed 18 November 2017).
35. 'China says sanctions won't help as Trump targets Venezuela', Reuters, 28 August 2017; available online at https://www.reuters.com/article/us-usa-venezuela-sanctions-china/china-says-sanctions-wont-help-as-trump-targets-venezuela-idUSKCN1B811D (accessed 18 November 2017).
36. Charles Fain Lehman (2017), 'Russia and China are propping up Maduro's regime in Venezuela', *Business Insider*, 14 September; available online at http://www.businessinsider.com/russia-and-china-are-propping-up-maduros-regime-in-venezuela-2017-9?IR=T (accessed 18 November 2017).
37. Josh Rogin (2017), 'State Department considers scrubbing democracy promotion from its mission', *Washington Post*, 1 August; available online at https://www.washingtonpost.com/news/josh-rogin/wp/2017/08/01/state-department-considers-scrubbing-democracy-promotion-from-its-mission (accessed 18 November 2017).

38. This is true both of 'anti-system' leaders such as Nigel Farage in the United Kingdom, but also of elected governments. For example, while UK Prime Minister Theresa May has pledged to maintain her country's commitment to spending 0.7 per cent of GDP on foreign aid – which helps to fund a range of democracy-strengthening activities – she has responded to public and media pressure by diverting some of these funds to deal with other issues, such as environmental protection. For an example of the media campaign around these issues see Mark Reynolds (2017), 'Foreign aid: Theresa May promises to use cash to rid seas of discarded plastic', *Daily Express*, 13 December; available online at https://www.express.co.uk/news/politics/892008/foreign-aid-budget-theresa-may-plastic-climate-change (accessed 11 January 2018).
39. Andreas Schedler (2002), 'The menu of manipulation', *Journal of Democracy* 13, no. 2, pp. 36–50.
40. Nic Cheeseman, interview with Zimbabwean election expert, Harare, Zimbabwe, June 2017.
41. Roessler and Howard (2009), 'Post-Cold War political regimes'.
42. Ibid.
43. Joseph Asunka, Sarah Brierley, Miriam Golden, Eric Kramon and George Ofosu (2017), 'Electoral fraud or violence: the effect of observers on party manipulation strategies', *British Journal of Political Science*; available online at https://doi.org/10.1017/S0007123416000491, pp. 1–23 (accessed 19 December 2018).
44. Anna C. Rader (2016), 'Politiques de la reconnaissance et de l'origine controlée', *Politique Africaine* 4, no. 144, pp. 56–7.
45. See Gus Hosein and Carly Nyst (2013), *Aiding Surveillance*, Privacy International, p. 21; available online at https://www.privacyinternational.org/sites/default/files/Aiding%20Surveillance.pdf (accessed 18 November 2017); and Damien McElroy (2011), 'UK pays £22.5 million for "questionable" Democratic Republic of Congo election', *Daily Telegraph*, 16 October; available online at http://www.telegraph.co.uk/news/worldnews/africaandindianocean/democraticrepublicofcongo/8830144/UK-pays-22.5-million-for-questionable-Democratic-Republic-of-Congo-election.html (accessed 18 November 2017).
46. 'Technology against tricksters' (2016).
47. Cheeseman, Lynch and Willis (2017), 'Ghana: the ebbing power of incumbency'.

FURTHER READING

Ake, Claude (2000), *The Feasibility of Democracy in Africa*, Council for the Development of Social Science Research in Africa, Dakar.

Alvarez, R. Michael, Thad E. Hall and Susan D. Hyde (eds) (2008), *Election Fraud: Detecting and Deterring Electoral Manipulation* (Washington, DC: Brookings Institution Press).

Berman, Ari (2016), *Give Us the Ballot: The Modern Struggle for Voting Rights in America* (London: Picador).

Birch, Sarah (2011), *Electoral Malpractice* (Oxford University Press).

Bratton, Michael, Robert B. Mattes and Emmanuel Gyimah-Boadi (2004), *Public Opinion, Market Reform and Democracy in Africa* (Cambridge University Press).

Bueno de Mesquita, Bruce and Alastair Smith (2011), *The Dictator's Handbook: Why Bad Behaviour is Almost Always Good Politics* (New York: Random House).

Carothers, Thomas (2004), *Critical Mission: Essays on Democracy Promotion* (Washington, DC: Brookings Institution Press).

Cheeseman, Nic (2015), *Democracy in Africa: Successes, Failures, and the Struggle for Political Reform* (Cambridge University Press).

Greene, Kenneth F. (2007), *Why Dominant Parties Lose: Mexico's Democratization in Comparative Perspective* (Cambridge University Press).

Hyde, Susan D. (2011), *The Pseudo-Democrat's Dilemma: Why Election Observation Became an International Norm* (Ithaca, NY: Cornell University Press).

Klaas, Brian (2016), *The Despot's Accomplice: How the West is Aiding and Abetting the Decline of Democracy* (London: Hurst).

Lührmann, Anna, Staffan I. Lindberg, Valeriya Mechkova, Moa Olin, Francesco Piccinelli Casagrande, Constanza Sanhueza Petrarca and Laura Saxer (2017), 'Varieties of Democracy Project annual report: democracy at dusk?', V-Dem, University of Gothenburg, 2017; available online at https://

www.v-dem.net/en/news-publications/annual-report (accessed 17 November 2017).

Mounk, Yascha (2018), *The People vs. Democracy: Why Our Freedom is in Danger and How to Save It* (Cambridge, MA: Harvard University Press).

Myagkov, Mikhail, Peter C. Ordershook and Dimitri Shakin (2009), *The Forensics of Election Fraud: Russia and Ukraine* (Cambridge University Press).

Norris, Pippa (2015), *Why Elections Fail* (Cambridge University Press).

— (2017), *Strengthening Electoral Integrity* (Cambridge University Press).

ACKNOWLEDGEMENTS

The authors would like to thank our editors at Yale, who have been a fantastic source of support. Phoebe Clapham, who commissioned the book, provided much-needed vision and inspiration, and encouraged us to think about this problem from a global perspective. The clear, constructive and consistently correct advice of Heather McCallum was critical to the evolution of a more readable and effective manuscript and to making sure that the book saw the light of day. Marika Lysandrou also provided thorough and insightful comments on an earlier draft which helped us to clarify many of our arguments.

Brian would like to thank Ellie for always being there; his parents for being an endless source of inspiration, support and parental wisdom; and Nic (Brian's DPhil adviser-turned-co-author) for transforming a wide-eyed student into a scholar. May every student find their own Nic during their education.

Nic would like to thank his wife Juliet, for supporting him in finishing this book while he moved jobs and obsessively watched the Kenyan elections of 2017. It would not have been possible otherwise. Thanks also to Laurence Whitehead, whose Democratization seminars at the University of Oxford have been bringing together people working on different parts of the world for many years, and in this way provided an intellectual melting pot from which this project emerged. The idea that presidents operate with a toolbox of strategies they can choose between also owes much to two of Nic's co-authors from a different project, Paul Chaisty and Timothy Power, whose understanding of comparative politics and the strategies adopted by presidents around the world has greatly informed these pages. He would also like to thank Brian, without whom this project would never have been finished.

Finally, this book would not have been possible without the hundreds of opposition activists, civil society leaders and election monitors who have shared their thoughts with us over the past decade. The willingness of people to take time out of their busy days to answer questions, provide information and recall often painful memories is humbling, and an act of generosity that we can never hope to repay. Unlike us, the people we talk to are not able to return to a comfortable home in a safe city where their human rights are protected at the end of every election campaign. This book is dedicated to them, and to the friends who have not lived to read it.

INDEX

ABOUT THE AUTHORS

Nic Cheeseman is professor of democracy at the University of Birmingham and founding editor of the *Oxford Encyclopedia of African Politics*. He lives in Birmingham, UK. **Brian Klaas** is a fellow in comparative politics at the London School of Economics. He lives in London.